"This arresting anthology of student nurses' Jeanne Bryner and Cortney Davis, illustrates th and often sheltered young people as they lea in presenting the healthcare of decades past—the disabled baby left to die in a linen closet, his unknowing mother sobbing nearby; the man dying, kept separate from his wife of over fifty years by the unbending rules of hospital isolation—these memories need to be preserved. With grace and lilting eloquence, these essays and poems show what it means to be a nurse in training. Nurses will recognize their own commonalities with these students while everyone will have entrée to the singular intricacies and challenges of studying nursing."

—BRIGID LUSK, PhD, RN, FAAN

director, Midwest Nursing History Research Center, and adjunct clinical professor,
University of Illinois at Chicago College of Nursing

"Introduces the reader to the personal stories of women and men during their arduous and, at times, exhilarating training for this most intimate of professions. These nurse-authors shatter the long-held image of nurses in white caps and starched uniforms and invite us into their world where, at the bedsides of patients, touch is an instrument of healing—holding the hand of a patient undergoing a procedure, or whispering 'I'm here with you,' in the ear of a dying patient as they take a last breath. We read of their fear as they open the door to meet their first patient, the scrutiny and support of their teachers, as well as the racism and sexism they confront along the way. *Learning to Heal* is a gift to all of us who, at some point in our lives, will have a nurse at our side in our most vulnerable moments—offering their skill, their comfort, and their humanity."

—LUCY BRUELL

editor-in-chief, Literature, Arts, and Medicine Database, and
associate director, H.A.M.E. Program

"In *Learning to Heal,* Jeanne Bryner and Cortney Davis have opened a marvelous window into the world of nursing education. In consistently engaging poetry and prose, this anthology captures the lived experiences of student nurses in multiple voices over many decades. As they progress along varied paths, they discover that the secret of healing lies in words and relationships, in human presence and touch."

—JACK COULEHAN, MD, MPH

editor of *Chekhov's Doctors: A Collection of Chekhov's Medical Tales*
(Kent State University Press)

"The meaning and challenges of work are not always visible to outsiders, but poetry can show us not only why work matters but what it does for and the costs it exacts from workers. The poems gathered in *Learning to Heal* make visible the dignity of a profession that is at once exhausting and creative, intimate and institutional. The nurse-writers who tell their stories in *Learning to Heal* reveal how their daily labor weaves specialized knowledge and routine together with tenderness and caretaking."

—SHERRY LINKON

professor of English and American Studies, Georgetown University, and a scholar of working-class literature and culture

Learning to Heal

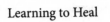

LITERATURE AND MEDICINE

Michael Blackie, Editor • Carol Donley and Martin Kohn, Founding Editors

Handwritten inscription: 3-15-23 / For Tammy, / So nice to meet / you & share our / meal / together. Bread! / Jeanne

Learning to Heal

Reflections on Nursing School
in Poetry and Prose

Edited by Jeanne Bryner and Cortney Davis

Signature: Jeanne Bryner

Foreword by Judy Schaefer

The Kent State University Press

Kent, Ohio

© 2018 by The Kent State University Press, Kent, Ohio 44242

ALL RIGHTS RESERVED

Library of Congress Catalog Card Number 2018008738

ISBN 978-1-60635-358-5

Manufactured in the United States of America

LIBRARY OF CONGRESS CATALOGING-IN-PUBLICATION DATA

Names: Bryner, Jeanne, 1951- editor. | Davis, Cortney, 1945- editor.

Title: Learning to heal : reflections on nursing school in poetry and prose /
edited by Jeanne Bryner and Cortney Davis.

Description: Kent, Ohio : The Kent State University Press, [2018] |
Series: Literature and medicine ; 26

Identifiers: LCCN 2018008738 | ISBN 9781606353585 (pbk. ; alk. paper)

Subjects: LCSH: Nurses' writings, American. | Nursing--Literary collections. |
Nurses--Literary collections.

Classification: LCC PS509.N87 L43 2018 | DDC 811/.608092161073--dc23

LC record available at https://lccn.loc.gov/2018008738

22 21 20 19 18   5 4 3 2 1

For our patients, whose vulnerability, trust, and courage
called us to the bedside

Jeanne Bryner: for Summar

Cortney Davis: as ever, for my family

CONTENTS

PART VI

Most of us need a teacher, someone who has traveled this way before.   205

FOREWORD

Judy Schaefer

My work, my job, as a professional nurse was to make beds, give baths, start IVs, and do whatever was necessary to make the pain go away and let the healing begin. How many beds? I never counted but at least a hundred thousand. I do know that while the IV I started might have been the umpteenth hundred for me, I understood that it might have been the very first for the patient. Nursing becomes a profession when educated and skilled hands meet flesh, mind, and soul. The art of nursing is expressed through the melding of nursing empathy, imagination, and creativity.

More than twenty years ago, Joanne Trautmann Banks wrote the foreword to the first international anthology of creative writing by nurses, *Between the Heartbeats: Poetry and Prose by Nurses* (1995). She wrote, "The truth is that when we are sick, very sick, it is often the nurse who is closest to our bodies, minds, and souls." Yet even with this privileged access to patients' lives, nurses—at that time—rarely wrote creatively about their work. But over the years, we have achieved something rich and significant. Now, more than two decades after *Between the Heartbeats,* we have a fully realized, international force of nurse writers. A gentle but strong creative bridge has grown to span the divide between nurses' professional roles and their literary responses to those roles. Just as healing tissue closes a wound, the divide no longer exists.

Nurses who *write* creatively *think* creatively. Can you imagine the anxiety patients feel, how fearful they are, pre-op? Can you imagine a patient's devastation when he or she is diagnosed with a serious illness, or the fear of a young and vulnerable student's first day on a busy ward? Imagination is in every nurse's toolbox, right there next to thermometers and sphygmomanometers. Of course the content of the toolbox keeps evolving with advances in technology, but a nurse's mind, heart, and hands are still the basic tools, regardless of how and where a nurse is educated or where a nurse might be practicing. The nurses in this volume demonstrate how imagination and creativity can elevate the discourse about professional nursing education to an art form—literature that gives us a glimpse into the early days of nursing school experiences.

Nurses choose to enter nursing education for a variety of reasons. Celia Brown in "My First Journey Abroad" writes: "For an Irish girl coming to Stoke, many adjustments were required. My teachers at home had already decided that my future would be better served as a scholar, and several of them were vocal in their disappointment. Nobody, not even my mother, seemed to understand that a nursing career, however improbable my choice, presented me, the oldest of ten, with a ready-made job. I was already a family caregiver; it was on that basis that I chose nursing."

In retrospect, how we were taught to perform even the simplest nursing tasks is refreshing and often humorous. Amy Haddad writes it succinctly in "Ablutions": "We were taught how to fold the washcloth just so over our cupped hands. The cold, wet tails of the cloth's corners were tucked in to keep them from dragging over the patient's body while we washed an arm or a leg. I would practice this technique when I washed myself in the morning, carefully mimicking my instructor's actions, standing in front of the mirror, watching myself wash my hand, arm, shoulder, armpit." I still fold a washcloth in this manner. While a simple maneuver, it was based both on comfort and science—comfort for the patient and the separation of soiled and clean supplies.

Nursing is a sophisticated scientific profession that requires knowledge of anatomy and physiology. In "My Most Selfless 'Patient,' My Greatest Teacher," Patricia Kalas writes, "As our cadaver was uncovered, I held my breath. As I focused on the figure on the table, I saw a pale, elderly gentleman with gray hair and a slender, healthy-appearing build. He reminded me a little of Reverend Riley from our church, the father of Margaret, my classmate from school in Gustavus, and a very admirable person. As I continued to consider the person before me, I began to wonder about him. What had happened to him? How did he get here—was this his intention?"

Scientific knowledge is put to use in student clinical rotations right from the start. Stacy Nigliazzo, in her poem "Rotation," recalls the challenge of her first day as a student in the OR: "It was winter / the surgeon's blade, / steady across a spider web inside the open abdomen. / What's this I'm cutting into? / The omentum, sir. / How many feet of small bowel in the gut? / Roughly twenty-five, sir. / And in the colon? / Roughly five to ten, sir. / Hold out your hand—."

Over time, education and experience blend to become nursing skill. Happily, for many nurses, that skill expands to include the literary arts that describe and thereby decode the self and the other. Belle Waring in "You Could Have Been Me" tells a story in powerful and illuminating poetry: "Ultrasound, imperceptible to anyone but bats, / will pass through liquid and bounce off solid / as sonar reveals a torpedo. / As it sees a malignant mass. / Doctors are whispering. / One looks over: You mind us talking? / Talk, I said. Sing, if you feel like it. / I walked straight out of that hospital / the moment the just-set-sun was casting a pearl shell over the city."

Student nurses must also master the intuitive skills necessary to care for and deal with a variety of individuals. Fear of not saying "the right thing," fear of being misunderstood, fear of not having all the answers—these concerns might rise up when a student first cares for a patient. Sr. Frances Smalkowski ("The Silent Treatment") describes one nurse's dilemma: "This fear made it hard for me to relate to my new patient. Someone looking at us would have seen Mr. Loy and me sitting side by side in silence. Occasionally I'd make attempts at conversation. These long periods of silence, as it turned out, were therapeutic—for me. Being outgoing by nature, I found sitting with Mr. Loy difficult, even painful. But, sitting beside him, I could see how irrational my fears were." Silence, once learned, is the *tabula rasa* upon which the art of nursing thrives; silence is a language spoken by all. It is the music that goes before every note of love that a nurse's hands can offer.

In this anthology, we see how the student moves from first-experience fears to comfort with patients, confidence with nursing skills, and preparation to face a future that holds a cascade of unknowns. Some of our nursing education is strict and formal; much of our ongoing education evolves from the very essence of who we are and who our mentors have been. And, as so many authors in this collection attest, our patients are our first and best mentors. When stories of our professional, educational initiations are shared from the nurse's point of view, a rare opportunity presents for the reader. Much can be learned here—not the usual "see one, do one, teach one," but instead I would encourage "read one, write one, share one." Nurses, quiet no longer. Artful discourse is how we learn and how we heal ourselves, as well as others. And in the process, we elevate our nursing practice in fulfillment of our earliest nursing educational hopes and aspirations, with gratitude to our families, our teachers, our colleagues and, always, to our patients.

ACKNOWLEDGMENTS

Our gratitude to the editors of these journals and publications in which some of the work in this anthology previously appeared:

Jeanne Bryner: "Life Flight" first appeared in the author's poetry collection, *Both Shoes Off* (Bottom Dog Press)

Joanne Clarkson: "First Patient" first appeared in an earlier version in the author's chapbook, *Believing the Body* (Gribble Press)

Elayne Clift: "Whiteout" first appeared in *CHEST* (Journal of American College of Chest Physicians)

Cortney Davis: "Selling Kisses at the Diner" first appeared in *Alimentum: The Literature of Food;* "Wednesday's Child" first appeared in *Pulse: Voices from the Heart of Medicine;* "The Nurse's First Autopsy" first appeared in the journal *Labor: Studies in Working-Class History of the Americas* (Duke University Press); "I Want To Work in a Hospital" first appeared in *Bellevue Literary Review;* "Surgical Rotation" originally appeared in the author's poetry collection *Taking Care of Time* (Michigan State University Press)

Theodore Deppe: "Little Colloquium by the Sea" is an excerpt from a poem of the same title that first appeared in the author's poetry collection, *Liminal Blue* (Arlen House)

Amy Haddad: "Ablutions" first appeared in *Fetishes,* the literary journal of the University of Colorado Health Sciences Center

Nancy Kerrigan: "From Beginning to End" first appeared as "My First Therapy Patient" in the author's chapbook *The Voices: The Poetry of Psychiatry* (Finishing Line Press).

Jeanne LeVasseur: "Each One Alone" first appeared in *Tar Wolf Review*

Veneta Masson: "Morning Report" and "Passages" first appeared in the author's poetry collection, *Rehab at the Florida Avenue Grill* (Sage Femme Press)

Madeleine Mysko: "Calvert and Pleasant" first appeared in the *Baltimore Sun* (under the headline "A Monument to Memory"); "The Sacraments of Sister Thecla" and "The Sister on the Chronic Ward" first appeared in *American Journal of Nursing* 111.5 (May 2011): 72 and in *American Journal of Nursing* 105.9 (September 2005), respectively, and are reprinted with permission

Stacy Nigliazzo: "Rotation" first appeared in *The Yale Journal for Humanities and Medicine;* "In My First Year" first appeared in the *American Journal of Nursing* 112.12 (December 2012) and is reprinted with permission

Sr. Frances Smalkowski: "The Silent Treatment" first appeared in *Pulse: Voices from the Heart of Medicine*

Eileen Valinoti: "Hospital Corners" first appeared in *Pulse: Voices from the Heart of Medicine*

The braiding of diverse voices and historical photographs was a collaborative effort. We respectfully thank Dr. Renee Carter-Perpall; Christine Fowler, Mercy Health Archives; DeAnn Russell, Hannah E. Mullins Archives; Davina Gosnell, RN, PhD, FAAN, emeriti dean and professor, Kent State University College of Nursing, and founding nursing program director of Hiram College (retired); Shirley Harrow, RN; Dr. Steve Tilley, Department of Nursing Studies, University of Edinburgh (retired); Alistair Tough, archivist, NHS Greater Glasgow and Clyde and Senior Lecturer, University of Glasgow; Mrs. Alma Topen, University of Glasgow; and Patricia Waring.

INTRODUCTION

Jeanne Bryner

When Cortney Davis asked me to join hands with her and coedit an anthology about student nurse experiences, I was excited and intimidated to receive such an invitation but quickly agreed to be her partner. Have I edited before? Yes, I have. In every workshop I've conducted, we created anthologies of the work, and every time, I grew as a teacher and human being. Holding poems and stories of children, university students, breast cancer survivors, elders, and community participants, I saw language tunneled, shaped, and examined in a different light, which empowered authors and enlightened readers.

Maybe stories are the last ground we can claim as our very own, and if we choose not to, well, we don't have to welcome you to our porch. Even in a blizzard, we don't have to leave the light on. To share even a morsel of our story is sacred, as sacred as breaking bread with a stranger, making a place for her at your table. When editors create a satchel for stories, a yoke of honor and responsibility gets bundled. For however long it takes, you cannot remove this yoke; you cannot set it down. Cortney and I set out to do our work.

Dear reader, if I say the words *student nurse* to one hundred of you, what image does your mind's eye behold? Do you see the hospital's pilgrims as *other* or as yourself, serving an apprenticeship in your chosen field, filled with trepidation and uncertainty? On our journey to become the best human beings we can be, we are all apprentices. We embark on *insufficient knowledge,* as Robert Frost so wisely stated in "Voices and Visions," a 1990s PBS special.

Cortney and I placed a call for work in *Poets & Writers* magazine, sent emails to our sister/brother nurse writers, wrote letters to national and international nursing organizations, placed phone calls, passed out flyers to nursing audiences, and held writing workshops for colleagues. Poles in the water, we waited for bites, and sure enough, our poles commenced to bend. I never met an angler who didn't stretch the truth about her catch, but the depth, the heartfelt stories, poems, and essays in this collection are as shimmery as a table heaped with rainbow trout. I mean to tell you we are so very honored to receive the communion of these voices. We truly are.

Let me begin with our respected elders as I have been raised up to do. Rosa M. Sacharin, Minnie Brown Carter, and Helen L. Albert provide an unyielding foundation for this house of voices you are about to enter. They have traveled a long way, pushed by winds that were not of their choosing. If I say the words *Kindertrasport project,* what images will your mind behold? Will you see thirteen-year-old Rosa in 1938 being taken from her German homeland with close to 9,500 other Jewish children to be saved from Hitler's death camps? Will you hear her crying in the night for her parents, her sister, and brother? Will you feel the weight of her doll as she carries it off the ship into England? And can you imagine the faces of strangers opening their homes to her? To the other children? Can you see her moved like a chess piece later to Scotland and working as a domestic for two years before she was allowed to reenter school, graduate, and then be asked, "What will you do now?" And by that time in her young life, knowing her father and brother perished in the camps, what should Rosa say to those who have saved her life? In such a life, there's little time for grief and, I suspect, even less time for dolls.

At ninety pounds, Minnie Brown Carter's family doctor told her he didn't believe she could become a nurse; the work would be too taxing for a person her size. But she gathered herself and went forward, her eyes always on her dream. A woman of color born in Lynchburg, Virginia, Minnie was accepted and educated as a World War II army nurse cadet at Hampton Institute Nursing School, Dixie Hospital, class of 1947. Here Minnie would rail against the indignities of entering through the hospital's back entrance door for *coloreds.* She and her classmates would raise their voices in protest and eventually be able to walk through the hospital's front doors. If I tell you that white patients refused baths from her or changes in dressing or even comfort, can you feel the rush of blood rise to her cheeks like a slap? I hope you can. I truly do. At age ninety-one, Minnie Brown Carter is the last African American WWII nurse cadet alive, and I am proud to report, still raising her voice to get veterans' benefits for the WWII nurse cadets.

Born in Alabama's segregated south in 1925, Helen L. McClendon Albert was one of eight black women admitted to Birmingham's Norwood Hospital School of Nursing where she'd graduate as the 1943 class valedictorian. When, initially, Helen was denied admission to that nursing school, Dr. W. B. Martin, her employer, went to Norwood and urged she be given a seat the next year. She had worked for Dr. and Mrs. Martin for several years, helping with housework, children, and laundry. Dr. Martin had a clinic in her hometown of Argo, Alabama. He was respectful of all persons and well respected. If I tell you that Helen, at the tender age of seven, and her widowed mother rose at 4:00 A.M. in order to catch a ride with other cotton pickers by 5:00 A.M. and they'd stand in the truck's bed so more people could fit in and they'd earn fifty cents for each hundred-pound sack, whose life would you say was blessed? Helen's or the cotton's?

Our shared goals for this anthology were diversity in age, gender, race, nationality, socioeconomic opportunity, and education. When I emailed my friend and nurse educator Dr. Steve Tilley about the project, he offered to help me identify nurses who might be interested in contributing their stories. Thanks to Steve's help, nurses Rosa M. Sacharin and Mary Gavan both agreed to contribute to the anthology. Born in Scotland, Mary Gavan is retired after forty years of palliative care nursing and also a well-known storyteller, traveling to places like Dubai and Iran to share stories of her Celtic heritage.

Nurses are taught to observe closely and to document meticulously, and so it's natural that we might also transmit the stories of our lives in writing. For morning care, in the decades leading up to the late twentieth century, we used to gather a basin, soap, and hot water to bathe our patients. We included several nurse stories in this anthology about this sacred activity, for those types of baths—like our white caps and clinic shoes—are no longer in style. Reusable metal or plastic basins have been replaced with prepackaged cleansers that do not require rinsing and are meant to decrease the transmission of hospital-acquired infections—but, dear reader, we grieve for the loss of steam rising on the overbed stands. We old-school nurses understand the reason for the update, but we wanted you to know how we learned to memorize the unmarked paths and hollows of bodies. Pesky particles of superbugs were somewhere floating in the future, but, being student nurses, we didn't have time to fret over that distant planet. We were too busy learning to navigate the craters and mountains of this one. Come early evening, we used to have a sort of folding in of our days. We'd load the cart with some fresh linens and start down the hall to give back rubs, change a soiled draw sheet, turn pillows, and tidy up the bedside stands. As the warm lotion went up and down a spine, much was shared, even if the patient couldn't speak or didn't want to speak or was hurting too much to speak. Our hands did all the talking, and the very act of touch—how we stroked the bodies of the sick—became our art form: a ballet of hands on aging flesh, a secret wish we carried in our heart's pocket for those patients waiting, yes, waiting for the *nurse*, waiting for us. Even as we worked, our own cells were dying, pushing us over some unseen cliff and into our chair of old age.

The nurses in this anthology have an age span of about seventy-five years. Our youngest contributors, recent graduates, are in their twenties and our elders are in their nineties. I grieve that we could not gather more stories, but student nurses are extremely busy, working nurses are overextended, and even retired nurses tend to have full schedules, so we are grateful to all who took the time to write about their student nurse days. They have come together in this space to bear witness to how they learned to crawl and walk, stand and speak as professionals, and be heard not just for themselves but for the most vulnerable entrusted to their care. To the legions of student nurses who will follow these writers who share their experiences in this anthology and who will soon care for their own patients, we urge you to listen and remember well these stories. We hope that everyone connected to healing professions will acknowledge and appreciate the shoulders they stand on. The few voices in this anthology must stand for so many twentieth-century nurses. Computers have changed how nurses' fingers record pain and administer treatments and doctors' orders, but not how our hearts process our patients' suffering and the shared relief we have when they are healed. When I learned to be a nurse, we students were encouraged to talk or write reflectively only in our psychiatric nursing class. It was combined with community nursing, as I recall, but I could never stop reflecting on the bravery of my patients day after day, year after year, and so I became a writer like the courageous nurses you are about to meet in these pages.

We did not go out beating the bushes for famous nurses but found out after we chose their poems, stories, and essays that these were highly respected and skilled practitioners. In the beginning, we just knew they had a good story that deserved to be shared. Many of our contributors did not start out desiring to become nurses, but then, suddenly or not so suddenly, they felt called to the profession. And a few left nursing for sociology or the priesthood or music but still identify as nurses and, for the most part, would return to nursing. One contributor who, as a student lacked the support of those who should have been her mentors, was unable to finish her studies in nursing. She still wonders how her life would have been different if she had. The dream deferred is an important ageless tale, and we are grateful for her sharing such a difficult truth.

We are, all of us, like a platoon put together by the fates. One of our tribe, Belle Waring, recently died of colon cancer. She was with us in the first creative writing anthology and continued to write poignant poems about her life as a nurse, so like any unit worth its salt, we carried her beautiful spirit with us, refused to leave her behind. Many of our contributors have had painful passages. Minnie Brown Carter's mother died when she was seven years old. Another one of our contributor's parents were killed in a car crash when she was thirteen, and Helen Albert failed state boards the first time she took them. "Honey," Helen told me, "I'm no test taker, but I'm no quitter, so I took it again, and I passed. Thank God." One test score does not a life make. These are the winds that shape us as we move through our days. Like our patients, we don't get to choose; we just learn how to walk through the fire and be forever changed. More than ever, our young nurses—no, our young people—need these stories, are starved for these real heroes, and do not even know they are hungry. Shame on all of us if we do not call them to supper.

How many times have I stomped my foot saying the world needs to hear more stories about the lives of nurses? And wasn't this project just a grand way to bring a new choir to the stage? We'd be asking nurses to become time travelers, and, from the beginning, I felt the journey would be life changing for me, for them.

Sometimes memory is a pocketknife, something shiny and folded and hidden. We bring it out when we need it. We marvel at the many ways it serves us over time and fails us as we age.

Over the years, memory becomes our Grand Canyon, lined with switchbacks, narrow paths dusty from mule trains carrying dreams and nightmares. All the uncertain footbridges between the chasm of ache and wonder remain here. If I say the words *student nurse* to you now—all of you who have read this little note about a handful of well-lived lives—what image will your mind's eye behold? We are heading into a Grand Canyon, so gather your gear and kerchief; you'll need both as we have sent someone ahead to make camp and start a good supper.

PART I

There are no choices here,

this is devotion, this work

has nothing to do with wages,

this work is a universe, yours

with dimensions drawn to fit

only you.

LUCIA CORDELL GETSI, "NURSING"

I have never been so afraid.

Welcome to our neighborhood. See the clothes we're taking off the lines? Nursing students, the world over must leave their old lives behind and put on the uniform of servitude. People are fearful, of course, in any new area of study, but nursing students know their actions or missteps may forever alter the course of a person's life. When we are students, first learning the art of nursing, fear of failure and exhaustion sew themselves inside our lab coat pockets. They weigh us down. Hours devoted to studies and clinical labs are grueling, but through the fog of fatigue we rise, for we have been called. Upon graduation, our uniforms will change, but emotional labor and rough shifts do not lose their intensity.

LINDA MAURER TUTHILL

A School for Hands

After the ward rounds, basin baths,
the rigors of making
occupied beds, bottom sheets
stretched drum-tight,
we student nurses sigh into afternoon.

The nourishment cart rattles
in the corridor, dispensing juice
and Lorna Doones or graham squares.
Aides refill metal water pitchers
beaded with sweat, ice already failing.

Expected to offer P.M. back rubs,
we pull flimsy curtains for a hint of privacy.
Fancy French massage terms:
effleurage, petrissage, friction, learned
in class, ping pong in our heads.

Our bodies rock, a rhythmic blur of blue,
as supple hands knead and stroke
from tail of spine to shoulders.
At this school for hands, we speak
with the warm vowels and consonants of touch.

Linda Maurer Tuthill, Johns Hopkins Hospital School of Nursing, 1963. Courtesy Linda Maurer Tuthill.

SAUNDRA SARSANY

For Now

Everything here is quiet
and I'm thinking
of the day I left home
for nursing school in 1957.

I had to say goodbye
to my family. When we
arrived, we were sent home.
Our school was new and not

ready. So back home
for two more weeks, then
start over again. Two weeks
into classes, I had my appendix

out. Finally, back
and in Nursing Arts lab, you
Miss Beamer, said my petticoat
(a can-can slip) made too much noise.

You sent me out to the restroom
where I took it off. My slip
was new and not ready to be mute.
You were very strict, very critical.

Saundra Sarsany, Trumbull Memorial Hospital graduate, 1960. Courtesy Saundra Sarsany.

We were so scared, called you
the witch. Maybe we can start
over again, Miss Beamer. Tea?
A ham sandwich between
dusting stars? A happy meal?

Saundra Sarsany, flight nurse, 1986. Courtesy Saundra Sarsany.

SAUNDRA SARSANY

I Became a Nurse

Because my Aunt Peg
was an Army Nurse in WWII,
because she let me play
with her nurse's caps,
lieutenant bars and med ampules.
Because I worshipped her,
because she gave me a picture
of the *Nightingale Pledge* for my room.
I knew then I would also be a nurse.
Because of Aunt Peg, I went to the library,
read every volume of Sue Barton,
Registered Nurse, over and over.
Because there were so many fields
of nursing. Because of her, I went
into nursing school at her alma mater,
found out how I loved caring for patients.
Because of Aunt Peg, I found my life
calling, calling, calling.

Saundra Sarsany's Aunt Peg Noderer, First Lt. Army Nurse Corps, WWII, 1942–1944, field hospital in England. Courtesy Saundra Sarsany.

BARBARA BROOME

I Am Not Superwoman

I can name a room full of people who say they always wanted to be a nurse. But, I'm not one of them. I grew up in rural Ohio, where my parents worked hard to make ends meet. Often we were without heat in the winter because we couldn't afford both heat and food, and food was more important. Those cold evenings, I was happy to huddle under extra blankets and watch TV.

In my eyes, my dad was the biggest man in the world. He worked full time at a bumper plant and part time as our township constable. My mother cleaned houses for teachers, a dentist, and lawyers, professionals who lived in what we used to call "town." In reality, it was only a village, but it seemed like a big town to a kid who never saw traffic lights. In those days, black families, intentionally segregated, lived grouped in one area and white families lived in the "richer" areas with conveniences such as running water and sewage. My family had pumps in the yard and outside toilets. To this day, I believe my early environment, so divided between poor and "wealthy," made me want to be "like them." Not really sure what *like them* meant, but I wanted to be able to take a bath in a nice tub with bubbles and hot water out of the tap, water that didn't have to be heated on the stove.

Because my mother needed help cleaning houses, I missed a lot of school. We were paid a whopping seven dollars per house. If I went with mom, we could clean two homes a day. Although we never made a lot of money, the families often gave us clothes and shoes, things I didn't have in my closet. These hand-me-downs were the only store-bought clothes I owned; the others were homemade, using patterns from McCall's, Butterick, and Simplicity. Mom taught me to sew when I was nine. Those corduroy jumpers and gingham skirts were made with patience and attention. One of my favorites was a gray jumper with pockets. I wore that

Barbara Broome, Dean, Kent State University College of Nursing, 2014. Courtesy of Barbara Broome. Photo by Bob Christi.

jumper until I couldn't hold my breath enough to fit inside it. The kids who made fun of me didn't know how long it takes to press a pattern and line up a zipper—we may have been poor, but I remember all the ways in which I was loved.

Maybe because I missed a lot of school, I had a love-hate relationship with it. I enjoyed school when I was able to attend because it was fun to learn, but I also hated it because I was the outsider and had few friends. In May 1966, I graduated from high school, and my only aspiration was to get a job. I found work in a collection agency—ironically one that had my parents in collection—but it was a job, and even earning less than $1.50 an hour, I was proud. In August, I was married and continued to work. Soon, an opportunity to work at a local hospital's business office presented itself for $3.05 an hour. I worked there until, two years later, my husband and I had our daughter, a bundle of joy. When I returned to the hospital, I landed in the admissions office until, three years later, we welcomed our son. With a new baby and a toddler, back to the hospital I went, but this time as the admissions supervisor, with responsibility for inpatient, outpatient, and all cost containment programs. Still, nursing was the furthest thing from my mind.

After seven years at the hospital, I left to become the office manager for a local health-care specialist. A year later, I was unemployed. Like so many, I never saw it coming. My self-esteem was shattered, and I was angry. For the first time in my life, I applied for and received unemployment compensation. But I *wanted* to work—and I realized the need for further education.

I decided that only I could control my destiny and not give others the ability to destroy me. Then, within six months of losing my job, my father died of cardiac arrest. I had a solid background in the business workings of health care, and now I was introduced to the challenges of caregiving in a dramatic way. I began

Barbara Broome (lower left, first seated student in row one) with her fellow nursing school graduates, Hannah E. Mullins School of Practical Nursing, 1994. Courtesy Hannah E. Mullins Archives.

to consider that nursing might be a path for me, but I was unsure. Wanting to be sure nursing was a *calling* and not simply an impulse based on my long-term association with hospitals, I stepped back from health care completely and took a job as a manager and buyer for an office supply company. In less than six months, I knew this career was not for me—nursing was. I applied to a licensed practical nursing program, Hannah Mullins in Salem, Ohio, and I was accepted.

I drove more than fifty miles a day to class after getting up, dressing my children, taking them to the sitter, and leaving at five in the morning to arrive in class by seven. My husband was working full time, and we both left the house by 5:00 A.M. It was a grueling schedule, but I was determined. My patients, especially my minority patients, often offered inspiration and encouragement, perhaps sensing that, like them, I had to work hard for my education and my future. My dedication paid off, and I was voted class president. At my graduation in 1985, it was me, a girl who used to scrub floors with her mom, the girl who wore handmade gingham blouses, giving the final class address. What an honor! After passing my licensure examinations, I worked at a local nursing home and in a year applied at the hospital where I'd previously worked; I was hired for the Intensive and Cardiac Care Step-Down Units.

My mother was so proud of me. She would tell others *my daughter saves lives.* "I am so proud of her; we scrubbed floors together, and look at her now." My husband and children had also been my constant cheerleaders, putting my semester transcript on the refrigerator, just as I did with their report cards. When I had good grades, my husband would take me and our kids to Dairy Queen. Those hot fudge sundaes were so good.

Unfortunately, my mom's health began to fail. She'd been diagnosed with cervical cancer and had received radiation. I emptied every drawer of my nursing skills to help my mother, but her cancer spread and she developed lung cancer. Love was not enough; she died Thanksgiving Day 1986, after being in the intensive care unit on a ventilator for over a month. In memory of my parents, I understood the value of advanced education; health care was changing, and I wanted to be ready to be a part of its evolution. As a nurse leader, I'd be able to implement cutting-edge research and guide students to become creative and critical thinkers. My dream was to assist my community, my students, and my patients to function at their highest level—to live, not just exist. I wanted to help others experience minimal suffering at their journey's end.

I called a family meeting. After intense conversations with my husband and children, we decided it was time for me to take the next step and become a registered nurse. I applied and was accepted to Kent State University and, while elated, I realized I had lots of hurdles ahead of me. Indeed, I was fortunate to have a husband and children who supported me. I continued to work full time as an LPN, go to classes, and be a student worker in Kent's Anatomy Lab and the Tutoring Center while still fulfilling my role as a wife and mother. Four years later, I graduated and received an Ohio Board of Regents Fellowship to continue my education. Mom and Dad never got to see me graduate; however, I always felt my parents' presence. They were with me every step of the way, urging me to do my best. They both lived in my heart, and unafraid, I took the next step and entered the master's program.

Hospital colleagues warned me that I was educating myself out of a job. Some made comments such as "those that can do; those that can't teach." I knew that taunts from others were merely projections of their own life frustrations: I had to stay focused. Once again, I worked full time while being a part-time graduate assistant. In two years, I graduated as a clinical nurse specialist in medical surgical nursing with a minor in mental health nursing. Then, I was hired as faculty at Kent State; my assignment was to start a nursing program at the regional campus.

I was over the moon because I was giving back to my community, and I loved teaching even as I continued working as a hospital nursing supervisor. My career path had been one of "stepped" experiences, and I could draw upon these experiences to help other students accomplish their goals. University employment meant I must make a decision: tenure versus nontenure. A tenured position required more education, and that's what I wanted. I applied and was accepted into the PhD program at the University of Pittsburgh.

This was indeed a true challenge on so many levels: travel to Pittsburgh, cost (I was an out of state student), family with teenagers, and a full-time faculty position. I am not superwoman, not even close, but I knew I had to do this. Focused on success and personal achievement, when I least expected it a challenge and an opportunity for growth arrived: my advisor urged me to write a National Institutes of Health Minority Supplement grant. I'd never written a grant before, but my advisor was determined that I needed to do this on my own. My will to survive kicked in and the rest, as they say, *is history.*

In my new role as Dean of Kent State University's College of Nursing, I face waves of frustrations and victories, but steering a mighty ship gives me a sense of accomplishment. And yes, I am proud of myself. I've been on the floor with a scrub brush, and now I'm standing tall. Opportunity exists, but we all need mentors who are active listeners, who see the promise within us, and who encourage us in our course of action. The work of education is difficult, it's one-day-at-a-time baby steps that lead to experience and success. And my path, like that of so many others, has been long and often difficult. But I'm now able to share my story with students, understand their life challenges, see their potential, and offer them guidance.

Truly, every time a student graduates, it is a gift.

ANNE WEBSTER

One Nurse's Education

In September 1958, I entered nursing school at Piedmont Hospital in Atlanta. My divorced mother worked as a stenographer and couldn't afford to send me to college, but I had received a scholarship for $175 toward the total tuition of $300 for three years that included uniforms, room and board, and medical care. As I moved into the student dorm on the sixth and top floor of the hospital, I was happy to be there, despite having little interest in nursing. My only other choice had been to take a secretarial job like my mother's, and I knew how she hated her work.

Though each room had a private bath, the quarters were cramped. We crowded three girls, three beds, three dressers, and three desks in a space intended for a single patient. One coat closet held all of our clothes. Still, we were excited to be out in the world and away from home.

Weekday mornings we rode a bus downtown to Georgia State University for lectures on anatomy, sociology, and psychology. In the afternoons we had classes at the hospital, such as nursing arts, where we learned basic skills like how to make beds with mitered corners. Using each other as dummies, we practiced "log-rolling" and giving bed baths and treatments, such as "pretend" enemas.

The second quarter, our college classes took place after lunch, enabling us to work with patients in the mornings and put our new skills to use. I was assigned to a med/surg floor where I had seven or eight patients for "A.M. care," which included giving each patient a bath and making his or her bed with fresh sheets. It taught me a valuable lesson in budgeting time, as it was a challenge to finish these tasks by noon.

That term, our subjects at Georgia State were bacteriology, organic chemistry, and advanced anatomy and physiology, all requiring a great deal of rote memorization. Often after the mandatory 10 P.M. lights-out, we sat in our pajamas in the dimly

Anne Webster, Piedmont Hospital School of Nursing graduate, 1961. Courtesy Anne Webster.

lit hallway, chanting the periodic table of elements and reciting the cranial nerves to the rhyme "On old Olympius' towering top, a Finn and German viewed some hops," our way of remembering the cranial nerves—olfactory, optic, oculomoter, trochlear, trigeminal, abducens, facial, vestibulo-cochlear, glossopharyngeal, vagus spinal accessory, and hypoglossal.

When we had survived the finals in those courses, it seemed a relief to have all our classes at the hospital. We continued to work with patients each morning and had lectures after lunch, plus giving A.M. care to patients on weekends. We were lucky to have a full day off twice a month. If I sat still for more than five minutes, my eyelids drifted downward.

But I didn't dare nod off during pharmacology, which covered dozens of drugs and their classifications, actions, and side effects. The teacher made it clear that even if a doctor ordered the wrong drug or the wrong dose of the correct medicine, the blame fell on the nurse who administered the medicine.

Our class in nursing arts became more advanced when we learned about sterile technique, spinal taps, and catheterizations. The instructor gave us each a checklist, and after we had completed a protocol satisfactorily in the presence of an RN or instructor, we would "check it off," and could perform the procedure without supervision.

We began our second year as upperclassmen and were assigned to work six weeks in every department, including Central Service, Dietary, Surgery, and Obstetrics. On my first assignment, I found myself fixing patients' trays on a conveyor belt and planning meals for those on special diets. In Central Service I learned to set up surgical instruments wrapped in green towels and to operate the giant autoclaves we used to sterilize them.

The three months that I spent on the OB floor were mostly on the night shift, where I learned to dread the weeks of a full moon. I often sat for hours in a dark labor room, my hand on a woman's belly, timing her contractions. When they were less than two minutes apart, I would call the doctor from the staff room, and we would push her stretcher down the hall to the delivery room, roll her onto the table, and strap her legs into stirrups. After we scrubbed and gowned, I would pass instruments to the doctor who sat on a stool between the woman's legs. At first I wavered between horror and nausea when the doctor injected a numbing agent around the vagina, then crunched through the perineum with shiny scissors to open the birth canal. But by the time I had assisted with one hundred births, little impressed or horrified me.

When assigned to a patient unit, we worked the evening or night shifts. RNs were scarce after the day shift, so two students shared responsibility for fifty-six patients. We had to hustle to give medicines and treatments on time. If we had questions, we called the supervisor, but only as a last resort since she covered

the entire hospital. Despite the terrible hours, I liked being in charge, and, even better, I didn't have to give baths.

I returned to the land of the living with my surgery rotation. The operating room cranked up at 6:30 A.M. and—barring an emergency—closed down by late afternoon. We students worked as "scrub nurses," passing instruments and sutures to the surgeons. Abdominal surgeries became technicolor magic when a doctor plunged his hands into an open belly, pulled out intestines, and lay them on sterile towels beside the incision before pointing out a liver or stomach in the dark abdominal cavity.

Our class split into two groups at the beginning of the third year when we were sent to other hospitals to study pediatric and psychiatric nursing. That fall my group went to Birmingham to work three months at the Children's Hospital. The patients were a welcome change from the often-cranky adult patients at Piedmont. The children bounced in their beds and held out their arms to us when we came on duty.

Many of the babies had congenital anomalies, such as holes in their hearts or cleft palates that required surgical corrections. Others with diarrhea often looked like withered old people. A tiny six-month-old, named Ricky Ricardo after the TV character, had staph boils on his buttocks, along with the usual diarrhea. I once took care of premature twins, babies born at home (whose mentally challenged mother had dropped them off at the hospital in a shoe box). The babies were so small I thought they looked like baby rats.

On returning to Atlanta, I was assigned to alternating evening and night shifts and attended classes during the day. My classmates and I thought we knew it all. We could dispense medicines while slightly tipsy from early dates, dodge interns who cornered us in the kitchen at 2:00 A.M., and handle complaining patients. Intensive care, cardiac units, and monitors didn't exist, so we did our best to take care of gray-skinned men in oxygen tents, fresh postoperative patients, and anything the emergency room sent up.

When we ran into problems, we weren't allowed to disturb the private admitting physicians at home. If a patient needed medicine that had not been ordered, had chest pain, or started bleeding, we called the intern and prayed he would answer. We soon learned which ordinary medicines we could give without orders.

Then, when the intern managed to appear, he would obligingly write orders to cover what we'd given.

After Christmas that last year, our class split up again; half of us went to Milledgeville State Hospital for psychiatric training. We worked in the admission building and attended intake examinations where a psychiatrist asked each patient a set of questions, such as the year, month, and day or the name of the president. Many of the patients seemed normal while others cowered or wept.

We escorted the women patients to the shower and helped them dress. On the men's wards, we played gin rummy and listened to lame jokes—easy duty after working nights at Piedmont. Even better was the fact that we had every weekend off, but not until we had paid a price. Each Friday afternoon the wards emptied out, and patients streamed into the cavernous gymnasium. On stage stood a small band of patients sawing out tunes on fiddles and strumming guitars. The student nurses were required to dance with any patient who asked them. For two hours we bumped bellies with old men in overalls, drooling boys, and some who claimed to be Napoleon, counting the minutes until we could pile into someone's car and head back to Atlanta.

When the wisteria began to bloom in March, we returned to Piedmont for our last six months of training. Now seasoned nurses, we gave up all pretense of attending class and instead staffed the hospital on evening and night shifts, ticking off the time until we would become real nurses, paid for our work.

In June, our class held a joint graduation ceremony with the class that had begun three months ahead of us. After that night, they became graduates and free women. But even with diplomas in hand, my classmates and I had three more months as students. The time ground by like a glacier moving down a mountain as I worked those final weeks, holed up on evening and night shifts.

When September finally arrived, my classmates and I were so glad to be free that no one seemed sad about going our separate ways. Only later would we realize that those three years of what we considered "hardship" had enabled us to do work that touched people's lives. A half century later, I regularly call my old roommates and count them among my closest friends. I proudly look back on my years of hospital training and treasure the lifelong friendships with my classmates and the precious moments I've spent with patients, all made possible by nursing school.

JEANNE LeVASSEUR

Each One, Alone

In the cupboard are the pungent
jars of alcohol, and near the wall
the table to which I will come,
fumbling under my gloves.
This is the first time I will reach
into a thick-webbed recess,
my left hand spooling
for the ping of an ovary
or the darker bell-note of tumor.
I, too, have apricots, a pear,
the trailing vines of a tree.
You are thirteen, shy, and lie so still,
it could all be painted—
the white table, shining fruit.
You pull a sheaf of hair across your face.
It serves as leaves and you are gone
deeper, swinging down into yourself
like church bells.

Jeanne LeVasseur, Pace University graduate, 1980. Courtesy Jeanne LeVasseur.

JEANNE LeVASSEUR

Becoming Real

It could be saving a life—the push-push of IV fluids,
paddles on the chest,
but for me it is a day like any other,
routine diagnosis—
Another Teen Girl Has Herpes.

So when she asks, "Will I love again?"
I am astonished by the reverberations.
Incurable, contagious—
how will she negotiate the ravishing transitions,
chambray shirt sliding from her shoulders,
torn jeans unzipped, the whole lush undressing
with someone new who must be told.

She sits, her head bowed.
So I say, she will know this new love
when it comes,
she does not need to know the words
now, they, too, will come.
And what is right will follow.

She sits at the table's edge
with her shining eyes
and I know enough to listen,
to stand beside her and take the tiny flashlight
they gave me in nursing school
and shine it on her glorious, technicolored future.

MADELEINE MYSKO

The Sacraments of Sister Thecla

When I was a nursing student, back in the late '60s, Principles of Nursing was held in a dim classroom on the first floor of our nurses' residence. There the freshmen students would sit in the old, theater-style tiers, intent on the instructions of Sister Thecla.

Sister Thecla was tall, thin, and slightly stooped. We "girls" were only eighteen, and thought she was old. But now it occurs to me that her posture probably reflected humility—or perhaps the discomfort of shyness—more than it did her age. Her voice quavered a bit, like that of a maiden great-aunt. Her face wore an expression of continual mild concern. She was not one of those nuns whose gaze you feared. Sister Thecla's pale eyes were often looking away, or down at her spotless shoes.

Sister Thecla taught us that nursing was "an art and a science." She taught us the proper order of the full bed bath, the modesties of the "local bath," the imperatives of the back rub, and the refinements of the draw sheet, the emesis basin, and the ordinary washcloth. Sister Thecla demonstrated that the art and science of nursing required all the scrupulous attention to detail of a priest celebrating High Mass.

At the center of Sister Thecla's demonstrations was an old mannequin that lived all its days on the hospital bed at the front of the classroom. I can still see the chipped, painted face of that mannequin—the trust in the eyes, the unreadable thin lips. I can see Sister Thecla turning that mannequin on its side, taking care with the sheets so as to avoid exposing the nakedness. And Sister Thecla's hands—how they were all tenderness, and how somehow, right before our eyes, they transubstantiated the cotton covering of the mannequin into the feverish, aching flesh of someone who was really sick.

Madeleine Mysko, Mercy Hospital School of Nursing graduate, 1967. Courtesy Madeleine Mysko.

The other night, Sister Thecla visited me in a dream. I hadn't thought of her in years, and yet there she was. I don't know how to describe the power of this dream, except to say that I cannot seem to let it go.

Right before this dream, I'd been admitted to the hospital, by way of the emergency room, after a bout of chest pain that radiated up into my throat. The pain had come out of the blue, so of course it was a scare. But by the time I scooted myself from the gurney and into a bed on the unit—where they'd watch over me until the stress test in the morning—the pain was gone, and the blood work was coming back negative.

The nurse was kind and efficient. After she'd gone over me thoroughly, she wrote her beeper and her cell phone numbers on the board at the foot of my bed. She encouraged me to call any time, "For anything at all," she said, smiling. "Really, anything." And then she was gone.

I wasn't afraid. And except for the clumsiness of being attached to a monitor and IV tubing, I wasn't uncomfortable. Though I'd been cautioned not to eat or drink, in truth I wasn't even hungry. The room was semiprivate, but the other bed was empty. It was the end of the evening shift.

A friendly nursing assistant came to take my vital signs. When I almost made the mistake of saying that the unit seemed quiet, she shushed me: "No, no, don't say that word." I laughed and told her I was a nurse myself and understood all about jinxes. I settled down then under the extra bath blankets she'd brought me. She turned out the lights.

I wasn't afraid, and yet, suddenly and inexplicably, I felt as though my heart had been broken. I felt abandoned, by whom I couldn't say. The tears ran down my face into the stiff pillowcase. I had such a lump in my throat—real pressure—that I was afraid something would show on the monitor.

This is nonsense, I told myself. *Get to sleep.*

Somehow I did.

And then she came to me: Sister Thecla, carrying her old porcelain basin, the linens, the lotions, and powder. She turned me on my side, her arms stronger than I'd ever imagined they'd be. Her hands moved slowly down the length of my spine, kneading in tenderness. *It isn't nonsense,* she said, leaning close. *You know that.* She made a gentle sound, a grandmotherly *tsk, tsk* close to my ear.

Oh my, she said, in that quavering voice from long ago. *Whatever happened to* P.M. *care?*

RACHEL RENEE GAGE

The Musical Sound Track in a Nurse's Day

Ding ding ding,
the soft call lights ring

Beep beep beep goes the IV pump
when the bag is almost empty

Click click click, hurried nursing clogs in the hall
and w*hir, whir, whir* as the pyxis dispenses meds

Whoosh whoosh whoosh
of the suction canister

and the constant *ring ring ring*
of the phone.

Sounds endless, fascinating,
(and since they are new to me)

offering a small amount of terror!
What symphony will tomorrow's rotation bring?

Rachel Renee Gage, University of Illinois at Chicago graduate, 2016. Courtesy Rachel Renee Gage.

M. BEN MELNYKOVICH

My Second Go-Around

After investing five years in the Dana School of Music at Youngstown State University but then dropping out before finishing, I found myself at a crossroad. My plans for singing professionally and teaching, while partially accomplished, were not to be. In college, I'd worked several jobs, including being an emergency medical technician (EMT). After dropping out of music school, I'd become a full-time EMT; later I became a paramedic. As much as I loved being a first responder, clearly the physical demands of this job could become too great a challenge as I aged. Should I try a second bite of the college apple? At my age? Nursing students were eighteen and nineteen years old. At twenty-seven, I was ancient. Agonizing over this with a friend, I said I'd be thirty by the time I finished the diploma nursing program.

"And how old will you be in three years, if you don't go to nursing school?" he asked.

His matter-of-fact question was the nudge I needed, and I applied.

Fortunately, I'd never been faced with failure or rejection in my educational endeavors. But when I applied to St. Elizabeth Hospital School of Nursing in Youngstown, Ohio, I was not accepted into the upcoming fall class. Heartsick was an understatement. All my deliberation and now, the class was full. But three weeks after making the "waiting list," I received a call from Sr. Mary Justin, the admissions coordinator. A spot had opened because someone changed their mind. Was I still interested in starting that fall? "You bet, Sister!" was my excited reply. And off I ran into the unknown, into my second go-around of education for my newly chosen career. Never did I expect this adventure into uncharted waters to be the life-changing epic it was about to become. A door had been

M. Ben Melnykovich, St. Elizabeth's Hospital School of Nursing graduate, 1981. Courtesy Mercy Health Archives.

opened, and now I was called upon to muster the courage to succeed in what I had chosen as my life's work.

Late August 1978, I met my class. There were eighty of us, of which four were men. Seventy-six women—heaven for a single guy! I did note a couple ladies, several years out of high school, but I didn't seem to identify with them. Instead, they reminded me of the age gap between me and virtually every other class member. This felt awkward at first, but those chronological barriers quickly melted away and we became one unit—living, working, moving, and learning inside the hospital campus grounds.

To this day, I clearly remember moving onto the hospital campus. Women lived in the nursing school dorm, and men were housed in older apartments on campus. Being part of the hospital campus helped me form bonds with the school and my classmates. My saving grace was the three-year curriculum sheet passed out on our first day. Every quarter's requirements for the program were listed: each class, each section. The three-year planner was my anchor, and I used it as my motivation. Each class, each section was a step closer to graduation, and, when completed, a highlighter line was drawn through it. It was my journal of progress; it kept me focused, lifted me when I felt beaten down.

The life of a male student nurse was not much different from that of my female counterparts. We were subject to the same rules and regulations, but the men on campus found it easier to game the system. Alcohol was forbidden in the dorms and, for the girls, very difficult to hide. But we men found having alcohol in our apartment easier, and it made our place the social hub for our female nursing buddies. The girls had housemothers with the skills of CIA agents, but we were beyond their reach.

Our apartments were staffed with a housekeeper who cleaned and provided paper products weekly. Sounds pretty highbrow, but not so much. The housekeepers were actually "agents" of the housemothers who took every opportunity to rat us out when we stepped out of line. Have no fear. This was only a speed bump on the journey of the misadventures we embarked on whenever possible. We found time to make play out of every possible aspect of school, intermingled with the difficult tasks of becoming caregivers. For example, we did funny things to skeletons while studying for anatomy exams. At that time I was a fervent smoker of Marlboro Reds, so they became a handy prop. One morning, our librarian, Mrs. Crawford, came into the school library; she found the familiar skeleton with a brand-new Marlboro clenched between his teeth. Somehow, the humor was lost on her.

Finished with evening clinical rotations, we'd regroup to play Uno and Yahtzee until the housemother chased the women off to their beds and the men out of the dorm. For me, the great game in nursing school was "Outsmart the Housemother." I used every devious talent I could muster. The housemothers may have been older, but they were far from feeble. My first foray into this game was ascending the "Sacred Stairs." The old Victorian mansion that was the women's dorm had a beautiful set of curved stairs that were actually referred to by that name. Because of the age of this original structure, traffic was limited. Once a year, it provided a lovely backdrop for the graduating seniors. The challenge of ascending these "Sacred Stairs" screamed out to me, and I did not shy away. With the help of classmates living in the dorm, I climbed those stairs many times, not so much to enter the Holy Grail of the women's dorm, but to defy the edict that had been thrown down like a gauntlet before me. The dorm custodian, Art, became a lifelong friend. He tipped me off, usually calling me. He'd inform me about the coming and going of the housemother on duty. This was a cat-and-mouse game I'd play until the day before graduation. In the late 1970s, it was part of being a student nurse.

Allow me to set the stage for nursing school life as we knew it. The original part of the women's dorm was a refitted Victorian mansion leftover from the days of Youngstown's steel barons. Lavish in its decor and old-time opulence, the women's rooms were not spectacular, but the lower level, which housed the parlors, was *the bomb.* Another featured part of the dorm, specifically the housemother's office, was Sheba, a geriatric German shepherd, who was the nursing school mascot. Since before WWII, there had been a Sheba at St. Elizabeth's School of Nursing. When one dog died, they got another to replace her. Our poor Sheba was arthritic and nearly blind, and she found all the parlors, especially the front one, ideal places to have her monumental bowel movements. It drove my custodian friend absolutely crazy, so much so that he regularly threatened to kill the dog but realized any such action would trigger a felony investigation. The housemothers just might insist on the death penalty. Reluctantly, he never implemented his plans to do away with Sheba.

One of our housemothers was clearly showing slow advancement into the area of geriatric eccentricities and, for this woman, Sheba had taken on a status much greater than a mere mascot. I remember entering the dorm one morning on the way to class and seeing the housemother dipping Sheba's paws into a bucket of soapy water, a mini bubble bath to clean Sheba's paws after the dog had been outdoors. Also, every morning I noted a sickening sweet smell as I passed the housemother's office. I assumed it was air freshener, but my female classmates set me straight. The housemothers, particularly this one, regularly sprayed Sheba with White Shoulders cologne. It was part of my education, learning not to question or be surprised by what I saw or heard or smelled coming from the women's dorm or the housemothers' office.

It was no big deal to be seen going out with a bunch of girls. We went to bars, restaurants, and just about everywhere together. I learned to be part of them and they looked out for me. All in all, we discussed our teachers, the weather, and our lives. We made sure we were ready for our classes and clinical rotations. But we never missed an opportunity to have some fun or to find play in the direst of circumstances. After a grueling day of clinicals, I was always amazed at how the women would race back to the dorm to watch their favorite soap opera, *General Hospital*. I was incredulous, especially after having spent eight mind-bending hours in *Specific Hospital* working as a galley slave, better known as a student nurse.

In the eyes of the housemothers, ignorance of the rules was no excuse. Women in the dorm had to be in by 11:00 P.M. with the exception of what was called a *two o'clock*. This, when requested by a student, provided an extended curfew. In my second year, I began dating a classmate. Watching TV in the parlor was a chance to catch some make-out time when no one was looking—and to watch TV when they were looking. One midnight in the parlor with my date, I heard a sound over my shoulder. It was Mrs. S. She was particularly stern, sort of a battle-axe housemother who always worked the 11:00 P.M. to 7:00 A.M. shift. In my most polite manner, I said, "Hi, Mrs. S."

She replied, "It's twelve midnight."

I thanked her, trying to figure out why she felt the need to give me a time update. In ten minutes, she came by again and announced, "It's almost a quarter after midnight."

Again, I thanked her, thinking she was likely *slipping off the reservation* like her elderly counterparts. Finally, she came in and told me it was time to leave and that she was not happy having to repeatedly remind me of the time. I questioned the early exit until I learned the rules that governed parlor visits. From then on, my girlfriend would have to use up one of her precious "two o' clock" extension requests if she wanted to stay up and entertain me after 11:00 P.M. Mrs. S. stood and watched me slither out of the dorm. Mentally, as I walked to my apartment, I knew this meant I had one more challenge in the "Beat the Housemothers" game.

Because it was a Catholic school, graduations were held at St. Columba Cathedral, with the archbishop officiating and participating in the distribution of our nursing diplomas. The beauty of this ceremony was a primary motivator for all underclassmen. It was mandatory that we attend the graduation ceremonies of the classes ahead of us. Watching young men and women, who only days ago wore the same uniform we did, now dressed in whites, rekindled our heart's fire for knowledge and fueled us for the next year, as we all approached our own finale.

In May 1981, I was lined up wearing a white uniform in St. Columba Cathedral, eagerly waiting the moment when, finally, I would be called a registered nurse. Formally, this was officially contingent upon my passing state boards, but symbolically, it happened in my heart at graduation. My joy at achieving this milestone was enhanced by the look on the faces of my parents and my brother at the ceremony.

Ever more, people would turn to me for help in times of need. I discovered in this second chance a life I could never have imagined and the many degrees of joy, satisfaction, and future fulfillment it would hold for me.

AMY HADDAD

Ablutions

The art of bathing a patient was taught early in our nursing program. We were shown how to fold the washcloth just so over our cupped hands. The cold, wet tails of the cloth's corners were tucked in to keep from dragging over the patient's body while we washed an arm or a leg. I would practice this technique when I washed myself in the morning, carefully mimicking my instructor's actions, standing in front of the mirror, watching myself wash my hand, arm, shoulder, armpit. We were forbidden to touch a real patient until we observed a demonstration of a bed bath and then bathed a fellow student in practice lab. Of course this meant we were on the receiving end of a bath as well. It was hard to say which was more awkward and embarrassing, giving or getting a bath. In less than a week, we would start our clinical experience in a nearby nursing home.

The evening before our first clinical day, we went to find our assignments, to review the charts, and to meet our patients. I felt professional, wearing my lab coat and name tag for the first time in public. I found "my" patient's name posted in the nurses' station—"Cecil Johnson, Room 220A 84 y/o CHF, COPD, CAD." I didn't know what all of those acronyms meant. All I really understood was the patient was elderly and a man.

I found the chart. It was enormous. I took my brand-new notebook and began to work my way through language that was foreign to me. In the medical history and physical section, I discovered that Mr. Johnson had chronic heart and lung problems. From all of this, I had to develop a care plan.

I went down the hall to room 220 and peered into the darkened chamber. It was only 8:00 P.M., and already most of the patients were asleep. Mr. Johnson was in bed A, the one nearer the door. I could hear his breathing even before I entered the room. As I stepped through the door, I saw the head of the bed raised

Amy M. Haddad, Creighton University graduate, 1975. Courtesy Amy Haddad.

almost as straight as a chair. I thought Mr. Johnson was asleep, but he must have heard me as he opened his eyes and turned his head to look at me.

"Hi," I said, "I'm going to take care of you tomorrow. Okay?"

"Okay," he said and closed his eyes again. I left without introducing myself.

At report the next morning, the "real" nurses who worked at the nursing home sat around a table and listened to what the students had planned for their patients that morning. The charge nurse called my patient's name first. I nervously read through my care plan that had taken hours to write the night before. Besides the bath and brushing his teeth, I was going to wash his hair, trim his toenails, conduct passive range of motion on his extremities, and get him up in the chair.

The charge nurse laughed and asked, "You got anything else planned for him?"

I was panic-stricken. What had I forgotten?

"No," I hesitantly stated.

"Good, honey, cause that's enough for one morning don't you think?" she said.

I hadn't caught the sarcasm. I didn't understand what doing too much meant. As report continued, the rest of my peers cut back on their plans for their patients.

When I went into room 220, Mr. Johnson was in bed, eyes closed, the same position he'd been in the evening before. I noticed today that there was someone in bed B—a small, quiet bundle. I pulled the curtain around Mr. Johnson's bed for some privacy. As I did, I watched him struggle to breathe. I stood by the side of the bed and leaned over him. His eyes quickly opened.

"I'm back. Remember me from last night?" I said.

"No," he almost whistled his response. He exhaled through his mouth each time. His bluish lips were in the shape of a large case "O." He eyed me warily. "What do you want?" he said.

"I don't want anything. I'm going to help you with your bath, you know, get you ready for the day," I responded.

"Too much bother," he said.

"Oh, let's just start by washing your face and brushing your teeth before breakfast. Wouldn't that feel better?" I said ignoring his refusal.

"Not hungry," he flatly stated and closed his eyes again.

I wondered if he thought by closing his eyes he could make me go away. Again, I ignored what he said and got two washcloths, one to wash and one to rinse and a towel to dry. When I gave him the first washcloth, he took it with a sigh and wiped around his face for a long time, back and forth, over and over around his eyes, forehead, chin. As he handed the cloth back to me he rubbed his chin.

"Whiskers," he said. I offered to rinse and dry his face, and he let me.

"Want to shave?" I could not believe I said this. We hadn't covered shaving in class yet. I had never shaved a face. I had shaved my own legs and underarms, but not a face.

27

"Okay," he said.

"Do you have a razor?" I asked.

"Somewhere," he said.

I found an old electric razor in the bedside stand, and finally figured out how to turn it on. It was filthy and full of whiskers. I'd seen my father clean his razor by blowing into the head, and so I blew as hard as I could to get rid of some of the debris. I touched Mr. Johnson's check and he turned his head so I could get a better view. He brought up his bottom lip so I could shave his chin, his skin thin and red. I pulled the skin on his neck taut and worked the razor up and down. It took a long time to notice any effect from the dull razor.

I noticed that his breathing became quite labored whenever he moved, even slightly. When I left him alone, he shut his eyes and seemed to focus on his breathing. The muscles in his neck stood out as he worked to get air. I saw the nasal cannula and tubing from the oxygen tank near the bed.

"Do you want your oxygen?" I asked. Before he could answer, I started to slip the tubing over his ears.

"Don't help," he said. "Take it off." I did as he asked. Next, I got out an emesis basin, a glass of water and his toothbrush. He opened his eyes and saw the toothbrush.

"What's this?" he asked.

"To brush your teeth."

"Oh, they come out," and he reached in and pulled out his dentures, full upper and lower plates. "There's pellets to clean 'em." He held them out to me. This was the first time I saw dentures outside of someone's mouth. My grandmother had dentures, but she seldom let anyone see her without her teeth. I took the teeth from him in my bare hand and delicately laid them on a tissue on the bedside stand until I could figure out what to do. I found the tablets to clean the dentures and a little plastic container. The dentures were covered with food, so I decided to brush them before soaking them. While they were soaking, I offered him yellow-colored mouthwash diluted in a little water.

"Why don't you rinse your mouth out with this?" I held the emesis basin up below his chin, expecting him to spit. He took the glass and instead of swishing it round and spitting it out, he drank it before I could stop him.

"Ack! Sweet water!" he gasped and then started to cough. The coughing really exhausted him. After he got his dentures back in place, he wheezed, "Okay. Enough. Let me rest."

"I can do everything else, I promise. You just relax," I assured him.

He leaned back on his pillows and, once again, shut his eyes. I got a basin of hot water and began the bath. I started with his hands and noticed that his nails were filthy. Without thinking, I said, "What have you been doing, digging potatoes?"

He said, "No, can't clean 'em."

What was under his nails? I didn't want to think about it. Also they needed trimming. I put his right hand in the hot, soapy water. "We'll let your nails soak for a minute, then I'll clean them."

I couldn't find a nail file, so I went to the locker room and got a nail file and clippers from my purse. I wasn't sure if this was the right thing to do, but I could always get another. Gently, I cleaned under each nail and trimmed them. Then I washed his hand, arm, and under his arm, letting one hand soak while I cleaned the opposite side. I washed and dried his abdomen, rolled him to his side, washed his back, and gave him a one-handed back rub since I had to hold him up with my other hand.

All that was left was cleaning his genitals. I wanted to lower the head of the bed. Somehow I thought it would be easier or more proper to do this part of the bath if he were flat in the bed. As I started to lower the head of the bed, he jerked and almost shouted, "No! Don't! Leave it up."

"Okay, I'm sorry." I raised the head back up.

I covered his arms and chest with the bath blanket. Thinking I should warn him before washing him there, I announced, "I'm going to wash between your legs, okay?" He hardly nodded in reply. Armed with a soapy washcloth, I lifted the gown and began to clean his penis and testicles. His pubic hair was sparse and gray; he smelled like old urine. I'd never done this before. We hadn't practiced this part of the bath, and I wasn't sure if I was supposed to conduct the whole business under the sheet and not look or what. Periodically I took what I thought was a clinical look under the sheet to make sure I had rinsed most of the soap. A sense of efficiency and matter-of-factness set in as I washed him, a new feeling, blocking out the pity and sadness that washed over me. I changed the water and took the basin to the end of the bed.

"I'm going to soak your foot for a while. Here, lift it up so I can get it in the basin," I instructed.

"Ahhh," he sighed, "Nice."

I took one look at his long, curved toenails and decided that I wasn't going to touch them. I let him soak in the basin for several minutes because, for the first time since I started his care, he seemed to relax a little. I cleaned his feet as best I could and finished the bath. With help and against his protests, I got him up in the chair next to his bed and changed the linen. He didn't want to stay in the chair.

I tried to cajole him into sitting up for a while. "It will be good for you," I encouraged.

"I'm all done in," he said leaning forward heavily, arms resting on his legs. He seemed weaker as I helped him back to bed.

"That wasn't so bad, was it?"

"Let me be," he said in an irritated voice, ignoring my question. He was wheezing more with each breath. I left him alone, sitting up in bed. It had taken almost the whole morning to finish his care. He hadn't even gotten breakfast, and now the trays were long gone. I made some toast and tea and set it on the overbed table.

"I brought you some breakfast," I said. He looked like he was asleep, so I quietly walked out.

After we'd finished with our patients, we met with our instructor in a small patient dining room across from the nurses' station. While each student recited what he or she had accomplished that day, there was a commotion in the hall and staff ran past the door. We already knew that no one runs in a nursing home. Although the staff ran down the hall, they walked back. The nurse stuck her head in the door as she passed and said, "Mr. Johnson died."

Everyone looked at me. The student next to me whispered loud enough for everyone to hear, "My God, what did you do to him?" She said what we were all thinking. What *had* I done? At that time, we all deeply believed in the potency of our touch, the almost magical power to heal and perhaps harm. If he died, I must have caused it, either by doing something or, worse, neglecting something. Our instructor cleared her throat and we returned to our reports. I felt foolish when it was my turn since everyone already knew the outcome of my care. My patient died. The last thing he said to me was, "Let me be." I had let him be. Maybe I should have checked on him one more time before our postconference started. I never thought to go back to his room.

As we were getting ready to leave, the charge nurse stopped by the dining room and asked, "Would your students like to prepare the body for the morgue?"

Our instructor turned to us and said, "You don't have to, but it would be a good experience for all of you. I'll help."

Three of the other students and I followed our instructor down to Mr. Johnson's room. The curtains were drawn completely around his bed. His roommate was gone. The tea and toast I'd brought him were in the wastebasket. For the first time since I saw Mr. Johnson, he was lying flat in the bed, completely covered with a sheet. His round chest rose up, giving some shape to his small body. Later, when I learned about chronic obstructive pulmonary disease and the term "barrel chest," I would always see Mr. Johnson, unmoving under the sheet.

We gently uncovered him, as if not to disturb him. He was wearing the patient gown I had tied around him only a few hours earlier. All of his effort to breathe was gone. All of the energy he used to push air out and barely inhale was dissipated. His mouth was slightly open, his eyes closed. He was a little grayer than before, but the main difference to me was not in his appearance, but in the stillness.

The other students in my group stood back from me and Mr. Johnson. This was a private experience since, after all, he had been my patient. Our instructor opened the "shroud" kit, a packet of materials to prepare the body for transportation to the morgue. The kit included cotton ties to keep the mouth shut. "Always remember if the dentures are not in the mouth of a deceased patient, put them in as soon as possible after death. It is very hard to get dentures in if rigor mortis has set in," our instructor advised as she tied the cotton strips around his head and jaw. Mr. Johnson now looked a little like Marley's ghost in Dickens's *A Christmas Carol*. I helped change his gown because Mr. Johnson had wet the bed. I didn't know then that this often happens when a person dies. He would be embarrassed, I thought. All these women standing in a circle around his bed—he wouldn't like any of this.

Once again, I went to get hot water, soap, and towels to clean him up. "Families should not have to view their loved one when they are soiled and dirty. Also, you should remove intravenous lines and any other tubes before the family comes to view the body," our instructor noted. Family? I had not thought about his family. I'd not seen him in any context other than as a solitary patient in a nursing home. My assignment. My patient.

The other students watched while I washed Mr. Johnson. They helped me remove the wet sheets and turn him. We tied his wrists together across his abdomen. Our last gesture was to fill out an identification tag that we tied to the big toe on his right foot. I looked at him one last time, still expecting him to gasp for air or move. We pulled the sheet over his face and left.

No one said very much on the way to the parking lot. My instructor called after me as I unlocked my car, "Don't worry. I'll find another patient for you to take care of tomorrow."

CORTNEY DAVIS

Selling Kisses at the Diner

It was my second year, my wild year.
I was a student on the evening shift, my boyfriend

would pick me up after work, take me
to an all-night diner where mostly old men lingered—

the homeless, the widowers, the boozers trying to get straight.
We would saunter in past midnight,

me in my proud uniform, white stockings and clinic shoes;
him stopping to slap the backs of the guys he knew.

The old men would sing to me, *I'll give you a dollar for a kiss,*
and I'd take their bills, bend to kiss their cheeks

as if I were Florence Nightingale or little sister to the hookers
who loitered outside the diner door. And yet,

pausing here and there to press my lips to those sad lives,
I recognized the power of my first foray into healing.

Cortney Davis, Norwalk Community College graduate, 1972. Editor's collection.

JOANNE CLARKSON

First Patient

for SW

He was how I first learned
nursing, to accept in white corridors
the summons of pain, and send it back
softened, moonrise on cliff stone.

Morning shift and lists of tasks
tremble in my hand. I must bathe him,
spoon pills between chapped lips, assure
a regimen of healing neither of us
yet understands. With a veteran nurse
I must change the bandage, rank
with seepage, where they sawed away his leg.

I have never been so afraid.
But this tremor is not for the pinch
of dried blood. Or for infection
never mine to cure. It's clumsiness
curled inside a hesitant hand,
for well-intentioned love is not enough.

How I envy my quick, competent
mentor, stripping away the darkened
gauze, unraveling its sterile

Joanne Clarkson, Grays Harbor College graduate, 2002. Courtesy Joanne Clarkson. Photo by James Clarkson.

replacement with one seamless twist.
She hands me the cleansing spray, cloth
to dab barbed wire stitching

across his swollen flesh. I press
and swab, smooth the new bandage,
apologizing under my breath as I wind
the final Ace, *tighter,* as she requires,
across the phantom pain.

But it is me his gaze follows
as I clear the tray, wash my hands.
I'll do better tomorrow, I promise.
But we both know this is not quite
true, for nothing is as tender
as the terror of first touch.

STACY NIGLIAZZO

In my first year

studying anatomy and physiology
I was assigned
a large cat swimming in formaldehyde
for dissection.
I named him Lazarus and cried
when I cut into his face, but marveled
at the bones unhinged,
and the pink muscles, and the gray
viscera.
I sliced one kidney in three parts
isolating the cortex, ureter, and veins.
I received high marks,
then tucked it safely back inside, lest he be left incomplete.

Stacy Nigliazzo, Blinn College School of Nursing graduate, 2006. Courtesy Stacy Nigliazzo.

MIRIAM CRAWFORD GRANT

The Titan in Room 406

A short television script based on my own student nursing experience

FADE IN:

EXTERIOR: VETERAN'S HOSPITAL, CHARLESTON, SOUTH CAROLINA

(The flags wave in the morning sky, backdropped by pink and golden hues as the sun rises to its throne, flags boasting honor, with their colors flying in the wind. All at high staff, proud and dignified. Driving to the hospital, MIRIAM, a student nurse, glances in the rearview mirror one last time. Her pearl earrings look larger than she expected.)

(When MIRIAM arrives, the parking lot is already filled with visitors and staff surrounding the gray fortress that is Veteran's Affairs. MIRIAM hurries toward the front entrance, patterning her steps to mimic the busy professionals, adjusting her name tag and smiling like a tiny tugboat cruising alongside the big ship. She appears wrought with fear.)

(She opens the doors and steps inside the lobby. The hospital "machine" is running. A woman carries a briefcase filled with files; a doctor in a lab coat leads a group of medical professionals to the elevator. A tiny, elderly woman pushes her husband in a wheelchair down the hall. MIRIAM stands out like a sore thumb in her uniform, the white fabric gleaming against her pecan skin. Her skin glistens from the humidity. White is the color of the student nurses. But she can't hide; she's already been noticed.)

(A security guard, a well-groomed, older man with gray hair, sits near the front entrance waiting for the student nurses to file in.)

SECURITY GUARD: Fourth floor. Take the elevator to 4 West.

MIRIAM: Thank you, sir.

INTERIOR: 4 WEST CONFERENCE ROOM
(MIRIAM and the other student nurses enter the conference room, where there is a large oval table. Sitting around it are 15 students and the clinical instructor, MRS. CARTER, early thirties, blonde hair, confident smile, wearing gray pants and a white blouse. This room looks like the global office on the TV show *West Wing*, a yuppie contrast to the hospital halls that are laced with cotton balls, alcohol preps, and the constant beeping from IV poles.)

MRS. CARTER: The folders located in the rear are for your clinical summaries. They are due in 24 hours.

ONE OF THE STUDENT NURSES: Can we email them to you?

MRS. CARTER: Typed or handwritten. But the clinical reviews must be hand-delivered here. After hours, slide them under the door. Read through the patient Privacy Act and sign your name.

(Students flip through what seems like a small novel.)

MIRIAM (VOICE-OVER): I was sitting in the only available chair near the door. This was now Day 2 of our clinical experience. My new classmates were not aware of how being in the veteran's hospital jolted my spirits. Not so long ago I walked

Miriam Crawford Grant with her mother, Vivian W. Crawford, after graduation from the Medical University of South Carolina Nursing Program, 2010. Courtesy Miriam Crawford Grant. Photo by Shawn Grant.

the long gray line at the Citadel Military College, one of the few women who had entered during its transition to a coed college. Those veterans had lots to say about females in their castle. I was once again terrified, like a military private on line with his drill sergeant. Readying for an attack. I turn to the end of the book and sign my name. No need to read anything, I have no intentions of even sharing my name.

(Students exit the conference room, and chatting nervously, follow MRS. CAR-TER to 4 West, down a short, busy hallway and past the nursing station filled with peeping eyes, everyone watching the new kids heading to the playground. MRS. CARTER pulls a computer from a hutch in the wall and starts typing BLOOD PRESSURE, PULSE, RESPIRATORY RATE, HISTORY, AND PHYSICAL.)

MRS. CARTER: If you have any questions, please step into the hallway. I or another staff nurse can help you.

(She walks away. MIRIAM'S hands start to sweat. She walks to Room 406, where a tiny note on the door reads "PRECAUTION. DON GOWN AND MASK.")

MIRIAM (VOICE-OVER): Great. Now how do I do that? I can't believe this is my first day on the floor. What happened to the book work, or another tour, or something else?

(She stubbornly stands there. MRS. CARTER approaches.)

MRS. CARTER: You take the gown like this. (She opens a clear bag filled with a blue vinyl-like back-opened hospital gown.) Easy. Then put on the mask. (Putting it on, then taking it off again, she looks at MIRIAM, who has tears in her eyes. Sensing an impending meltdown, MRS. CARTER moves in closer, pulls magical healing tissues out of her pocket.)

MIRIAM: This is hard for me—

MRS. CARTER (interrupting): These first days are the worst. Nothing will ever be as hard as it is today. It only gets easier from here. (MIRIAM scrubs the tissue over her eyes.)

MIRIAM (VOICE-OVER): There was no need to explain my pain to her—these first clinical days are the hardest part for all students, regardless of their past. That moment before you open a patient's door, that moment when you fear being "found out," fear feeling like a fraud. Taking my Citadel ring off of my right index finger, I place it in my lab coat. I don the gown and mask. I push open door 406.

(Dimly lit and cool. MISTER, a round older white man, is lying in bed. A large window is almost obscured by towels, bed pads, a urinal, and greeting cards. An IV pole hoists a bag of clear fluid that flows through transparent tubing into his pale arm. He looks at MIRIAM in silence, a half-eaten breakfast tray in front of him. MRS. CARTER has long since disappeared.)

MIRIAM: Good morning, sir. My name is Miriam. I'm a student nurse. How are you? (He nods.) I just need to check your blood pressure and a few other things. (He obediently holds out his arm.) Do you know why you're in the hospital? Can you tell me why? (He looks at MIRIAM in silence. She wraps the cuff around his arm. Her hands tremble as she inflates the blood pressure cuff firmly around his arm. 132/80.) Not too bad. (He looks at her. A subtle smile appears on his face.)

MISTER: Where are you from, gal? (His voice is firm but gentle.)

MIRIAM (VOICE-OVER): He called me "gal"! He's from the South.

MIRIAM: I'm from right here. Charleston, South Carolina. Graduated from The Citadel. Now I attend Medical University for nursing school. (He shifts in his bed, struggles to sit up. Looks at her.)

MISTER: I got Agent Orange. You know, in Vietnam. Out in the field. What branch did you serve? They make you go in the Army over there, right? (He smiles, hesitantly.)

MIRIAM: No, sir, I didn't go.

MISTER: Well, I don't blame you. Gotta pick your battles.

(She places two fingers on his wrist. The strength of his beating heart pulses through. MIRIAM straightens up, stands tall. Nursing school is a battle she will win.)

PART II

An invocation. Though the words do not always

Seem to work. Still, one must try. Bow your head.

Cross your arms. Say: *Blessed is the day. And the one*

Who destroys the day. Blessed is this ring of fire

In which we live. . . . How bitter the burning leaves.

BRIGIT PEGEEN KELLY, "BLESSED IS THE FIELD"

How many languages are there? I wondered.

Yes, that's us bent over our books by the desk lamp, making note cards, memorizing nerves. We're serving an apprenticeship, and there are many moments of angst, many forms of fire we'll pass through. We must learn a new language as nursing students, must not melt under the heat of constructive criticism or social injustices. We must not be ashamed of our ignorance and learn to love ourselves as we evolve. And we must share our observations and knowledge with others, even though it may create friction, for this is the path to finding our professional voice.

KELLY SIEVERS

Heads Bowed

Aspergillus. One

patient in ICU, weakened

by steroids, breathless.

Lungs showered

with fungus, each cell

beneath microscope

shaped as an aspergillum—

the Bishop's hallmark

holy water sprinkler

blessing us students

heads bowed, newly

capped in white

silent as candles,

stilled vessels

filled with breath

briefly blessed.

Kelly Sievers, St. Mary's Hospital School of Nursing graduate, 1968. Courtesy Kelly Sievers.

Whispered

Brugmansia's scopolamine,
chemist's distillate known to divide
mind from body, memory
from pain. Twilight of heaven
or hell of hallucination. A history nurses
whispered in obstetric wards—a mother
laboring in "twilight sleep." She jumped
from her hospital window, a chimera

of drugs coursing her veins: morphine
wagging a tail of scopolamine. I dreamed
glass and slam and echo. I found
the window, its frame nailed shut.

How quick her escape—
the elegant corolla of her body
a poisoned bell thrumming
with fevered rage. She flew
into or out of battle, toxic
with our sorcery.

Brugmansia: *Solanaceae family (nightshade), known for possessing a diverse range of alkaloids. These alkaloids can be desirable, toxic, or both. Common name, Angel's Trumpets, refers to the large, pendulous trumpet-shaped flowers.*

JEANNE BRYNER

Debridement, Burn Unit, 1978

My fine teacher, my good captain
her left hand light, then firm
upon my shoulder. *This must get done.*

He's twenty-one (my brother's age),
a gas well explosion, 80%, second, third
degree. Help the nurse, his doctor, your patient.

He's been medicated, so he won't feel much.
They handed me scrubs, gloves, a mask.
The tiled room, no bigger than a closet.

A door closed. I knelt by the metal tub
and saw he'd gone to a cruel planet
where monsters steal your face.

He was their apple, and they bent
to their work. So much blood,
not like Jello or ketchup, a metallic smell

like guns. I held his arm or leg or whatever
the hell they told me to. He never quit screaming,
his mouth without lips, his eyes without tears.

Jeanne Bryner, Trumbull Memorial Hospital School of Nursing graduate, 1979. Editor's col-
lection.

How much I wanted to be brave,
but my heart switched gears.
I saw my uncles, Papaw, their black aprons.

Butchering time on the farm, heard the hogs
such a squalling in November's pen.
Granny shooed us to her kitchen, busy baking

mincemeat pies. She gave us raisins, leftover
dough.   Small hands made shapes of men
row   after   row   after   row
bodies that brown inside ovens,
           sweet cinnamon ones.

MINNIE BROWN CARTER

Inequality, Work, Perseverance, Sleepless Nights, Service

From 1943 through 1948, approximately 179,000 women enlisted in the United States Cadet Nurses Corps, and an estimated 124,000 graduated as registered nurses. Of that number, only 3,000 were "colored" women, even though this was the first uniformed service to include a nondiscriminatory clause. I am proud to say that I graduated in 1947 as a U.S. Cadet Nurse and so launched a rewarding and successful career as a registered nurse.

My student experiences were interesting, intimidating, painful, sad, supportive, and fulfilling. Initially, I almost didn't make it. My family physician told me that I probably would not succeed in nursing school. I weighed only ninety-nine pounds and had a heart murmur. My family didn't want me to go. But I pleaded with them, and thankfully a relative who was familiar with the school and the program reassured them. They finally let me travel to Hampton, Virginia, to enroll in Dixie Hospital at Hampton Institute (now Hampton University) for my nursing training. My first day there, I was ushered to the infirmary for a complete physical, an EKG, heart exam, blood pressure check. One week later, I wondered if I had made the right decision.

Dixie was a Catholic Hospital, located across the street from the college. The hospital staff consisted of two "colored" physicians, two "colored" head nurses, two "colored" nursing instructors, and a building filled with Caucasian, German, and other foreign physicians, nurses, instructors, and staff, all speaking a variety of languages. My anxiety level increased.

Our nursing student dormitory was located across the street from the hospital; however, all "colored" nursing students had to enter the hospital through the back door of the building. Only months later, after we picketed in peaceful

Minnie Brown Carter at age ninety, 2016. Courtesy of Minnie Brown Carter.

protest, did we succeed in getting the "Whites Only Entrance " and "Colored Entrance" signs removed.

As a woman of color, I encountered seemingly insurmountable obstacles in my nursing training. I endured long hours of study and hard work, crowded living conditions, and military-style rules and regulations. Forty-eight-hour workweeks were the norm, as our schedules were based on a combination of both clinical and classroom experiences. In the classroom, we were seated alphabetically. My last name was Brown; therefore, I was always in the front row and always called on first by my instructors. We had strict rules and were threatened with being "sent home" if we did not maintain a B+ grade point average or better. We took classes and worked twelve-hour days, six days a week.

We could be dismissed if we failed to salute the chief nurse whenever she appeared on the floor (sometimes as many as fifteen times a day) or if we failed to be present with dying patients as a comfort while they were taking their last breaths, a vigil often extending throughout the night. This was especially true for patients in the "iron lung."

Many of our patients were white, and they did not want "colored" nursing students administering to them. Often, they were reluctant, refusing treatments and medications we offered; many were very mean spirited. I have tried to forget

Minnie Brown Carter with her fellow nursing school graduates, Hampton Institute Nursing School, Dixie Hospital, Hampton, VA, 1947. Courtesy Minnie Brown Carter.

the hurtful words I heard during those years. Nevertheless, we continued to smile and provide them care, and little by little, they accepted our services.

I remember some embarrassing moments during my training. Once I fainted in the operating room, due to a combination of no breakfast and the sight of so much blood! The head nurse commanded, "Just move her aside and let the next cadet take her place." Often exhausted, I sometimes fell asleep in the classroom and even once standing in the food line!

The years passed, and all the inconveniences and struggles of my training helped me become strong and confident in my skills. I became accustomed to working in a variety of difficult situations, which helped me tremendously during my nursing career, in many different settings and challenges.

During our third year, there was a staffing shortage due to the war overseas. We worked as head nurse supervisors and acting chief nurses, which prepared us to become future leaders. Also, as part of our training, we worked in the pharmacy, preparing medications, learning medication names and dosages. Our training also included off-site experience. We were sent to St. Phillip's Children's Hospital in Richmond, Virginia. We worked with polio patients and those in the iron lung. These experiences I will never forget. Once our formal classroom work was finished, we had to study for the State Board of Nursing examination while still maintaining our clinical hours and B+ grade point average.

There were also moments of fun during my nursing training years. On weekends we were bused to the USO Centers to socialize with the soldiers, sailors, and servicemen from the nearby Norfolk Naval Base and Ft. Eustis Army Base. We dressed up in evening attire, a welcome change from our stiff, starched white uniforms. Only the cadet nurse students were allowed this privilege. The other students on the campus became jealous when we told them about our social evenings off campus. Our excursions were very relaxing and gave us the opportunity to get acquainted with the men in the uniformed services.

As World War II was ending, I graduated from my nursing program. I was offered the position of head nurse at Dixie Hospital and the opportunity to continue my education in the five year nursing program at Hampton Institute, but I declined and opted instead to begin my career in Washington, DC, where my family had relocated. I became part of the early integration of "colored" nurses into the federal government hospitals. I was appointed to work at the National Institutes of Health, DC General Hospital, and St. Elizabeth's Hospital (now closed), beginning my career as a staff nurse and continuing to move up as Nurse Supervisor, Nurse Coordinator, and Acting Nurse Director. I served as an official agent in the community, as our Church Nurse and on Health Fair programs.

I was married in 1954 to Thomas L. Carter and was blessed with two beautiful daughters and now four grandchildren whom I adore. They keep me up to date with today's technology: I have an iPhone, computer, and Kindle tablet, which I use daily! How long ago and far away those early years seem now—that time when a frightened young woman walked through the door of nursing school to receive the education, master the skills, and fulfill the longing to serve, which became the beacon guiding my life.

Editors' note: Minnie Brown Carter's contributions to nursing, her participation in the quest to recognize women in military service, and her honors would fill more pages than we have here. For a number of years, she has been working with other former cadet nurses to get a bill passed in Congress to enable the U.S. Cadet Nurses of World War II to receive veteran status. HR 3423, the U.S. Cadet Nurses Equity Act of 2007, is their eighth act introduced into Congress. The U.S. Nurse Cadet Corps was the largest and youngest group of uniformed women in service to our country during WWII and the early postwar years. By 1943, the Corps was playing a major role in shoring up the ranks of the nation's health care providers. By 1945, the Corps provided the majority of nursing care in our nation's hospitals.

EILEEN VALINOTI

Hospital Corners

"And now, as we finish up, we'll need to put our blankets away. I want you to fold them like this," announced my yoga teacher—a bit sternly, I thought. With swift, deft hands, she began to demonstrate. Something in the tone of her voice and the sharp jut of her chin brought me back to Miss Coyle. . . .

Miss Mary Coyle, RN, was the nursing arts instructor in my first year of training, more than fifty years ago. She taught our group of thirty—twenty-seven eager eighteen-year-old women and three young nuns—the basic nursing skills, including how to give a bed bath, administer an injection, and prepare hot and cold compresses.

Twice a week, my classmates and I filed into her classroom, which was set up to resemble a sickroom. Its features included basins, bandage trays, a large bath thermometer, and a hospital bed on which reclined a lifelike mannequin whom we called "Mrs. Chase."

One morning Miss Coyle announced that we were to learn how to make the hospital bed.

Some of us yawned and shifted in our seats.

Miss Coyle frowned. "A badly made bed is uncomfortable to lie in, and a wrinkled bottom sheet can lead to pressure sores."

Now we sat up straight. No one wanted to be responsible for pressure sores, although we weren't sure what they were. Miss Coyle did not elaborate. Chastened, we left our seats and stood as directed in a circle about the bed. After carefully moving Mrs. Chase to a chair and stripping the bed, Miss Coyle began to demonstrate.

First, she placed a large rubber sheet on the mattress, then covered it with a crisp white sheet.

Eileen Valinoti, St. Catherine's Hospital graduate, 1960. Courtesy Eileen Valinoti.

"Now you anchor the bottom sheet by making the hospital corner," she said, "lifting the sheet about eighteen inches from the side of the bed and folding it at a right angle, then tucking it in." Miss Coyle worked briskly, creating the perfect hospital corner in one elegant maneuver as I struggled to match her words to her nimble movements.

When she'd finished, the bed looked perfect. Only the boldest patient, I thought, would dare to disturb it. Now each of us would demonstrate our technique.

"Miss Murphy," Miss Coyle said, directing me to the bed.

My heart pounded furiously. The image of the "hospital corner" vanished from my head. As I fumbled helplessly, the rubber sheet slipped and slid, and the crisp white sheets grew damp and wrinkled in my perspiring hands. In the end, all I could manage was to bunch the bottom sheet into clumsy little clumps beneath the mattress, just as I'd always done, and my mother before me.

At last, Miss Coyle put a restraining hand on my shoulder and addressed the class. "Manual dexterity," she said, with a puckered smile, "is an essential requirement for a nurse."

With a rush of shame, I put my hands behind my back; they felt enormous and useless. I looked at Miss Coyle's small, sturdy ones—capable, no doubt, of wonders.

After class I brooded over the phrase "manual dexterity." Could one acquire it or was it an inborn trait? My father hated tools of every description—and they hated him. An encounter with a hammer and nails invariably resulted in a smashed finger and howls of pain. For my mother, the greatest challenge was to sew on a button. Growing up, I'd learned to make do with safety pins.

Every evening after that class, I would practice my bed making in the nursing arts classroom. Often I stood perplexed, studying the length of sheet in my hand—was it the requisite eighteen inches? Alone in the room except for Mrs. Chase, I despaired of ever making a proper bed.

One afternoon as twilight fell in the gloomy room, a classmate, Sister Catherine, stopped in to retrieve a book. She stared at me in astonishment: Not even the nuns spent their spare time in the nursing arts classroom. Without a word, she placed her hands over mine and began to guide them. We worked together in slow, easeful motions. The weight of Sister's warm flesh and her calm, soothing presence steadied my nerves. As she murmured words of encouragement, I finally made a satisfactory bed on my own, complete with all the right angles. Sister waved away my thanks.

"I'm late for prayers," she said, hurrying out the door.

I rushed out after her, happy to leave my perfect bed to the impenetrable gaze of Mrs. Chase.

Now, listening to my yoga teacher's stern instructions, I felt my stomach muscles tighten. No matter that in my nursing career I had made thousands of beds with great success, had folded countless sheets, blankets, pillowcases, and linens and had never gotten a complaint.

I found myself looking anxiously out of the corner of my eye at my classmates to see how they were following the teacher's directions. *Did she say to fold the blanket in thirds, or was it fourths?* I wondered anxiously.

Then I saw that everyone was laughing and chattering and happily folding their blankets every which way. My stomach relaxed. The teacher had ended the class by covering each of us with a blanket as we lay stretched out on our mats—a gesture, I'd supposed, in the spirit of Buddhist compassion. Compassion, I had thought, half dozing beneath my blanket, lies at the heart of nursing, manifesting itself in the many small acts in a nurse's day: holding a patient's hand during a painful bone-marrow aspiration, murmuring "I'm here" into the ear of a dying patient, brushing the tangles from an Alzheimer's patient's white hair before her daughter comes to visit. Making a hospital bed, giving an injection, and starting an IV are all vital tasks that can be taught in a classroom like Miss Coyle's, but performing these tasks with compassion makes all the difference.

Looking back, I'm proud that I learned the essential skills of nursing, that I overcame my insecurity and mastered the hospital corner. But my greatest gift to my patients, and my greatest joy, was when I performed these skills with compassion—and in those moments became the nurse I'd always wanted to be.

PATTAMA ULRICH

Me and the New World

1.

I visited a bamboo shack, hospice care, the slum in the middle of the divine
   city,
Bangkok, before my journey, the journey to marry a man I loved and longed
   to be with for eternity.

The skinny bony men were dying of HIV/AIDS, but they were smiling.

There is no money to buy such dignity, but caring hands could make a divine
   city.

2.

In the new world, I resisted being called *immigrant.*

I wanted a new career in caring, healing others like a sprouting plant.

I was excited to see the new world, but soon I lost my identity.

The medical terminology.

The marriage terminology.

*Pattama Ulrich, Ohio State University College of Nursing graduate, 2004. Courtesy Pattama
Ulrich.*

The new world terminology.

How many languages are there? I wondered. I have to learn.

I wondered why there is no book on the new world identity.

The confusion of being illiterate in marriage and caring.

3.

On a clinical practice day, I saw the first, then the second tower,
how humanity was lost in New York City.

My new world shattered. I stared, stood stiff and still before the TV screen,
   insanity.

I remembered the bamboo shack in the Bangkok slum, the caring and dignity.
   But that day in September, I forgot what it meant to be human.

4.

The summer study at Children's Hospital revived my kindness. The children
   brought back my memory.

The mother who adopted so many unwanted medically handicapped children.
   The unconditional love and caring shown endlessly in their eyes.

I asked the mother, *why?*

They deserve love and caring like my own child, she replied.

5.

One family left their daughter, "failure to thrive."

More medical terminology.

End-stage liver disease took a boy, then a girl the day before their livers arrived.

Again, the new world shattered. Those parents, shattered.

The student nurses, doctors, patient care team, shattered.

Children, their yellow eyes and skin, extended abdomens like balloons stretched too tight with water.

Fatigue and endless pain took the light and hope from their eyes. They were dying in rain, I believed, the excess fluid of internal rain.

Would nursing and caring remind me, remind my new world of the humanity, loving, and kindness we must have to survive?

I could see every vein. I could see every vein.

PAULA SERGI

The Structure of Nursing School in an Otherwise Chaotic Life

All my changes were there.
  —Neil Young

I didn't always want to be a nurse, but I always wanted to be someone important, to make an impact on the world somehow, and to get out of the silly town where I was raised. My only childhood brush with nursing came when I wanted to play combat with my brother and his friends in our backyard. My brother didn't want me around, but one of the guys suggested I could be the nurse. I was grateful to have any role with the boys because their games always seemed more adventurous, more fun than the games I played with my girlfriends.

Home life was a bit chaotic as my widowed mother tried to deal with four children, the two eldest rebellious and wild. There was a tendency for things to fall apart: the furnace, bedroom windows, and leaky eaves. We didn't have curfews, but almost always had a meal at 5:00 P.M. Lawn care and laundry were managed, but with a lot of anxiety and coaxing. Money was scarce and worried over. I couldn't wait for my real life to begin.

In 1971 I entered the University of Wisconsin in Madison, just as the protests against the Vietnam War were becoming more radical. I'd read about how professors and students held "teach-ins" to educate and discuss objections to an escalating situation. Only a year before, the army-math research building on campus had been bombed.

The week before classes began, I switched my major from English to nursing for practical reasons. I knew I'd be paying for college, and at that time there were few teaching jobs available. What would I do with a degree in English? Nursing would be a safer bet for job security. Besides, I told myself, I could always read

Paula Sergi, University of Wisconsin graduate, 1975. Courtesy Paula Sergi.

literature on my own, but I doubted I'd pick up a book on chemistry or anatomy just for fun.

My midwestern sensibility prepared me for the rigors of school at the university. Focused and hardworking, I'd been a diligent high school student and an officer on student council. I expected to study hard and wasn't surprised when I needed to spend two to four hours a night on my schoolwork. I took a work-study position at the library and managed my time well.

What did surprise me was that there were nursing students more serious than I was. Some of my classmates arrived early to class to secure front row seats so they could tape the lectures. Although I wasn't among the most ambitious, I did pride myself on taking excellent notes. The style of education, lecture and reading, memorization, and visualization of the material, worked well for me. It wasn't until years later that I realized I'd been an academic nerd. My children pointed it out.

Meanwhile, a new world opened to me. The elective classes were enriching and exciting. A philosophy professor asked questions I'd never even considered. A fellow student in an English class knew more about Shakespeare than I did. There were lots of smart men around and plenty of opportunities for fun. I met a redheaded Jewish man from Argentina in ballroom dance, which served as my physical education requirement. I hadn't known that there were Jewish people with red hair or in Argentina.

One day there was excitement in the air. The dorm was emptying. From my room on the sixth floor I saw a crowd of people walking toward State Street a block away. I'd heard about previous protests against the use of napalm, a chemical weapon used in the Vietnam War. It seemed important to add my presence, and I was curious. I joined the crowd of protesters. We walked shoulder to shoulder. I was jostled and couldn't see the police but knew they were there from the shouts of the crowd. When I heard the words "tear gas," I headed back to the dorm. But lots of other people sought shelter there in the lobby, and the police threw a canister of tear gas into the crowd. I headed back to the safety of the sixth floor. It was all so wonderfully dramatic, both in the actual event and in the newspaper headlines the next day. I felt my place in history.

I also found time for socializing. One young woman in class didn't look like the rest of the nursing students but more like Joan Baez. She had long dark hair and wore blue jeans and muslin blouses, avoided the front row seats, and sometimes walked in late. I needed to meet her and so approached her one day after class. As we walked in front of the old nursing building, we spotted a tangle of beads on the sidewalk. She picked it up and said, "Someone lost a necklace." I was confused, because it was clearly a rosary, and I told her so. "What's a rosary?" she asked, and thus began a long friendship marked by curiosities and a sincere appreciation for what we didn't know about one another, about worlds we'd never known existed. She introduced me to my first fresh tomato and mushroom, my first bagel and cream cheese. And to jazz.

My high school boyfriend was a year ahead of me at the university, on a football scholarship. I guess that was nice the first couple of weeks, but my roommate introduced me to another guy with whom I became fascinated. He was a chain-smoker, tall and handsome, and not enrolled in school. I liked him even after learning he'd spent a year in prison for armed robbery. Poor man was misunderstood. He was reckless with booze and money, exciting and forbidden, a gambler and risk taker, and he was attracted to the stability and common sense he saw in me. I learned to smoke pot and drink tequila, to start the weekend on Thursday night when the bars offered cheap pitchers of beer.

Looking back, I realize that it never occurred to me that my partying behavior could have any ramifications on nursing school. Everyone was smoking pot, and it wasn't unusual to find it at afternoon block parties. I'd moved from the dorm to a house near Mifflin Street, famous for its summer bash where the mayor, a twenty-seven-year-old, could be seen. As far as the drinking went, well, that was a pastime throughout the state, not just on campus. As I write this, a new list of the top "drunkest cities in America" reveals that twelve of the top twenty cites cited are in Wisconsin, the first four within an hour of my home. Here in Fond du Lac we're merely number seven.

How did I keep my act together in college? Nursing school kept me grounded as changes occurred everywhere around me. I needed to focus on writing papers and continued to study for long hours. Academic life ultimately took priority over partying. There was a built-in structure. There was always food in the cafeteria. Our meal cards guaranteed three squares a day. Class schedules and syllabi ruled my life. I managed to keep up with class work and grew interested in the sciences. How very cool to paint bacteria on an Apgar plate, to see the human body dissected and preserved. We nursing students were allowed to view cadavers after the medical students dissected them. Weirdly, I had a craving for chicken after viewing muscle groups, but kept this to myself. The academic part of school also held my attention. I enjoyed the scientific principle and the idea of predicting outcomes. Like chaos theory, so much motion opened up many possibilities. When finished with school, I could work in pediatrics, surgery, a clinic, or public health.

And the professors: middle-aged women who wore reasonable shoes and tidy hairstyles. I remember hitchhiking to the VA hospital in faux leather boots with wedged heels during a snowstorm, working in wet socks all day. But the instructors seemed unfazed by crisis, by blood spurting from various orifices of demented old men who grabbed at student nurses. The instructors calmly demonstrated injections, blood draws, and dressing changes and emphasized the concepts of critical thinking and evaluation. Healing didn't just happen: it could be predicted and measured.

I wanted to be one of those women with clean, short fingernails and a grasp on practical knowledge. When one of my instructors announced her engagement and upcoming marriage (at what age? Maybe thirty-five!), another light turned on in my brain. One could marry after establishing a career. That fact was comforting to me, and later I mimicked her, marrying at thirty-two.

My job was to figure out how to be both a capable professional with heavy responsibility and a person committed to questioning authority, to throw caution to the wind at times, to be open to the beauty of the unpredictable. I learned to live with a foot in two worlds as both a serious academic and a playful student. I kept a journal to help me reconcile the flat facts of life and death as well as personal challenges. Was I really in love again, or was last weekend's flirtation just another fascination? Both ideas seemed equally important to me at that time, but I learned how to value and handle both. As it turned out, I graduated with honors from the university.

I like to think I still maintain a balance. I feel devoted to science as a way of explaining some mysteries, and that keeps me grounded in an otherwise crazy world. I believe in climate change and the need to reproduce results. What science doesn't or can't explain I make up through writing poetry and call that another way of knowing. I write to play around with the storytelling of science. While working in the university hospital just after graduation, I noted the tremendous strain on patients and families dealing with serious diagnoses and treatment. I worked on many units, including gynecology-oncology, and I had to imagine myself as competent and professional even when I didn't feel that way. Some days I felt like an imposter, taking the bus to work in my uniform and white shoes after a night of blue jeans and folly. When I wrote a poem from the patient's perspective, it helped me feel like I knew what I was doing, after all.

Though I no longer work as a nurse, I recall that work with a sense of pride. It's real and visceral and empowering. Nursing is deeply spiritual in its service to others, and I feel lucky to have done it, to have discovered satisfying adult behavior, even as I flirted with the foolishness of things. The lessons I learned in nursing school still help me sort fact from fiction as I deal with the serious challenges of the daily business of living in a complex world. Reframing my perspective through writing is key.

JUDY SCHAEFER

After the Code, Student Nurse

Finally time to pee, stampede
of white coats, rolling cart, stand

                clear, clear the bed, *when icicles*
                When icicles hang by the wall

Couldn't save this one
Toe tags and body bags, hand
Finally time to pee
warmest toilet in the January building
Time to sit, ah-yes relief
                of steady stream, *when icicles hang*

Sweet warm rush of privacy
Couldn't save this one
                When blood is nipp'd and ways befoul

Warm cocoon like mother's womb
So easy to stay here, cuddling

                self's slow body, slow soul, *nightly sings*

Biting back vomit, sobs
swallowing the slow studied idealism
Swallowing, couldn't save this one

Judy Schaefer, Harrisburg Area Community College graduate, 1977. Courtesy Judy Schaefer. Photo by Daniel Schaefer.

Push off the commode, stand
Pivot to the basin, scrub
              gently wash each hand, *then nightly*
              Then nightly sings the staring owl

Return, try to walk, pivot, transfer, stand
go back now, down the hall, call lights on

JUDY SCHAEFER

I've singing lessons

So let me out of class
Early please
It is time to go
No calculus
Anatomy

Throw a syringe like a dart
Remain alert to peristalsis after breakfast, lunch, and dinner
Smile when you enter the room
See one, do one, teach one

Sing for a lesson
It is time to go
So let me out of school
Early
Please

Nonetheless, this deference was insufficient. Assigned to a male surgical ward, I encountered a ward sister who, although young, was of the traditional belief that student nurses must be broken and molded to the cause. I never did discover what cause. In those days, names were always surnames and rarely spoken. As individuals, we were subsumed under our function. We existed as the doer of deeds and not the holder of family names.

The ward sister, a title from the days of Florence Nightingale and since replaced by charge nurse, was addressed only as *ward sister*, never by her name. She identified me as *that* student nurse. I felt cursed even though none was voiced outwardly. Now I marvel at the antipathy she lavished upon that title.

As a university nursing student, I was not beholden to the hospital training system. I was supernumerary to their labor requirements and was there to learn. Indeed, I had the right to organize my learning needs. That right, however, soon proved to represent delusional thinking on the turf of this ward sister. She eloquently expressed her distaste at my presence, at the university course, and at the probable outcome of my nursing career.

To minimize our contact, therefore, she confined me to the afternoon shift while she worked the morning shift. One December afternoon, she commanded me to assemble and hang the new Christmas decorations. A former patient had left money specifically for this purpose, and she had bought the very best decorations. After she departed, the other nurses went about their tasks. The solitary task of assembling these decorations separated me from the nursing team.

Left alone, I felt abandoned. The knife stab of grief showed on my face, but no one noticed until the cleaner passed by. I had never spoken to the cleaner—in those days, workers exchanged talk only within their peer group. Yet this woman moved across the rigid class lines and spoke to me, taking time from her duties to listen to my woes. She recommended a solution: involve the convalescing patients.

Heartened by her advice, I enlisted the help of those at the foot of the ward as they were closest to discharge. Delighted to help, the men worked willingly. After a few hours, I stood back to view the decorations. Instead of cascading swirls, instead of interlocking circles, instead of bands of cheerful color, I saw squished up bundles masquerading as carefree Christmas celebrations. Perhaps the large hands of manual laborers were a less optimum choice for assembling dainty decorations. The cleaner whispered, "She will kill you for this mess."

Next afternoon at report, the ward sister glowered witheringly at me. As soon as I heard her voice rise, I tuned out. As a daydreamer at school, I was accustomed to adults going into tirades that held little interest to me and so had perfected the technique of listening to tones, not words. The first time I heard Mozart, I thought he, too, knows the art of tuning out the words and juggling only the tones.

When ward sister's tones settled, I was confirmed as a person of no consequence: she refused to assign me a task. Abandoned again, I stood alone. The cleaner came over and said, "You can work with me." Grateful for the company, I followed. Thanks to her tutelage, I gained certificates in *Damp Dusting* as well as the *Care and Thrifty Use of Electricity*. Yes, the hygiene and the economy of the hospital were deemed safe in my hands.

Nursing was not. Daily, the ward sister refused to sign my nursing practicum book. Her denial threatened to dislodge my sanity, but three people rallied to my cause and showed me the generosity of their spirits. The first of this trio was the cleaner who showed me how to work and chat with the patients. Listening to her, I began to appreciate that she was a healing agent. Later research showed that cleaners of floors and bedside furniture are indeed significant healers in such a ward setting.

Their role in healing arises from the fact that the cleaners talked with the patients as individuals, not as surgical cases. For the patients, this cleaner placed bets on dogs, horses, and pigeons; such information extended my extracurricular syllabus. In addition, she brought in the gossip of the neighborhood, the gang fights and the stabbings. In word and deed, she was the advocate for the outside world, one to which the patients would return. From her, I learned that the community is greater than the institution of the hospital. Moreover, I saw that healing requires personal contact and mundane conversation. I learned that ordinary humanity often outperforms other healing techniques. I recognized a generosity of spirit when one human being reached out to another without gain or guile.

The second who showed me the generosity of their spirit were the men who helped with the decoration debacle. They described themselves as "lucky to be alive" because they had been "waving to the angels" when their situations were acute. I was too new to clinical nursing to appreciate their long worded diagnoses and their postsurgical dilemmas. Thanks to surgical intervention and good nursing, however, they lived for another day and looked forward to discharge.

On the one hand, I found it salutary to hear their praise and to realize that gratitude is a sister to compassion. On the other, this combination of compassion and gratitude presented me with a dilemma. I heard the truth of their gratitude, but I failed to connect it to the experience I was enduring. For me, their truth was a concept but not the reality of the ward experience for junior student nurses such as me.

To nudge me out of this dilemma, they gave me ways to cope. As manual laborers, they had little work status. They were accustomed to shoveling muck on building sites, lifting hods of brick, as well as broom sweeping the paths and gutters. They fetched and carried in skilled trades as carpenters and bricklayers. As underdogs, they had learned ways to stand up for themselves without losing their jobs. I began my crash course in work survival. They were good tutors, for I became more focused: no longer did I let intravenous drips run dry. Besides, they spoke privately with the ward sister and something shifted in her attitude.

Although she still confined me to the afternoon shift and away from her presence, she did assign another student nurse to oversee me. My second week on that ward began with the promise of nursing tasks. The assigned nurse referred me to the men at the foot of the ward. This was a gift indeed, for they taught me, from a patient's perspective, basic patient care: how to give bedpans and baths and change beds.

They also taught me how to give injections. "Throw it like a dart," they commanded. But dart throwing had eluded my secondary school curriculum. Mindful that I was practicing on their derrieres, they rustled up kith and kin to take me to pubs to learn dart throwing. These lessons also necessitated drinking pints of beer, which did little to enhance my aim. Gallantly, my companions resolved that deficiency by declaring: "You have a curved eyeball." Face saved, I persevered.

In time, the beer, the darts, and the curved eyeball harmonized and I was entrusted to give injections. I felt launched on my nursing career. These men gave me more than access to practical skills—they gave me confidence in my ability to nurse. This newfound asset helped stiffen my erstwhile jelly field of a backbone. I now eyeballed the rest of the nursing team.

I was a force to be reckoned with, willing to use guerrilla tactics to hold onto my sanity and survival. This was my introduction to the politics of power imbalance. I became aware that I, too, wanted power—not the power of domination, for I lacked the personality of a leader. I wanted to pursue my learning and sustain my survival without harassment.

I told my story to anybody who would listen and many who did not. My story encapsulated the victimhood I endured with respect to that ward sister in particular and the institution in general. For years to come, I milked my victimhood story.

I remembered standing back and watching the men mangle the decorations that evening. I recalled the next day when I arrived early for report in order to witness the initial reaction of the ward sister: absolute horror. Her horror morphed into silent rage. A rage so intense that I thought she would have a stroke. I recalled how I hugged myself, gleeful that I had managed to rattle the bars of her cage. *Gotcha.* Internally, revenge thrilled me. Externally, I stood with my head hung, demure drop of the shoulders and wringing hands, acutely aware that by exhibiting the model of contriteness I was infuriating her further.

Eventually, my nursing and my attitude matured. The depth of this understanding came about slowly as my assigned university tutor worked assiduously with me. Specialized in psychological nursing and well acquainted with the survival options of student nurses, this tutor encouraged me to see the range of conscious and unconscious motivations on my part.

Intellectually, I was willing to discuss this. Emotionally, I was still holding on to my victimhood story. I needed this brief episode to showcase the trials to which I was subjected by the dominatrix of this domain. Adding understanding ruined my tale of woe and burst asunder my persona as an innocent student nurse.

My tutor listened. From her, I experienced the greatest gift: the gift of being heard. Being heard unconditionally was a novel experience for me. My account did not become a football to be kicked around with differing interpretations and explanations. No, my story reigned as is. As a result, I trusted my tutor and her thinking.

During this practicum, my university studies dictated that I journal my experiences. One incident I recorded was the passing of one of those men at the foot of the ward. Instead of achieving his expected medical discharge, he died on the ward.

When I returned from days off, the ward sister informed me of his passing. She waited and watched my reaction. I was astounded. My utter surprise emanated from the fact that he had acted without the ward sister's permission. I regarded her as the fulcrum of all activity in this ward. Thus, the unilateral act of dying without her permission ranked high as guerrilla tactics. He had scored a bull's-eye. Tactically, however, I could not share my delight with the ward sister. Thus, I had nothing to say. Nor did she comment further to me.

After the report, I went to the remaining men at the foot of the ward. They explained about his relapse and the efforts undertaken to save him, but it was not to be. They talked about the process of his dying, but I wanted to know the *reason* for his death. Why had he chosen that moment to die?

In my journal, I debated what could have happened to enable him to challenge the ward sister so effectively and succeed. My tutor picked up the limited context in which I placed his death. She returned to the moment of my hearing the news from the ward sister and questioned me further on my reaction and the ward sister's motives. I refused to countenance that the ward sister might have some concern about my reaction to his death.

By this time, my tutor was well acquainted with my worldview. She appreciated that I was one of that 30 percent of the population who need to know the reason. How this man died was immaterial to me; *why* he died at that moment was critical. I was convinced he had willed his death. I regarded him as an active agent in his demise. The disease was merely the road taken to fulfill his decision.

Thus began years of discussion around death and dying. My tutor and I had opposite views. What we shared in common, however, was the need to question. She prompted me to think for myself and gave me the power to voice my thoughts, however inadequately expressed. She appreciated that a student has knowledge and is instrumental in gaining an understanding of the topic. Over time, I grew to respect her as much as I did the cleaner and the men at the foot of the ward. She became the third person in my trinity.

This trinity enabled me to survive and thrive throughout a five-and-a-half-year course. From them, I learned about power. I gained an understanding that power is like an amoeba that oozes haphazardly into all crevices. To be effective, however, power needs both boundaries and cautious use. From this trio, I learned to be patient when using power. Indeed, patience counts even more than the execution of power.

To this trinity, I owe a debt of gratitude. They guided not only my nursing practice but also my postgraduate work and specialization in palliative care. More than that, their generosity of spirit enabled me truly to experience all aspects of humanity and to know that humanity is the crux of nursing.

CORTNEY DAVIS

Nursing 101

Silver scissors glistened, the fluted jewel of a nursing pin
nestled against her breast. I was restless,
watching the shirt move over the boy's back

three seats forward. She hushed us, a hiss of cotton against silk,
then she said *pain* and *shot,* and there
in that bright arena, a crescendo of moans like sweet violins.

I learned how cells collide then meld and peel into spheres,
multisided like soccer balls or Rubik's Cubes.
I stabbed oranges until my hands ran with juice, then patients

until my hands rang with grace. I learned the quick save:
airway entered upside down and turned into breath. I learned
to kiss death, my lips seeking those slack mouths, while a boy

waited, flicking his bright cigarette, the burning eye that led me,
my shift over, to his embrace. Even there,
I longed for the corridors where patients slept in silence

thick as grief. Where the night nurse moved in my favorite dance—
pianissimo, pale through hospital halls.

YOLANDA PEREZ-SHULMAN

My First Clinical Day

Before I entered nursing school, hospitals were places of mystery to me. I didn't understand medical "talk," the strange names of medications, or what the various procedures entailed. The first time I was introduced to "hospital" was when I was eleven years old. My sister and I stayed in the lobby of Long Beach Children's Hospital while my parents visited my new baby brother who was born five weeks prematurely. My parents would bribe us to behave with a chocolate bar or small toy from the hospital gift shop.

In high school, my father took me to my grandmother's hospital room when she was recovering from surgery. She seemed weak but was able to get up and walk around. When she stood up, I noticed that her calves were so skinny her compression stockings hung loose. Then, when I was in college, my mom took me to see my aunt at UCLA Medical Center. I remember the bright windows and the background buzz that seems ever present in a medical center. There was something very cool about being there, but when I saw the IV in my aunt's hand, my stomach turned. The last time I went to a hospital was to visit my college friends who'd just had a baby boy. Their hospital room was filled with balloons, flowers, and giggles.

I attributed my assumed "hospital-phobia" to the fact that I'd been named after my father's youngest sister who had died of cancer when she was thirteen years old. My parents named me after her believing that when they heard her name, now my name, their sadness would be overcome by happiness. After I learned the source of my name, I avoided any risky activity that would land *me* in the hospital. But as I would learn in nursing school, nothing can protect us from the randomness of life's events.

In spite of my aversion to hospitals, I enrolled in nursing school at Massachusetts

Yolanda Perez-Shulman, Massachusetts General Hospital Institute of Health Professions, 2009. Courtesy Yolanda Perez-Shulman.

General Hospital (MGH). If you told me that I'd be wearing scrubs and attending nursing school in Boston at the age of thirty-four, I'd have advised you to get a psych evaluation. But biology had been one of my favorite subjects, next to history and architecture. A picture book of the human body was my childhood favorite. I studied the pictures of an army of white blood cells battling an infection.

I enjoyed the classroom portion of my nursing education—but eventually we students had to face our first clinical day. One afternoon after a full day of classes, our clinical instructor, Sharon, met us for a quick tour of Bigelow 11, the general medicine floor of MGH. Bigelow 11 would be our clinical site for the semester. As we walked past the various landmarks, halls, and rooms we would have to remember, Sharon gave us instructions. "Don't hang around the nursing station. We are guests. Clean up after yourselves if you use the lounge."

She asked our clinical group of five if anyone had never been inside a hospital before. I sheepishly raised my hand. I lied. Even though I'd been in various hospitals a few times in my thirty-something years, compared to my classmates, I was a novice. Most of them had mothers, sisters, aunts, or cousins who were nurses. And some classmates had mothers, fathers, or grandfathers who were doctors. A few classmates had worked in hospitals or in research prior to attending nursing school. But *my* parents, my aunt, and an uncle, were teachers. I felt as unprepared for the hospital environment as if I'd never set foot in one before.

When our tour was over, Sharon sent us off. "Get a good night's rest and be ready to go tomorrow."

The night before my first clinical experience, I spent hours getting ready for the big day. I packed a granola bar and put a crisp twenty-dollar bill in the front pocket of my backpack. I laid out my teal scrubs on a chair in the living room. I'd have to change there since I'd be waking up at five, and I didn't want to disturb Adam, my husband, who'd graciously agreed it would be a good idea for me to go to nursing school. He didn't even mind the student loans.

I managed to eat something in spite of my growing anxiety. What would I face in the hospital? Around eight thirty, I took a children's Benadryl to help me fall asleep. My shoulders were tight, and the knots in my muscles made my neck feel as thick as an ox's neck.

At five, the alarm went off. *What are you doing?* I asked myself. *You cannot be serious!* I'd worked at some important places in my life. The summer after I graduated from college, I interned with the National Park Service at Jamestown, Virginia. I was selected for an internship at the U.S. Embassy in London. I was a cast member at Disneyland in California. Nursing was never on the list of things I wanted to do when I grew up.

I went through the motions of getting ready, trying to provide some routine in my day. It was a dark cold October morning and I shivered waiting for the

D-line subway. At Park Street, I made the switch to the Red Line. There were a few other classmates there too—I recognized their teal scrubs. We sat next to each other but said nothing as we approached the entrance of MGH, the oldest public hospital in Boston. The ether dome, the iconic symbol of the hospital, has been the site of the first public demonstration of anesthesia. People came from around the world to be treated at this Harvard teaching hospital.

In my first week of nursing school, an instructor noted what an honor and privilege it was to care for another human being. During a class presentation, a classmate, Liza said, "I get a rush listening to another person's heart—their life source." Facing this clinical day, I realized the responsibility of nursing. This would be the first time I would care for another person as a nurse, not as a big sister, babysitter, friend, or wife.

At 6:30 A.M., the lobby at MGH was bustling with people coming and going. Various groups of nursing students from other schools staked out meeting spots. Boston College students wore maroon scrubs, while students from Northeastern, Simmons, and UMass all wore navy scrubs. I was dressed in bright teal, a color that reminded me of a California beach day. I remember how my mother had urged me to become a candy striper in high school—her dream, not mine. Down the hall, the air was filled with the scent of freshly brewed coffee, tempting me as I walked past the "Coffee Central kiosk" to get to the elevators. But the last thing I needed was an upset stomach on this first day of clinical. Killer bees already swarmed inside my stomach.

I ran into a clinical group member, Alice. Her smile calmed me.

"I could barely sleep last night," she said as the elevator opened. There was no turning back. We were at Bigelow 11.

The city's early morning quiet was replaced by beeps of telemetry and flashing screens. A few nurses sat around the nursing station. Their pockets were filled with alcohol wipes and tape. They wore stethoscopes like necklaces. Their clogs were scuffed and smudged.

Our clinical group gathered in the back corner. Sharon gave us our assignments. We were expected to do vital signs: take the patient's blood pressure, temperature, heart rate, and oxygen saturation level. Next, we were responsible for bathing the patient if they were unable to get out of bed. And we were to obtain a history and physical.

"Do not touch any machines or give the patient any medications unless I am with you or the RN on duty is," Sharon warned.

I went into the lounge for a drink of water. The window faced west, over Beacon Hill, the Charles River, and Cambridge. I got a glimpse of the CITGO sign and the Fenway on that cloudy, overcast day. The nurses' lockers were covered with pictures of their children, boyfriends, and pets.

Suddenly, I wanted to go home. But I couldn't. My husband had generously taken on supporting us for the three years I would be in school. I'd had a good paying government job at Boston City Hall. But all I wanted in life was a job and career where I could help people.

My assignment was the patient in the room at the end of the floor facing I-95 north. The patient, I'll call her Gail, had been hospitalized for an emergency cholecystectomy. I quickly looked up information in my portable med-surge book. Why were the words so difficult? It was much easier to say "gallbladder removal" than coalee-sis-tectomy!

I knocked on Gail's door and walked inside. "Hello, I'm Yolanda, a nursing student." I was so tense I barely mumbled. "I'll be working with you today."

She looked at me, confused. "What? You have to speak up."

It felt like I was yelling. My face was hot, my hands trembled. I took her vital signs, her blood pressure, heart rate, temperature, and oxygen level—all normal.

Her room looked north over Charlestown, the Boston Harbor, and I-95. "What a great view," she said with a smile. She asked what was next and agreed to answer my questions for the medical history.

After her vital signs, she got up and sat in the chair, and tried to puff up her "bed-head" hair.

"I ate too much Chinese food the other night. I knew I shouldn't, but I had a craving." She tapped my hand. "Next thing I know, I'm here at MGH and I need surgery." She lifted up her johnnie to show me the incisions on her abdomen.

She answered all my questions; then I performed my exam. Her heart, lungs, and bowel sounds were fine— just like those of my healthy classmates when I'd practiced on them in class a few weeks ago.

Around 10:00 A.M., I went to the lounge for a snack. A few of my clinical group members were chatting. Alice, Marlena, and Kate remarked how easy this first day was. "Everybody here is so nice." We laughed about being unable to sleep the night before. It was strange, but the hospital floor truly was quiet and calm, nothing like the frantic action you might see on TV or in a movie.

· · ·

I'd spent the last twenty-four hours thinking and worrying about the gravity and acuity of hospital patients, yet I knew that all the studying in the world would not make me a good nurse. I had to remember the human touch. I understood that hospitals are places in which tragedy occurs. But I was learning that there is *life* in hospitals too. People can still smile, laugh, and share a story. I'd arrived in the morning feeling like a giant phony wearing scrubs and carrying a stethoscope. On the T, riding home, I felt a sense of relief to get this first clinical day out of the way. My eyes and feet felt heavy, but my spirit was energized. I was one day closer to being a nurse.

RACHEL RENEE GAGE

Buzz, Buzz, Buzz

My professor is a mosquito buzzing in my ear and around my head
I want to escape
Buzz, Buzz, Buzz
Complaining, nagging, belittling
Buzz, Buzz, Buzz
No positive words, no positive reinforcement, no uplifting thoughts
Buzz, Buzz, Buzz
Negative comments, disengaged and critical comments
Buzz, Buzz, Buzz
Buzz, Buzz, Buzz
I need a bigger flyswatter

HEATHER FOSTER

Marriage as Sterile Technique

Your hands better be clean when you start.
Not just the clean that lets you sit down
at the table for supper. I mean clean
like when you scrubbed up
to your elbows with chemical foam, singing
"Happy Birthday" twice, to visit your preemie
in NICU. Clean like showering twice
between men, surgeon clean.
And for god's sake plan ahead.
Have your sterile field draped and prepared.
Have those other dirty people
leave the room. Two-person show—you can never be
too careful. Lay out your things in the order
you need to touch them. Don't lean over.
You're practically crawling with doom.
You'll leave a hair, a drop of sweat, a ravenous strand
of necrotizing strep. All it ever takes is one.
Focus. The entire one-inch border is unclean. Open everything
away from yourself. Keep yourself out
of the other person's body.
If your gauze ends up crooked, over the edge
of the wrapper, start over. You've ruined everything.
When you're gloving, cover the strong side
first. Keep your hands
in your own no-no zone—chest to crotch.
Protect your fucking field.

Heather Foster, Union University graduate, 2016. Courtesy Heather Foster.

If you brush away a stray hair, start
over. If someone gets too close,
start over. If you look away even once.
If you sneeze. If you cough.
Contaminated.
If there's an itch you have to scratch. If you
breathe. Start over, start over, start over.
Everything in the room wants to swallow your patient alive.

LADY AMAKA OFFODILE

From a Far Place

In 1988, a young Nigerian woman, I had just graduated from the University of Benin when I decided to move to the United States to start a family with my husband. I'd had the privilege of traveling to cities in the United Kingdom, Ireland, and Italy on vacations, but none of those trips prepared me for my arrival in New York. Navigating my way through JFK airport to the busy city streets, squeezing through heavy human and vehicular traffic, traveling the six- to eight-lane highways, seeing several choices of unfamiliar foods and drinks . . . ahhh! needless to say I was very grateful to have my husband by my side to help. Within the next four years, we had our three children, and I started my career as a certified public accountant (CPA) in Cleveland, Ohio.

My job as an auditor flew me to different client sites across the country, such as cities in Ohio, Michigan, California, Texas, and others. The clients paid for our team's expenses: flights, lodging, food, phone calls, and rental cars. I enjoyed the job, but it required a lot of traveling, long stressful hours calculating numbers, and chasing after staff who would rather not deal with us auditors. I was successful as an accountant, yet I struggled to find a deeper level of job satisfaction. I yearned for a career more emotionally fulfilling, involving less travel, and offering a more flexible work schedule.

In 2002, I quit my job as a CPA and enrolled in the accelerated bachelor of science in nursing (BSN) program at a local university. Wow—what a challenge and what a change! I'd been working with computers, numbers, reluctant clients, facts, and figures, but now I would be working with a different type of clientele—patients, family members, doctors, therapists, and other hospital employees. I'd go from working in a cubicle by myself to working in a large hospital, caring for people at their most vulnerable moments.

Lady Amaka Offodile, Kent State University College of Nursing graduate, 2004. Courtesy Lady Amaka Offodile.

I graduated in 2004 with my BSN. Looking back, my nursing education was a difficult challenge. As a Nigerian immigrant, I was unfamiliar with the U.S. health-care system in general. The nursing school admission requirements, curriculum, graduation, and licensing criteria here differed from those in Nigeria. For example, to gain admission to a school of nursing in Nigeria, you must have a grade B equivalent or better in mathematics, English, biology, physics, and chemistry; score high at the Joint Admissions & Matriculation Board national exam; and pass both the written entrance exam and the in-person interview at the applicable school of nursing.

Science had never been an academic strength of mine, and during my nursing education I seemed to be studying twice as hard as my classmates just to maintain good grades in my courses. I sought help from my professors and even paid for tutors. On top of those stresses, I had three children in middle school. I remain forever grateful to my children and my husband, who have continued to support me. From reviewing my homework, explaining scientific concepts, to typing my reports quicker than I ever could, members of my family supported me in every way possible. My husband even ran the schedules of our children's extracurricular activities, despite his own busy schedule as department chair at the university, allowing me time to study, work, or sleep. Even now, as a loving mother and a compassionate nurse, it affects me when I take care of young adults as patients. When my son was sixteen years old, I cared for a beautiful girl of the same age who had sustained a traumatic brain injury from a motorcycle accident. She and her boyfriend were riding without helmets when they crashed into an oncoming vehicle. Her boyfriend died and she was in a coma for several weeks; then she was transferred to our long-term acute care hospital. Thank God she recovered and was discharged to a rehabilitation center; it was hard for me not to imagine myself in her mother's predicament.

In addition to classroom learning, my nursing education program required several hours of clinical experience. Working with human beings as a nurse continues to be more emotionally rewarding for me than working with numbers and computers as a CPA. As students on clinical, we were assigned our own patients and a preceptor. Under supervision, we performed nursing tasks and interventions for our patients. I remember my very first clinical patient, a ninety-three-year-old female in a medical-surgical unit of a local hospital. She had been diagnosed with multiple debilitating diseases and so activities of daily living, such as transferring, toileting, bathing, and dressing, had become nearly impossible. I listened patiently as she shared her personal life story. She never had a child and had retired thirty years earlier after her husband died suddenly of a heart attack. When it was time for her medications, I taught her about the pills I administered and answered her questions about their sizes, colors, and shapes. Again, as I gave her a warm bath,

I listened intently as she shared some of her experiences regarding hospitalization. She had no family or friends. She felt alone, scared, and unsure of the future. Some of the doctors, nurses, and other hospital staff performed their services so hurriedly that she hardly had the opportunity to chat. At the end of the clinical session that day, I returned to that patient's room to inform her of my departure back to school. The patient's face lit up as she stretched out her arms for a hug. "Thank you for the way you washed my feet," she said with a radiant smile. She stated that not only had she not received a warm bath in the past few days due to staff shortage, but also no one had "taken the time to clean between my toes and lotion them since I have been in this hospital." What a learning experience for me, who could still take daily baths. After that, bathing my patients became much more meaningful for me. To this day, I still think about her and do my best to provide the best nursing care that I can—because I never know how my presence and actions will impact those patients assigned to me.

For the past twelve years, I have worked in various nursing fields. My first job was in a medical-surgical unit. From there, I worked in two different long-term acute care hospitals and then in a transitional care unit and home health care. For the past few years I've been working in a post-acute care center in Cleveland, Ohio. I have had the unique privilege of holding the hands of lonely, frightened patients; educating patients and families on disease processes, wound management, medications, and nutrition; consoling the nervous and brokenhearted family members of dying patients; and helping other nurses balance the stress of professional and personal life. I can honestly say that I have also experienced my fair share of discrimination, racism, insubordination, and neglect in the workplace from patients, doctors, managers, and fellow employees. I have had to go the extra mile to prove that I am qualified, competent, and capable of performing multifunctional RN duties, especially providing total nursing care for the patients assigned to me. I endeavor to speak slowly and clearly, yet some people tune me out under the pretense that they don't understand my accent, to which I have always insisted that if they listened well and paid attention to what I am saying, they would understand me. Pronunciation, intonation, idioms, synonyms, and exceptions to the rule make the English language difficult. When coupled with cultural differences, communication constituted an extra stress factor for me. Transliterating thought into the correct English grammar resulted in slight delayed responses, which were often misinterpreted by my listeners. After administering the pain medication as ordered, I once said "sorry" to my postoperative patient who was in severe pain. She looked puzzled. I couldn't understand why and so I asked. She said: "You didn't cause my pain." In my Nigerian culture, saying "sorry" does not mean accepting responsibility or admitting guilt. We equate "sorry" to "empathy." The word just means the speaker places a high value on the other person, emotionally feeling their pain and wishing the pain would go away. I have since then learned not to say sorry to any patient. I recently decided to further my leadership opportunities by returning to school. In January 2016, I began working toward my master of science in nursing degree, while still practicing as a registered nurse supervisor.

Throughout the years, I have battled challenges on the job; however, the positive experiences have far outweighed the negative. Nursing indeed is transcultural, multidimensional, and universal. Every time I drive to work, I always thank God for the opportunity, and I pray for my patients—because being a nurse is one of the best decisions I have ever made.

LINDA MAURER TUTHILL

Relics

I grab a snub-nosed scissors
from its hook by the bathroom sink,
see a gleam of history.

Issued with my student uniform,
these scissors scurried with me
through a maze of corridors
to morning report. I shivered
wondering what assignment loomed.

Do white medication cards
and pink treatment cards
multiply in my slotted tray?
Can they *all* be due at 10 A.M.?

"Pace yourself, Miss Maurer,
pace yourself!" Miss Donough urged,
but my pace was stuck on slow.
In my uniform pocket, I felt
the bulge of bandage scissors,
took comfort from hardware
more stable than myself.

Five decades later I remain
scissor bright, steely resolve,
hinge swinging with the memory
of a first-year student.
My trenched hands, rope veins
gnarled by the warp of years.

JEANNE BRYNER

These Also Were My Teachers, Senior Year, 1978

Not the surgeon's huff and bellow
Jesus Christ spit from his mouth
his cases mixed up, a new orderly
brought second case first,
a sugary woman's gallbladder
instead of a boy's hernia.

Not the fast talk of the nurse
anesthetist, her dyed auburn hair
perfect under her bonnet. Not the rope
arms of three seasoned surgical nurses
Betty, Tillie, and May, how they
studied my fawn eyes, my lamb white hose.

But, how I shuffled, shut
outside their huddle, green
tiles, a cold room, its fire pit
any elder can toss you in.
A pup, they handed me to him
tucked me under his arm.

Three and a half hours, fat
and fascia, open abdomen, the old way.
And me? Gutted by his tongue.

Forty journals later, here we stand
November's breath brushes our skin.
Those three nurses? I touch them
with my pen. Aaah, see? They're my
squinty aunts limping off the train.
We hug, pancake makeup smell,

wool coats. Yes, we gush, even
cry, it's been a long pushy ride.

Honey, we've missed you, Aunt Betty
squeezes me like a Christmas doll.
They're sorry for Mama's death,
another cancer, their baby sister gone.
I am fixing to fold Aunt Tillie's walker,
help May with her lumpy bags.

At home, in my clean kitchen
a cake waits, coffee ready to brew.
Tonight, they'll share yarns,
the farm, its shaggy barn
a pony they used to ride,
sister secrets about Mama

stories I never knew
    tales to mend my heart.

PART III

To live in this world

you must be able

to do three things:

to love what is mortal:

to hold it

against your bones knowing

your own life depends on it;

and when the time comes to let it go,

to let it go.

MARY OLIVER, "IN BLACKWATER WOODS"

I can put the words down, like a hand against suffering.

The blood red towel drying near the dorm's heater pipes? Please focus on the towel's color. All lives depend on blood and our paths to professionalism are often shaped by lineage, geography, and political arenas. Rosa Sacharin was transplanted to England because she was Jewish and her life was in peril. Helen Albert and Minnie Brown Carter were discriminated against because they were black. As nurses, we are always dealing with blood: drawing it for testing, hanging bags of it for our patients, and fearing it for what it may carry. Still, we can never deny its ruby-like beauty nor divorce who we are or where we come from. The longer blood hangs around, the darker it becomes. But without blood, there's no heartbeat, no soul.

GEOFFREY BOWE

Student Nurse: An Early Experience in Mental Health

With long hair
and stumps for the legs
he'd lost
jumping in front of a train
my patient
would not have been out of place
in a hippy commune.

I was shocked
when he talked
of wanting to use
the amputated end of his femur
for the handle of a walking stick.

It was early summer.
Strands of light
wove themselves
in and out of cubicles.

For my part,
writing poetry
was in my every breath.
Each step I took
was a stanza.

Geoffrey Bowe, graduate, South West Cumbria School of Nursing in Barrow in Furness, Cumbria, England, 1983. Courtesy Geoffrey Bowe.

The patient
understood my art,
listened to me
as if listening
to an old guitar.

His fingers twitched
longing to find paper and pen.
Soon his thoughts flowed,
a burst artery of the soul.

His mother
had also jumped in front of a train
and now
his truth was written.

MARILYN MITCHELL

A Hundred Thousand Hospital Beds

Between your life and mine there are a hundred thousand hospital beds
made crisp with the gruesome knowledge of pain.
Trickling blood, gushing blood, soiling so many fresh linens.
Living in proximity is not the way to serve.
Yet it goads me, exhorts me to remember
the tight, white twisted bun and gentle red lips of Mrs. Thompson,
the heavy-lidded relief of dying Mrs. Murphy.
The discussion of the weather long ago
by a woman blackened ceaselessly
with her own wild cancerous flesh.
How can the nurse I became ever forget?

Marilyn Mitchell, SUNY Stony Brook's University graduate, 1980. Courtesy Marilyn Mitchell. Photo by John W. Mitchell.

ROSA M. SACHARIN

Nurse Training in Scotland 1943–1951

I was born in Germany in 1925 and my early life was deeply affected by the unrest there. On December 1, 1938, when I was thirteen years old I left Germany for England on the first "Kindertransport" (rescue efforts that transported Jewish children to Great Britain from Nazi Germany). After a short stay in a camp I was sent to Edinburgh, Scotland, in late December 1938. War broke out in 1939; I moved to Glasgow in 1941. I had problems adjusting and, when I was nearly eighteen years old in 1943, I found it difficult to know where I fit in and indeed what I could and should do. I had been introduced to the concept of nursing but knew nothing about what being a nurse actually entailed. The decision to apply to a nursing school was a difficult one. In fact, the initial contact with the hospital training program was made on my behalf in 1943 when the outcome of the war was still unclear; I didn't know whether I would remain in Scotland after the war. The career choices were limited to the essential needs of the war—nursing was one of them.

I received a letter from the matron of the Royal Hospital for Sick Children, Glasgow, inviting me for an interview. I went, reluctantly. The hospital, a very impressive looking building, stood on a hill with a view of Glasgow University. The matron, Miss Clarkson, was friendly, and although I was anxious, the interview went well. When asked if I had any questions, I asked how long I would have to stay before I could leave. She smiled and said: "Miss Goldszal, if you don't like us or we don't like you, you can leave after three months." When I received a letter of acceptance, I wept. I was to start my three-year training on August 3, 1943.

Only five probationers started that day.

Miss Sorrie, Sister Tutor, a kindly lady, helped us with our uniforms, particularly with the caps, and when we were ready went down to a large classroom in the basement. Miss Clarkson entered, welcoming us with the following address:

"Nursing is like the army: The senior staff—matron and assistant matron—are the officers. Sisters are the noncommissioned officers, and you are the 'privates.'" We were also called "probationers," referring to the initial period in which we had to prove our ability as student nurses.

The first week was spent in the classroom where we learned the basics of our role. We were then allocated to various wards. I was sent to a thirty-bed children's surgical ward where I carried out basic nursing tasks such as bed/cot making, bed

*Rosa M. Sacharin (*back row, second from right) *with nursing colleagues, circa 1950. Royal Hospital for Sick Children graduate, 1946. Copyright, National Health Service Glasgow and Clyde Archives, University of Glasgow, Scotland.*

bathing, and hair care including delousing. The children ranged in age from birth to thirteen; toddlers wore restrainers and, at that time, children were bedbound.

The initial training period in this ward lasted three months. During that period I participated in a variety of procedures, including removal of plasters during orthopedic clinic sessions—hard physical work since these involved hip spicas and large leg plasters. The plaster shears were heavy and this added to the strain of the work. It was of course also important to avoid hurting the child or causing injury. Apart from short meal breaks, the routine work had to be carried out.

On one occasion, when I was very tired and due to go off duty, I was told that as a junior nurse it was my duty to fine-tooth comb the children's hair. I had to complete this task before I could leave. When I was just too tired to complete my task of hair care or delousing and still had half the children in the ward to attend to, I decided to stop and told the ward sister that I was going off duty since I'd already exceeded my span of duty and was too tired to continue. In fact, I was weepy. She was surprised, but made no comment. I was surprised that there were no repercussions to my behavior.

We were expected to know every child's name, age, diagnosis, and any treatments given. While on my first night duty, the night Sister asked me to give report. I'd prepared myself for this, but I was so frightened that I could not utter a single word. When we had walked through half the ward, she stopped and said,

"Nurse, will you not tell me about the children?" It was kindly said, and I relaxed and proceeded to give my report. At the end, she thanked me. I was grateful for her understanding.

Nevertheless, I had difficulty adjusting, and after three months I went to Miss Clarkson and handed her my letter of resignation. She asked me to sit down, looked at me, and said, "I think we will send you to the country branch." I didn't object but simply accepted her decision. The move to the country branch in Drumchapel was immediate.

The hospital at Drumchapel was set just outside of Glasgow and at that time was quite rural. It could accommodate about a hundred children, some of whom were long-term while others spent a short time there to recuperate. Some of the children were bedbound; during the day, they were brought outside the building for fresh air and sunshine. Those who were well enough were dressed nicely and free to run about and play. It was a happy place. One morning, as I stood in the ward, still uncertain of my role, I heard my name called: "Nurse Goldszal, come and help me!"

Nurse Moira Campbell was a third-year nurse, tall and with a friendly and joyful approach to life. The children loved her. I joined her as we completed the ward tasks; we even had fun caring for the children.

Rosa M. Sacharin (back row, far left) with nursing colleagues, circa 1950. Royal Hospital for Sick Children graduate, 1946. Copyright, National Health Service Glasgow and Clyde Archives, University of Glasgow, Scotland.

It was then that I looked at myself and realized that my attitude was wrong—perhaps I could find a role in nursing. I returned to Yorkhill Hospital after three months at Drumchapel and although apprehensive, I finally settled down to follow the course of training.

I gained experience in medical, surgical nursing, operating theater, and outpatient admission hall (now called Accident and Emergency Department). We had to attend lectures given by physicians and surgeons as well as lectures given by the tutor who dealt with more advanced nursing techniques.

We were tested after each lecture and any absences had to be made up. At the end of the three-year training, we sat for the hospital final practical and oral examinations as well as for the state final examination. For the oral component, visiting examiners, both nurses and physicians, tested our knowledge. It was a stressful time, but I was able to cope.

To celebrate the end of our training, there was a final ceremony during which we were presented with our hospital certificates. I received my certification as a Registered Sick Children's Nurse from the General Nursing Council. Following registration, I worked as a staff nurse in the outpatient clinic on West Graham Street in Glasgow, a clinic established in 1888 and closed in 1953.

GENERAL (ADULT) NURSE TRAINING

After a period as a staff nurse, I applied to Stobhill Hospital for training in general (adult) nursing. As a children's nurse, I had to train for an additional two and a half years in a course that generally lasted three to four years. At my interview, the matron asked if I would be able to complete the course. I said, "Surely, the fact that I have successfully completed a course caring for sick children indicates my ability to do any other type of nursing, including the General Adult Nursing Course."

It should be said that there was quite a struggle for recognition of the Sick Children's Nursing course—we were often not recognized, as it was considered less technically challenging and more akin to babysitting. However, I was accepted and found caring for adults simply an extension of my previous course. I had no difficulty relating to adults of all ages, but physically it was more difficult due to their size and weight. However, there was always ready help given by male nurses, at least in the male wards. Most, if not all of them, had been in the Army Medical Corps and had ample experience in caring for severely wounded soldiers. Their humanity shone through in their approach to patients, and I benefited from their example.

The course content was based on the syllabus set by the General Nursing Council of Scotland, just as the Sick Children's Nursing course had been, but when comparing the courses regarding the close relationship between theory and practice, the former was far superior to the latter, both in content and practice. Following my final state examination and qualifying as what was then called an SRN (State Registered Nurse), I worked for three months as a night nurse in the operating theater before moving on to further my nursing education, applying for midwifery training in Ayrshire.

MIDWIFERY

The midwifery course consisted of two six-month sessions. The first six months prepared nurses to work as midwives in institutions, while the second six months enabled midwives to work independently. There were limited places available for training; I chose Ayrshire because there was a better chance of access to deliveries and fewer medical students competing for those deliveries. As nurses, we had to achieve a minimum of ten normal or uncomplicated deliveries.

The tutor prepared us for the work. We studied anatomy and physiology pertaining to the pregnant female, the theory and practice of delivery of the infant, care of the newborn baby, possible delivery complications, and postpartum care and complications. We had practical demonstrations in labor wards and practice using "dummies" in the classroom. Fortunately, we had no difficulty in getting the required number of deliveries, recording every case from admission through the process of labor and delivery.

For my second six months, if successful, I would be permitted to act on my own in the community. While still under the auspices of a hospital that provided additional theoretical preparation, we were moved to the District Midwifery Service, where we awaited calls to attend women in labor. I had a special bag with essential equipment, which was always inspected before I went on calls. To satisfy the conditions for service in the community, we had to provide written evidence of each case we attended. Both courses were well conducted and certainly prepared me effectively for the tasks ahead.

One of the rules regarding patients at home was that a district midwife had to be present at the delivery of the baby. It often occurred that the workload of the district midwife was such that she couldn't always be present. In this case, the student midwife had to contact the office for instruction and permission to conduct the delivery. I had to do this on two occasions and in both cases managed to handle the labor and delivery successfully. It was stressful but also gave me a tremendous sense of achievement.

After qualifying, I was asked to work as a district midwife. It had been a good training and, while I felt confident to work in that field, I wanted more experience within a hospital setting. Maternity hospitals were organized in different units: prenatal, labor wards, and nurseries. However, there was one small women's hospital in Glasgow with a small integrated maternity unit adjacent to the main hospital. This hospital was run by female doctors only. In those days, female medical students were often not accepted by their male colleagues. By creating their own domain, these female doctors were able to practice their profession. I applied to work there and was accepted. It was ideal for my role.

The maternity unit had two, later three, small labor rooms, one room for antenatal cases, one room for postnatal patients, and a small nursery. It was perfect. I wanted to work in an area where each of the different units providing maternity services was an integral part of the whole, rather than divided into separate units.

One example will highlight what this entailed. I was assigned to attend one woman in labor. She already had two boys and now wanted a baby girl. As labor progressed and the baby was about to be born, my patient became difficult and would not cooperate in pushing—she was frightened that her baby would be a boy. After much difficulty encouraging her to cooperate, the baby was born. And it was a boy. I realized by her behavior that there would be problems, and in fact she refused to accept her lovely, healthy boy. She wouldn't touch the child or feed him. The infant reacted to this rejection by vomiting every feeding given to him. It took great patience on my part to help the mother accept her lovely child.

Mothers stayed with us for fourteen days and during that time if all went well, both mothers and babies went home. Helping my patient to accept her little boy, I'd been able to use my skills as a midwife as well as the rich knowledge of infant and childcare that I'd obtained in my pediatric nursing course at the Royal Hospital for Sick Children in Glasgow. That kind of integrated care was exactly how I wanted to practice nursing.

ADDENDUM

While the main purpose of this essay is to describe my nurse training, it's also important to discuss its limitations as an educational, social, and political tool. Nursing, at least its philosophy, was then based on the assumption that those who chose the profession did so to help fellow humans in times of illness and stress. Nursing school administrators and teachers assumed that such students were capable of tenderness and had the ability to cope with illness, suffering, and death. As I look back on my profession and its value to society, I realize that no one mentioned the negative aspects of nursing training. Nor did I ask.

In the beginning, I felt that I was forced into something I didn't want to be or do. The information booklet only informed me of the course content and requirements regarding clothes, shoes, stockings, and other personal belongings. The limited introduction to the course and the emphasis on regulations, in particular the inferior role I was to play, made me rebellious. This was not what was expected of me; the purpose of training was to inform me of my inferior role in the scheme of caregiving. And to teach me to obey.

Since I was a rebel by nature, this type of environment fed my independent attitude and led to some friction. Since I was working in an environment that was different from the "outside world," I had to recognize the justification of this new and different form of behavior in order to function effectively.

It wasn't easy; there were times when I felt compelled to make known my own views. The theoretical course content was limited to learning the basics of anatomy, physiology, health and nutrition, medical and surgical conditions, *materia medica,* and of course all relevant nursing procedures. During my training, we did not receive lectures in psychology, although in my sick children's nursing course we were told of Sister Marie Hilda and her work with children affected by emotional trauma during the war. As previously mentioned, I was also given the opportunity to attend the seminar on psychology in Edinburgh in 1945.

Finally, it is worth stating that while I had problems accepting nursing as a career, I'm grateful to Miss Clarkson who perhaps recognized my early difficulties and guided me gently to pursue a career as a nurse.

While I followed the prescribed courses, I was also fortunate to have been given opportunities outside the routine courses, some of which were well beyond my understanding at the time but nevertheless acted as a stimulus to greater achievement and ultimate satisfaction in my nursing contributions.

ROSANNE TROST

Lesson Learned

Almost fifty years ago, I was a third-year nursing student doing my emergency room rotation at DePaul Hospital on the Fourth of July. I expected to see patients with injuries from fireworks or burns from backyard cookouts, but I wasn't prepared to see a young couple run into the ER carrying their daughter, who appeared to be seven or eight years old. The father had bloodstains darkening his light colored sport shirt, and his hands were covered in blood. The mother's bloody hands trembled as she attempted to soother her daughter.

"Laurie, you're going to be okay. Mommy and Daddy are staying right here with you."

The parents' eyes were frantic with fear, yet they spoke calmly to Laurie. I wondered how they could stay so calm as they tried to console their whimpering daughter.

Laurie's right arm was wrapped in a heavy white towel, soaked with more dark red blood than I had ever seen. I thought, *This is serious.* Miss Lang, my nursing instructor, helped me ease the young patient onto a stretcher, and we wheeled her to the exam room. Laurie looked so small and pale.

The parents followed, clinging to each other and eerily silent, but their expressions spoke volumes. Dr. Murphy walked into the room, nodding to Miss Lang and me. Always a humorous man, today he was somber as he introduced himself to Laurie's parents. I thought he would ask the parents to go to the waiting area—this was the era of strict hospital visiting hours, even for pediatrics. Instead he said, "We going to give Laurie a shot to ease her pain. You're welcome to stay with your daughter." They both nodded. He smiled at Laurie and gently patted her head.

Dr. Murphy asked me to give Laurie an injection of Demerol while he removed the bloody towel from her forearm. My hands shook as I drew up the medication.

Rosanne Trost, DePaul Hospital School of Nursing graduate, 1964. Courtesy Rosanne Trost.

Miss Lang began carefully to clean around the gaping wound with an antiseptic solution.

I leaned over our patient and said, "Laurie, you are doing so well. The medicine is going to make you feel better." She opened and then closed her eyes. Dr. Murphy asked the parents about the accident. In a quiet voice, the father replied, "Laurie fell on a jagged fence in our neighbor's backyard. He'd planned to get the fence replaced. This should never have happened."

Laurie's mother put her arm around her husband's shoulder, murmuring to him. Then she told us how the neighbor had run to their front door with Laurie in his arms. "Call an ambulance. Laurie's arm is bleeding," he cried. "Get an ambulance!"

In the neighbor's arms, Laurie had been very still. Too still. "When I saw all of that blood," Laurie's mom said, "I feared the worst." I understood that fear—I remembered that same fear when my little brother had been bitten on the neck by a Great Dane . . . a "friendly" Great Dane. My brother healed physically but still fears dogs, no matter their size. His scar is a constant reminder to me of how quickly tragedy can happen and how long lasting the effects can be.

Laurie began whimpering, "Mommy, I'm scared. My arm hurts real bad."

Dr. Murphy instructed me to give Laurie another injection of Demerol. He soothed our patient, saying, "You are so brave. I'm proud of you. Your mom and dad are right here."

Both parents were calm and loving as they supported Laurie, but I saw her mother turn away and wipe tears from her eyes. After the second injection, Laurie seemed to relax a bit. I marveled at how the medication had given her relief. Thank goodness. I also felt some relief.

The suturing was complicated. Miss Lang assisted Dr. Murphy as he carefully closed Laurie's wound, beads of perspiration glistening on his forehead. Miss Lang motioned for me to come closer. In my mind, I could hear her saying, *This is on-the-job training. Observe everything.* I'd always admired and respected her, now more than ever.

Soon I became engrossed, attentive both to the process and to our patient. When I glanced up at the father, I noticed how pale he was—I worried that he might faint. In spite of his own apparent suffering, he continued soothing his daughter.

"You are so brave. Mommy and I are proud of you, sweet girl."

With her eyes closed, Laurie whispered, "Daddy, I left my teddy bear by the fence." Miss Lang's eyes met mine as we heard the little girl's lament—such a typical comment in a normal setting, but so unusual in the ER.

Laurie seemed to doze, but at times she would cry out and her body would shudder. She looked so tiny and vulnerable, her pretty red hair streaked with dirt and dried blood. As he continued to suture, Dr. Murphy reassured the parents.

"These reactions are due to the trauma of her accident. We have her pain under control, and we're almost finished."

At last, the suturing was complete. Miss Lang and I began dressing the wound with four by fours, then larger bandages, followed by an ace wrap, very careful to minimize Laurie's discomfort. When I whispered to Laurie, "You are so brave!" she smiled, a weak smile that showed her missing two front teeth. Such a little girl. Now with such a big laceration.

Dr. Murphy spoke quietly with the parents. They looked fatigued, but I noticed the relief on their faces, how the color had returned to the father's face, how the mother's frown seemed to ease.

Dr. Murphy gave them wound care instructions. "The nurses will show you how to do it, and they'll give Laurie a tetanus shot. We'll also give you a prescription for an antibiotic to prevent infection—that was a nasty laceration. And you'll have a prescription for pain."

They thanked the doctor and Miss Lang and me over and over, even as they continued to reassure Laurie with kisses and soft words.

As preparations were made to discharge Laurie, Miss Lang motioned for me to follow her into the ER hallway. She leaned against the wall, and I noticed bloodstains on her lab coat. She complimented my work with Laurie. "You're an excellent student. Keep up the good work! You supported this scared patient and helped allay her apprehension. Dr. Murphy complimented your performance." I savored the compliment.

"There is still one important lesson you must learn and remember. You praised the patient, which is important, but you didn't acknowledge the parents' contribution. Just think how traumatized and helpless they felt. Yet they put their fears aside, and supported Laurie. I want you to go back in there and tell them what a great job *they* did. Praise them for staying by her side and for not falling apart. They could have waited outside the exam room, but they chose to stay."

Years later, when I became a mother, I understood with all my being how Laurie's mother must have agonized as she watched over her suffering daughter. How wise of my instructor to offer me this important lesson. I wanted more than ever to become the nurse she was. Straightening my student nurse cap, I walked back into the room. I was happy to see Laurie sipping ice chips. Her parents were smiling.

"I want to extend my appreciation to you for staying next to Laurie and comforting her. You were so helpful, not only to your little girl, but you made our job easier. We knew she felt better with you by her side and so could concentrate on treating her. I know this was not easy for you. Thank you."

The parents simply replied, "Thank you," relief and gratitude in their expressions. For the first time, the mother sank down onto a chair by the wall, closed her eyes and silently wept. Laurie held tight to her father's arm with her good hand as they discussed the missing teddy bear. Little by little, thankfully, things were returning to normal. I watched as Laurie, in a wheelchair with her parents by her side, left the ER and headed for home.

. . .

I learned a valuable lesson in the ER that Fourth of July weekend. Care for the patient must include compassion for the whole family. Some families, like Laurie's, might be able to stand by, to support their loved ones. Other families might not be able to—those family members also need compassion. Often patients come to the hospital alone or perhaps accompanied by a friend. No matter, it is our job to give care and compassion freely. Someday, we each might be in a similar position. We too might need a nurse's smile, her kind word. That lesson stayed with me throughout my nursing career.

PATRICIA KALAS

My Most Selfless "Patient," My Greatest Teacher

In the summer of 1967 something happened that is so difficult to put into words. However, this event has probably affected me professionally more than any other of my student nursing experiences.

My mother, Betty Place, was an RN, a graduate of Mt. Sinai School of Nursing in Cleveland, Ohio. She was in the WWII Army Nurses Program and graduated just as the war was ending. She married her high school sweetheart, John Place, who had just returned from serving in the navy. Mom started working at our community hospital, Trumbull Memorial Hospital in Warren, Ohio, and worked there for over forty years. As I grew up, I remember how proud I felt when I saw Mom in her freshly pressed, crisp white uniform. I also remember being so impressed, watching her fold her freshly starched cap and showing me how she bobby-pinned it on when she got to work. She was proud of her cap: she washed and starched it every weekend and then gently patted it onto the refrigerator door to dry. I loved seeing it there. I knew Mom missed us when she left for work—but I also knew how much she enjoyed helping people recover. When she came home from work, she looked tired but content and always had big hugs and kisses for us. I knew even as a small girl, I would follow in my mom's footsteps.

In the fall of 1966, as an eighteen-year-old high school graduate from a rural area, Gustavus Township in northeast Ohio, I was heading for Ann Arbor, Michigan, and the University of Michigan School of Nursing. I remember packing clothes, pictures, and toiletries into the trunk of our blue and white 1963 Ford Galaxy 500. My mom and dad and two younger brothers, Mike and David, and I got into the car, and Dad drove out of the driveway. I remember looking back at my home as we started down the road. I knew my life was soon to have a new horizon, and I hoped and prayed that I was prepared for the days ahead—and that in my heart I would always cherish and remember my beautiful childhood.

Patricia Kalas, University of Michigan graduate, 1970. Courtesy Patricia Kalas.

We drove straight from home to Ann Arbor, a four-hour drive, much to my brothers' chagrin. I think Dad was afraid if we stopped I'd want to go back home. As we drove into Ann Arbor, the thought of going back home did cross my mind. First we stopped at a small campus restaurant for lunch. I have no idea what I ate—I just remember seeing many college students and thinking, *am I ready for this?* Then, we drove through campus to find Moser-Jordan Dorm, my anxiety mounting. I realized how huge the campus was compared to my little farm community that had only a small church at the center, the place where everyone knew and cared for each other.

Finally we pulled up in front of Moser-Jordan Dorm and saw many other students carrying in their belongings. I soon learned that Moser was for the male students and Jordan for the females; I was on the fourth floor of Jordan. With all five of my family members helping, I carried my belongings to room 453. I was disappointed not to be in the nursing dorm—Couzins Hall—which was right across from the school of nursing.

When we walked into my room, there were two girls sitting there waiting for me—I was in a triple! Lolly was from Philadelphia, an electrical engineer major. Judy was from Flint, Michigan, a French/Education major. We all felt the same anxieties as we set out on our amazing adventure. Even though we three had just met, my new friends made it possible to wave good-bye to my family without crying as they headed home, although I know I saw a tear in my dad's eye. Lolly, Judy, and I became lifelong friends; we still keep in touch after fifty years.

As classes started, I found that it wasn't much different from high school. The elective classes were great, but the introduction to nursing classes showed me that I had made the right decision, and that nursing was my destiny.

Nursing students went to class year-round with short breaks three times a year between semesters. I really missed home, especially on family birthdays. I missed our church family and our big community homecoming on the Fourth of July. It was especially hard going back to "U of M" the first summer of 1967. I'd been home for only one and a half weeks and had so enjoyed the peace and quiet and slow pace of my break—sitting by my dad's big pond, listening to the birds and watching the fish jump, and visiting friends and family. Also, ahead of me was a single summer course I was dreading. It was Physiology and Gross Anatomy. I had lived a very sheltered and blessed life and had never been exposed to death. I'd never even been to calling hours or a funeral. I was fearful and anxious even to think of touching a dead human body. I didn't know how I would react or even if I could surmount this hurdle on my way to becoming a nurse. But I knew I had to.

I remember, as if it were yesterday, walking to the lab after our first anatomy lecture. The lab was located in an old building behind the hospital. As I walked in,

I felt as if I was in a tunnel. The walls were a dark beige-brown; the lighting was dim and the floors were well-worn smooth concrete. There were no pictures on the walls. It was dreary—not uplifting at all for the experience ahead. As I got to the room number on my class schedule, I saw others quietly waiting. When the lab door opened, no one wanted to go in first. As we entered the lab, we gave our names and were handed a card with a number. We were to go to that numbered table. The smell of formaldehyde was strong. Hesitantly, we all headed to our assigned tables. I could tell everyone felt the unease and tension.

There were approximately thirty metal tables, each one covered with a damp canvas sheet. All the shapes beneath the sheets were slightly different. I wanted to be anywhere in the world but in this lab. I didn't want the canvases removed—I didn't want to see what was beneath them. When everyone was in place, the medical students started to remove the canvases. Someone at the other end of the lab started to cry, and I also heard a faint scream—but no one fainted or left the room. As I looked around, I realized all of us were experiencing feelings of anxiety and dread.

As our cadaver was uncovered, I held my breath. The room, my lab partners (Lynn, Pat, Cheryl, and Julie), the medical student (Brian), and the "person" on the table all seemed surreal. As I focused on the figure on the table, I saw a pale, elderly gentleman with gray hair and a slender, healthy-appearing build. He reminded me a little of Reverend Riley from our church, the father of Margaret, my classmate from school in Gustavus, and a very admirable person. As I continued to consider the person before me, I began to wonder about him. What had happened to him? How did he get here—was this his intention? Was he in the medical profession? Was he married? Did he have children and grandchildren? Did he have a happy rewarding life? I hoped so.

In Biology II in high school, we had dissected a frog. That was hard for me. But now we were actually cutting and dissecting a fellow human being, studying muscles, bones, nerves, and the circulatory system. It seemed so unreal. Yet every scalpel cut and incision made me more aware of humanity and of the great mystery of our bodies. I observed how we, the entire class of nursing students, used the gentlest touch to show respect for *our patients*.

As we studied our patient's brain, I thought how miraculous it was. I wondered what had been learned and stored in all those twisted and turning gray tissue masses. This man's brain would have held his childhood memories, memories of his family, his home, and even his beloved pets. It held the memories of his teen years, his young adulthood, and his mature years. It held his hopes, fears, joys, and sorrows. As we touched and held this magnificent organ and studied each lobe and its functions, we forgot to be anxious and instead became ever more intrigued and amazed. A lifetime of learning, memories, and love had been stored in this small organ. His brain was the essence of who he was.

Next we studied his heart. I was again fascinated at the wonder of our bodies, how all our organs rely on one another, each doing a special job that all other parts of our body require. This goes far beyond the complexity of even the most highly technical computer system. Our bodies are phenomenal. I began to fully appreciate the intricacy of each of us as we are born, grow, live, and die.

As the semester drew to a close, I knew this was a summer I would always remember—not for the smell of formaldehyde or the body fluids on my gloves, but because of this special person who was my first patient. This man on the table was completely unselfish in giving his body so we nursing students could learn. I hope he realized how special he was and the impact he would have on me and my classmates for the rest of our lives.

For my next three years as a nursing student, I thought of my first patient often, as I learned of each illness's effect on our bodies. As an intensive care RN for the next forty-two years and for the remainder of my life experiences, I still think of my first patient and say *thank you*. He helped me realize the true circle of life, and how we all might appreciate and honor our bodies, our minds, and each other. And, thank you Mom for showing me this wonderful career—again teaching me the circle of life.

REV. ROBERT J. KUS

The Pin

In the early 1940s, a young couple from Cleveland, Ohio, met, fell in love, and got married. The young man, Bob, was a Bohemian-American soldier stationed in Washington, D.C., and the young woman, Pat, was an Irish-American RN from St. Alexis Hospital School of Nursing in Cleveland.

For reasons unknown—perhaps because she'd had rheumatic fever as a child—physicians told Pat that if she were to ever become pregnant, her life would be in danger. Despite this warning, Bob and Pat very much wanted to have a child.

On March 30, 1943, in the early hours of the morning, Pat gave birth to a baby boy at the old Glenville Hospital on Cleveland's East Side. I was that baby. Pat, my mother, died in the early evening on that same day. The only thing I have heard about my birthday is that in the evening, the nurses moved all the babies from one nursery to another so I could be alone in the nursery with family. I have no idea who came to see me that day, but I can just imagine the nurses on hand consoling my grieving family.

I also heard that my mother, aware of her doctor's warnings, could have ended the pregnancy, but she would not hear of it. I also learned, many years later, that the nurses and physicians took up a collection to buy Pat a beautiful red marble tombstone in Calvary Cemetery in Cleveland.

My paternal grandparents, Ted Sr. and Marcella "Marty," raised me in a tiny white house, which was more like a lakeside cottage, on Raymond Street in the suburb of Maple Heights, Ohio, until I was six. In the little house were my grandparents, my cocker spaniel Woo-Woo, and my uncles Ted and Norm. Although the house was tiny, the love was infinite. I could not have asked for a more nurturing environment.

Rev. Robert J. Kus, Cleveland Metropolitan General Hospital School of Nursing graduate, 1966. Courtesy Rev. Robert J. Kus.

Sundays were for attending Mass at St. Wenceslaus Church, listening to polka music on the radio, and then having a big Bohemian dinner with pastries we bought on Saturday from the Bohemian bakery.

Though we went to Mass each Sunday—where sermons were in both English and Czech—we were not particularly religious. Nevertheless, when I was four or five years old, I decided that I would be a Catholic priest one day; that desire never left me. At age six, I went to live with my father; stepmother, Mary Jean; and half-brother, Larry, in Cuyahoga Falls, Ohio, outside of Akron. Eventually, we added two girls, Jeanette and Christine, to the family.

For reasons I have never known, my dad asked the Irish side of my family, the Foleys, not be in contact with me until I was twenty-one years old. I never knew of this promise until the day I graduated from nursing school. I speculate that my dad's promise was to protect my stepmother, Mary Jean, from any feelings of insecurity she might have felt.

All through my childhood, I found the company of adults much more fulfilling than that of children my own age. I also loved being inside more than outside, art more than sports, and solitude more than socializing with same-age friends. I always had a passion for "the underdogs" of society, and this passion remains with me today. I also fantasized about serving others and making a difference in this world.

At the age of fourteen, I went away to a high school seminary called Maryknoll in the hill country outside of Scranton, Pennsylvania, where I spent four years getting an excellent classical education. At the end of high school, the Maryknoll fathers advised me to go experience the world before beginning the nine-year course of study to be a priest. I took them up on it and, desiring to be of service to others—no doubt influenced by knowing that my mother had been a nurse—I enrolled in Cleveland Metropolitan General Hospital's School of Nursing. There were thirty-three students in my class, thirty women and three men.

I loved nursing school from the start. At each new clinical rotation, I would think, "Yes, this is the field for me!" I felt that way about every field except burn nursing, for I hated having to hurt patients while doing burn care. I also wasn't as enthusiastic about caring for stroke patients because I'm a "fast-moving" person, and the patience it takes to be a nurse in that area was not my strong suit.

Before our class, the school always had the men nursing students study OB-GYN last. I protested that as discrimination, and the school changed that policy. I also challenged sexist practices that were prevalent, although I don't think our nursing instructors ever considered such behavior discriminatory. For example, before making assignments, some instructors would ask the patients, "Would it be okay if we gave you a male student?" That put doubts into the patients' minds that perhaps having a man for a nurse would be uncomfortable or not as good as having a female student. Another issue was how some staff and instructors would ask male students to help lift patients more frequently than asking the women. When I pointed out these discrepancies, the staff and instructors were more than willing to change. I have to admit, I was sort of a rebel.

In nursing school, I also learned the power of gender. I first encountered this phenomenon when I was assigned to a female surgical ward. Unbeknownst to me, some of the patients were "fighting over me," and this caused a bit of envy on the part of other patients. I was innocent in the ways of the world and unaware of any of this until the staff, who was having a blast watching the drama unfold, informed me that patients were asking, "How come she always gets that male student and we get the women all the time?"

For all the years growing up, I had never heard from the Foley part of my family until fifteen minutes before I became a graduate nurse, still a few months before our class learned if we would become RNs.

It was a sunny day in May 1966, and I was twenty-two years old. Along with thirty plus other nursing students from Cleveland Metropolitan General Hospital School of Nursing, I was waiting in line to enter the nondescript hospital cafeteria for graduation ceremonies.

As I waited, a clean-shaven, mild-spoken, middle-aged man came out of nowhere, approached me, and said, "Are you Robert Kus?"

When I said, "Yes," he gave me a little box, the size and shape that might hold a watch. I don't remember if the box was wrapped, but it was tied with a blue bow. This gentleman must have told me his name, but I have no idea what it was. I only remember that he said, "I have followed you for these past twenty-three years, and I knew your mother. I know she would like you to have this gift." With those words, he left, and I never saw him again.

When I opened the box, I was truly amazed, for in it was my mother's St. Alexis Hospital School of Nursing pin. On the front was the name of the school, some engraved lilies, and the motto "Vita Aliis Vota," which means, "a life devoted to others." On the back of the pin was engraved "P. Foley."

Through the years, I have treasured this pin. Unfortunately, in my many moves, I have misplaced it. That, however, is not important, for what it represents is always with me. This pin symbolizes not only the woman who gave her life for me but also the beautiful profession and calling of nursing, of which I am forever a part.

Since that graduation day, I have learned a little about the Irish members of my family tree: blackjack dealers in Las Vegas, liquor store owners in Minnesota, cops, nurses, a prisoner, and an assorted variety of other folks. Though I have been blessed with the opportunity to play many roles in my life—RN, university professor, sociologist, writer, police chaplain, and now a Catholic parish priest—I have always had a strong nursing identity and never hesitate to let people know I am an RN and to encourage others to explore this profoundly rewarding profession.

I know that my mother gave her life so I could live. Therefore, I understand that I have a special and unique obligation to live my life to the fullest, and to make the most of the gifts God has given me. I'm pretty sure my mom would approve of the paths my life has taken, but then, that's the kind of family I come from: "We're proud of anything you choose to do. Just strive to be the best you can be."

MADELEINE MYSKO

Calvert and Pleasant

As I drove through the intersection of Calvert and Pleasant Streets today, I was thinking of the Mercy Nurses' Residence. It's gone now. Or perhaps I should say *it has been removed,* because that's how I picture it: the old place wasn't really torn down after all, but was rather plucked up by the hand of a greater power. I have this sense that someday I'll be traveling in another part of the city and there it will be: the old Mercy Nurses' Residence, put to good use as low-income housing or a retirement home for nuns.

When I was a student back in the sixties, that dark old building already had a history. It had once been an orphanage, and so I slept in a bunk bed where decades before a little boy must have slept—the headboard was carved with a row of cowboys on horses, galloping across a plain.

There was irony in the wild freedom of those cowboys, because in my day, student nurses weren't free to gallop anywhere but across Pleasant Street to the hospital. Once a new student arrived, trailing behind her father lugging the suitcase (move-in day being the only time *ever* that males were permitted beyond the front parlor), it wasn't so easy to get back out. On that first day, the good Sisters of Mercy laid down the rules, which were based on the lay of the land: no venturing east toward the "red-light district," or west, where "hobos" camped in the park, or south toward the harbor, where dangers crouched in the shadows of the warehouses. As for north, we were permitted to go only as far as St. Ignatius for Mass on Sunday. Henceforth our activities would be confined to the nurses' residence, where the housemother kept one eye on the door.

Some girls could not be confined, of course. Some girls got out. I wasn't one of them—obedient Catholic girl that I was—but I heard the stories, whispered between floors in the lurching elevator with the accordion gate or in the low-ceilinged recreation room before lights-out.

One story went that a certain Miss S. discovered a window without bars, just above street level in the Nursing Fundamentals classroom. On St. Patrick's Day, Miss S. lowered herself to freedom on a couple of sheets and jigged across the street to purchase a six-pack with her fake ID. Another story went that Miss S., Miss C., and possibly Miss L. escaped through the same window and danced in the street with the rest of Baltimore on the night the Orioles won the World Series.

I marvel whenever I read about the sixties in Baltimore, particularly about the political unrest. *Where in the world was I?* And then the image floats up: *the*

Mercy Nurses' Residence. If I did breathe the air of that turbulent time, it must have been out in the courtyard, that open square at the heart of the residence, which was reminiscent of a small prison yard. Into the courtyard a student nurse might step for a breath of air, but in every direction the view would have been of windows looking nowhere but across at each other. Above would have been the sky that carried the weather over the rest of the city.

By the end of the turbulent sixties, that sky looked down on feverish unrest—a country wracked by war, a city wild with grief and dissent. But I had graduated by then and had taken a job out in the county. Looking back, I believe I was a good nurse at the age of twenty-one. But I wasn't much of an activist. In truth, I rarely read the newspapers.

Why is it that I'm riveted now to this memory of a long-ago nurses' residence? Perhaps it's the epiphany in it—realizing I wasn't really sheltered those years when I was a student nurse, for my training required a hard look into the face of suffering, the placing of the hand against another's pain. At the age of eighteen, the Sisters of Mercy taught me the art and the science of our profession. They also taught me to hold back my tears, at least until the end of the shift when I could return to the nurses' residence and fall into that bunk bed with the galloping horses.

It's taken me all these years to grow up—to get out, so to speak. I'm surprised when others refer to me as an "activist." But when I write about my concerns— wounded veterans who aren't getting the health care they deserve, the working poor who cannot afford to buy medicine for their children, all those soldiers killed in Iraq, soldiers the age of my own children—I know I'm empowered, and comforted too, by what I learned so long ago on the corner of Calvert and Pleasant. I can put the words down, like a hand against the suffering. I can hold back the tears, until the work is done.

HEATHER FOSTER

Dissection

It doesn't happen the way it seems to in the movies.
Cutting open an eye, the humor
doesn't shoot across the room. It's thick,
a loose jelly, like a tray of shots
before it's time to pull them from the fridge.
It's a night class, A&P. We sit at high tables in pairs.
The campus is quiet except for us.
The night we get the eyes, I've been having a spat
with a friend. His wife says I'm getting too close.
I tell my partner, Nurse Bill, *The woman doesn't*
take off her clothes in bed. It's depressing.
He is fondling the optic nerve.
We've been given disposable scalpels
sharp enough for bone. We've signed waivers.
We cut straight through the sclera,
divide each eye in half.

The front—like any other eye—
ciliary body, iris,
the lens a little marble disc we flick across
the desk. The eye is dead.
Everything seen through the cornea
appears as though covered in milk.
We are so careful. I never have been so careful.
By the time we get to the retina, Nurse Bill
has taken my side. *Who does that bitch*
think she is? Smash that retina. See how easy
it is to go blind? This is therapy. One squeeze
and the whole thing dissolves in your hand.
Nurse Bill says, *This once, I scrubbed in*
on a surgery—some woman had clawed
her own eye out, luxated
globe—a man had broken
her heart—it was ruined,

transected optic nerve.
They couldn't save it.
They gave her a glass prosthetic.
I was observation only back then.
I carried the eye to be wasted downstairs,
and the whole way I swore it could see me.

Now the back—because this eye was cut
from a cow—beneath the retina, there's a thick
iridescence—*tapetum*
lucidum—the blue brightens, nearly
neon at the edges, nearly glowing, *aurora*
borealis in an animal's skull, against
the black back of posterior hull.
It's what allows a cow to see things,
to be seen, in the dark,
what is making these six eyes catch
starlight, visible without streetlamps,
at the foot of my drive tonight,
when I finally pull in, fresh from class.
Coyotes. Not a dozen yards
from where I sit nightly, calling him,
formaldehyde stinking the skin of my hands,
telling him what I'm wearing, how I'd
touch him. Lying. What does he know?
If he closes his eyes, what's the difference?

ELLEN HUNTER ULKEN

Of Nursing School

In September 1958, before an interstate highway existed on that route, my mother and I drove from Fort Benning northeastward, through the hills and dales of the Georgia Piedmont region to reach the state capital. Atlanta had a small-town feel in those days, and we drove right up to the hospital on Peachtree Road as if we knew the way.

Students and mothers lined up along a wide corridor that fronted the director of nurses'—Miss Genevieve Garren's—office and those of her nurse assistants. We would see much of that hallway over the next three years, each time we checked in or out of the hospital, but on that first day, we felt like aliens in an undiscovered world. As part of registration, we students got a dose of the still experimental Sabin oral polio vaccine. I remember thinking how painless to swallow a bit of liquid to acquire immunity instead of receiving a dreaded injection. We met the nurse administrators: Miss Garren, Miss Henley, and Mrs. Fitzgerald, who smiled at us in welcome as they checked us off the list.

Mother helped me move my belongings into my room, where we chatted with my roommates-to-be and their moms. But all too soon, Mother and I said goodbye and she made the drive back to Fort Benning. She, my father, and my little brother would soon be moving to Bremerhaven, Germany, my dad's next U.S. Army assignment. Except for one or two brief visits, I wouldn't see her again until three years later, after I had graduated from the nursing program.

Anne Hughes and Karen Miller were my roommates. The combination of our last names, Hughes, Hunter, and Miller, defined us. Knight and Lemon checked in across the hall, and Matthews, McBride, and McCollum lived one room down. For most of the next three years, Anne, Karen, and I shared a room, a bath, one clothes closet, and lots of grief and laughter. Today, half a century later, we're still friends.

Ellen (Hunter) Ulken, Piedmont Hospital School of Nursing graduate, 1961. Courtesy Ellen Ulken.

Karen, tall and blond, fixed her wispy, light hair into a twist. Dark-eyed Anne kept her raven locks short and curled. I tried to turn my light brown mane blond like Karen's, but old pictures reveal an orangey result. Our simple hairstyles reflected lives with time devoted elsewhere, although we probably spent more time with our hair than on any other beauty routines.

On that first day, a bank of elevators had lifted us to the sixth (and top) floor of a new Piedmont Hospital where the student nurses lived. We occupied rooms that would become patient rooms as soon as a nurses' dorm was built two years later. North/South hallways met those that ran East/West. At the intersection, the room designed as the Central Nurses' Station served as our living room with a TV and piano, though we rarely had time to watch or play.

In room 638, we divided the three beds. Anne claimed the single cot. Karen, who didn't fear falling off, took the top bunk of the double-decker, and I took the bottom. After lights-out, all through training, when Karen wanted a laugh she would hang her arm over the side of her bunk, clutch her hand into a claw-looking fist, and scare me half to death. The beds remained our own, as if assigned, until we moved in our senior year to affiliated hospitals.

Our room, near the intersection of the hallways, provided close access to all amenities. Next door stood a walk-in shower, so near to us that the bathtub in our suite was usually dry. (When I had procrastinated hitting the books until there was no one left awake to visit with, I sometimes used the tub, propped with pillows, to study after my roommates went to sleep.) The light switch for the shower room was situated on a wall outside of the stall. A common trick was to turn the light off while a classmate was in there, naked, wet, and soapy. Karen loved to put me in the dark, and I think I got her back a few times.

The community kitchen stood at an angle across the hall from our room and across the other hall from the TV/piano room. Each evening, dining services sent up coffee, bread, and butter. We learned to drink coffee steaming with whole milk from water glasses too hot to hold, breathing in the aroma during the cooling time, a comforting ritual. Coffee mugs, so ubiquitous today, were absent from our cupboards. Solaria stood at each end of the North/South hallways—one for students, the other for Miss Garren, who lived in a private suite near her sun porch.

We had to stay quiet enough, within our "hospital/dorm" room, that neither Miss Garren nor Flossie, the housemother, could hear us giggling. We kept our quarters tidy and made our beds before leaving for duty each day.

For the first six months, we took science courses at Georgia State College (now Georgia State University). Those carefree days gave us a fleeting taste of university life. We took the bus across town to the college three afternoons a week, until Diane McCollum invited us to ride with her and her two roommates, Libby and Judy—six girls in a sedan. We were lucky. I think Diane had the only car among our classmates. On Fridays we rewarded ourselves with a festive hamburger from Seven Steers on the way back to the hospital.

The standout memory for me is of the anatomy lab where we dissected fetal pigs. Each day we pulled the wretched porcine babies from large jars filled with pungent formaldehyde, laid them out over a long slab of steel, and tried to find their various veins and muscles. I named my pig Otto after a high school boyfriend who jilted me. Our instructor shook his head when I insisted that Otto was malformed. When I couldn't identify any of the veins and muscles inside Otto, I went to my neighbors' pigs to discover the designated anatomy.

On alternate days and during time not spent at Georgia State, we went to class in the hospital Nursing Arts Lab, which looked something like a large ward containing multiple patient beds and a variety of medical equipment. Practicing on mannequins and each other, we learned to care for bed patients, to manage their baths, and to make the bed with a patient in it. We learned to take vital signs, perform various treatments, and administer medications by mouth and by hypodermic needle.

Students rotated through the hospital constantly, two new classes per year, one in June and one in September, so that rookies like us were perpetually being groomed to take care of patients. Eventually, they let us loose in the hospital, under supervision, to work with real people.

An important milestone arrived when, after six months, we donned blue dresses with white, starched bibs and aprons and reported to the floors to attend to patients. For P.M. care, which is easier and less time consuming than A.M. care, we gave our assigned patients a back rub, fresh drinking water, a bed straightening and pillow fluff, and whatever treatments were ordered. We took their vital signs—at last on humans other than ourselves. Anne still remembers that she was inordinately proud of her new name tag: *Miss A. Hughes, S.N.* (student nurse).

Within a few months, we had a "capping ceremony." We each got two caps so that one would always be clean, ready to fold and wear. According to Karen, before they had been through the laundry for several washings and starches, our caps were flimsy compared to those of the older students and graduates. Nevertheless, we were proud of our classic Piedmont caps. We could now measure progress toward the overarching goal, the day we would graduate wearing all white uniforms, pinned at the breast with a golden insignia, *Registered Nurse.* But for the next two plus years, we joined a small army of blue-and-white-clad women who could be seen attending patients in every department of the hospital.

Each morning, before reporting to the patient floors, we went to "Line-Up." For ten minutes after our six-thirty breakfast, we sang songs for Miss Garren, our stout director, who stood in the front of a basement classroom, near the cafeteria, facing us in her white uniform, stern expression. We sang two selections from an old songbook. Students got to pick standards of the era like "Grandfather's Clock" or "Carry Me Back to Old Virginia." If anyone chose "Sweet Genevieve," Miss Genevieve Garren would not allow it. All other songs from the two hundred pages were permitted.

As long as we worked day shift, we went to Line-Up. In a three-year training program, we skipped over the sophomore year. Freshmen became juniors and then seniors. As juniors and seniors working evenings and nights, our singing days were over. By then, we carried large trays of medicine up and down the halls to the patients and we monitored IVs. Then, before IV pumps, the drops had to be counted to deliver the correct dose. Our job was to deliver "the right dose of the right medicine to the right patient at the right time over the right route." We learned to pay attention.

After Line-Up, we rushed to our units, where each student would be assigned six to eight patients for "A.M. care," which resulted in clean patients, clean bed linen, fresh drinking water, and uncluttered tray tables. Treatments had to be done, whether foot soaks, sitz baths, hot packs to the spine, or whatever the doctors ordered. For ambulatory patients, making their beds was easy, and those patients washed themselves. But for bed patients, the process took quite a bit longer. Bedridden patients had to be bathed, back-rubbed, and sometimes fed. We had to be finished with our work by nine o'clock in order to report to class on time. Most of the bed baths went lickety-split.

We became pretty nimble at making beds in the days before fitted sheets. Through three years of nurses training, fitted sheets never appeared in our hospital, though they were invented in 1959. Four corners of a flat sheet had to be tucked in before the draw sheet, the top sheet, and the bedspread could be applied. There could be NO FANNING OF THE SHEETS, lest an errant germ fly up and float into a wound. Pillow covers had to be renewed—lots of pillows for the many orthopedic patients we treated. Every piece of linen on or around the bed was changed every day. The head nurse or the instructor nurse checked each patient behind us to make sure we hadn't flubbed our jobs.

The head nurses assigned each student her fair percentage of ambulatory patients because they made fast work. In those days, people came to the hospital for tests. They might be admitted for x-rays of the bowel or the gallbladder or for a minor surgical procedure. (Eventually, insurance companies refused to pay for these hospital admissions, a reason why today almost everyone hospitalized is acutely ill.) If patients underwent surgical procedures, rendering their beds empty as they were rolled off to the operating rooms, students made up the beds and tidied the rooms so that these patients returned from x-ray or the OR to an immaculate space.

We discovered what stress felt like while trying to get six or eight patients ready for the day between the morning hours of seven and nine. Once, our instructor nurse, whom we loved, found my work incomplete. In my rush, I had put new covers over a bed patient and neglected to remove the old ones. Miss Garner found my patient sweltering beneath two layers of top sheets and spreads. She fetched me from another room, told me what I had done, and took me to the scene to show me. I burst into tears right there in front of the patient, embarrassed and miserable. Miss Garner understood how upset I was and kindly finished taking care of my patients for me that day. She knew I had learned an important lesson—to double-check everything when caring for patients.

It was the only time I broke down during nursing school. Other challenges followed: time constraints, occasional mistakes, and confrontations with head nurses. I learned to bear up, to organize, to do my best work and stay calm. And I became one of the world's fastest bed makers.

With two part-time semesters at Georgia State behind us, we were cloistered at the hospital, our home and our universe. We worked six days a week. Sometimes we worked night shift until 7:00 A.M. and attended a 9:00 A.M. class, struggling to keep our eyes open until we could scramble to our rooms to sleep and prepare for another eight hours of night duty. Vacations consisted of one or two weeks during each year of training. In our home hospital we rotated through the emergency room, the operating room, central service, obstetrics, and the medical/surgical units. During senior year, we traveled to the Georgia State Hospital in Milledgeville for three months to study psychiatry, and to Children's Hospital in Birmingham, Alabama, for three months to learn pediatrics.

At Piedmont, we called the patient units "floors." When you visualized the "floor" of a certain service, the nurse who ran it dominated the atmosphere. Some of the head nurses were cranky. The efficiency of a floor was often consistent with the personality and governing style of its head nurse.

We became inured to excrement, bedpans, nausea, vomiting, bloody wounds, and their companion odors. What at first assaulted our senses became the routine sights and scents of the sickroom over time. Eventually, a sensitive nose could identify the smell of infection or of a cancer gone wild.

In labor and delivery, I felt dismayed by the patients' mighty screams since I was ignorant of the intense pain that accompanied their exertions. I'm ashamed to say that true empathy had to wait a few years until I labored with the birth of my own baby. But I loved the nursery—the sweet babies—and could have spent the whole three years there.

The operating room was probably the most exciting arena in the hospital. We had great surgeons. Some were known to explode, however, if an instrument came to them at the wrong angle. You could get blasted in the OR. Most of us spent a short interval there to learn the basics, but Karen happened to be assigned to the OR when they were shorthanded. She had two rotations in surgery, braving the fire, wearing whites for several months, and becoming a great scrub nurse.

Anne was the brainchild of room 638. Sitting cross-legged on her cot in her slip while playing cards, she would recite the muscles—all of them—but she especially liked the ones with the long names. *Sternocleidomastoideus* and *gluteus maximus*. We loved that our butt muscles had names and decided that for some of us, our *glutei* were more *maximus* than for others. Anne absorbed information like a dry sponge and the medical language fascinated her. *Latissimus dorsi* rolled off her tongue like a poem. Karen and I learned much by osmosis.

Our hospital delivered the infants of women who had been confined to an Atlanta home for unwed mothers. The Florence Crittenton Homes comprised a chain of safe homes across the country for mothers and children. The plight of the Crittenton patients deeply affected the student nurses. We cared for these young women who arrived at the hospital in labor, ready to give birth and then give up their infants. In a few cases, mothers kept their babies, but in the early 1960s a child born out of wedlock was still the stuff of scandal. Most of the Crittenton babies went up for adoption. Mothers could have only one visit with their infants, if adoptive parents were then going to take them. Sometimes, a mother declined the session with her baby to shield herself from attachment and regret—another sad chapter in the struggle for women's rights.

Over time, we students learned "detachment." When an elderly woman with cancer died, of course I was sad, though she had suffered greatly and death had freed her from her pain. "My back, my back," cried Mrs. Pappas, over and over again. Even with pain shots, she couldn't find a comfortable position. I accepted her fate. But when we lost a dark-eyed twelve-year-old boy with acute laryngo-tracheobronchitis, a long word for croup, it took me weeks to recover. I repeatedly remembered his struggle to breathe, the empty ampules and syringes, the tracheotomy—too late—the helpless treatment team surrounding his bed, his sobbing parents. Neither our arsenal of drugs nor the respiratory equipment of our era could save him. Emotional walls went up in my brain and stayed put like a fortress against future bombardments.

We were taught to revere our staff physicians. When one of our doctors walked into the chart room, every nurse stood up in respect, ready to assist him. They were all men, just as our nurses were all women. The first male student was admitted to the nurses training program at Piedmont Hospital in 1974, long after our class graduated.

Sometimes the doctors lectured us on an aspect of their medical specialties.

Dr. Hamm, a favorite plastic surgeon, volunteered to operate on our protuberant ears or acne scars—whatever cosmetic defect bothered us—as a graduation present. Three classmates accepted his offer.

Our old heroes still preside over Piedmont Hospital on Peachtree Road: the founders' portraits line the walls surrounding the lobby of the hospital.

On a rare day off, Karen, Anne, and I waded in the cool waters of nearby Peachtree Creek or sunbathed on the roof of the hospital, striking crazy poses with classmates, taking pictures of our young, spirited selves. In the evenings Anne and I had dates, driving off with fraternity boys from nearby Georgia Tech, or, in my case, with a certain young intern from Grady Hospital. Karen, already promised, went out with her betrothed when he was in town. Otherwise, she peered over the mezzanine balcony to see what our escorts looked like and made fun of the awkward way I carried my purse.

During the entire first year of training, we had to sign in by 7:00 P.M. on weeknights and 10:00 P.M. on weekends. As junior students, 10:00 P.M. was the curfew on weeknights and 11:45 on weekends. We all remember the long hall we had to walk from the hospital lobby past the huge Central Service Department, down and around the corner to Nursing Service, where Miss Garren reigned during the day from behind her desk, and where Mrs. Paul ruled at night, both paragons of white, starched authority, the sign-in sheet on a table near the desk. Sometimes the office was empty. But you never knew as you rounded the corner, who *might* be sitting there. Occasionally, we had a few nips of punch at the fraternity parties to which we'd been invited, rendering our walks a little crooked. Life was a risk.

A student nurse could get kicked out of training for a number of infractions, but if she got married or pregnant, she was automatically dismissed. We lost classmates to both conditions. We started the program with twenty-three students in our class and finished with eighteen. No one minded making outrageous rules for women in those days, and it didn't occur to us to protest, nor would protesting have yielded any justice.

Miss Garren caught me smoking in the stairwell while I was on duty. No one would have believed that this large woman would ever take the stairs so quickly, but she did. "Miss Hunter," she said, "I'll see you in my office at 3:00 P.M." I figured my nursing career was over. I wondered how I would explain my dismissal to my parents on another continent and how long the letter would take to reach them, since then it was too expensive to call. And where would I go when Piedmont was no longer home? But when I met with Miss Garren, she basically told me, quietly, not to smoke in the stairwell. Later, some said that she smoked cigarettes too, though none of us ever saw her.

Many people smoked in that era; the habit was widely accepted and the tragic health consequences of smoking and secondhand smoke were not yet known.

Our nurse teachers did warn us away from drugs. We had access to patients' medications and sometimes "borrowed" a Darvon to battle menstrual cramps or a headache, but we steered clear of the hard stuff. "It's all addictive," said our instructors. "Don't take any of it." I'm forever grateful for the admonition.

My roommates and I consoled each other through the tough times, while our youthful exuberance insisted on episodes of fun. We played cards across the breadth of a cot in our room after work. We joked, cussed, and gossiped about the doctors and the hospital staff with whispered laughs, careful not to alert the attention of Flossie, the housemother. We splurged, if budgets would allow, and walked across Peachtree Road to Papa John's (not the current-day pizza parlor) for a hamburger.

We fussed at times. Anne and I smoked cigarettes, and Karen, who couldn't stand the smell of them, gave us hell about it, and said we stank up the whole closet full of clothes. Sometimes, one of us would sleep during the day, having worked the night shift, while the other two found a way to keep quiet within the room or stay out of it altogether. Except for cigarette smoking, we learned the meaning of respect and cooperation.

After graduation, I worked at Piedmont for a few months while waiting for the results of the Georgia State Board of Nurses exams. As soon as notification arrived that I had passed, I flew to Germany for a joyous reunion with my family and went to work on an infectious disease unit in a U.S. Army hospital in Frankfurt.

In 1984, the Piedmont Hospital School of Nursing closed its doors. Twenty-three years after our graduation, a three-year hospital training program for nurses had become educationally and financially unfeasible. The nursing staff hosted a "Great Graduate Reunion," inviting all Piedmont nurses back to town for a spectacular weekend with tours of the hospital, cocktails, dinner, speeches, and grand visitations. Hughes, Hunter, and Miller were part of the celebration. We stood together in the lobby of the nurses' dorm and gazed at a large oil painting of Miss Garren, a gentle rendering of a formidable lady. We remembered how we feared her.

In the whole world, Anne and Karen are still two of my favorite people. Although we live in far-flung Georgia and Florida towns, we see each other yearly or we keep in touch by phone and email. And when we meet, we measure our memories with laughter and affection while the intervening decades melt away.

We talk about the old days when we were young and eager. Faced with issues of illness and suffering, a measure of maturity took an early hold on us. The years of nursing school, three emphatic years—remember, six days a week—are forever embedded in our souls. For life, we would carry in our pockets, like bandage scissors, the skills we learned and the pride of a worthy profession.

STACY NIGLIAZZO

Rotation

for Richard Alford, MD

I remember my first day
as a student in the OR. It was winter,

just as cold inside.
We scrubbed

and cloaked ourselves in green gowns.
Shoe covers were required.

Out of the box they looked like pale boats
wrecked

against the concrete floor.
The tread was silent.

    Black blood oozing—
    pink flesh torn away—

the surgeon's blade,
steady across a spider web inside the open abdomen.

    What's this I'm cutting into?
    The omentum, sir.

    How many feet of small bowel in the gut?
    Roughly twenty-five, sir.

    And in the colon?
    Roughly five to ten, sir.

    Hold out your hand—

an orphan with an empty bowl,
complicit without question.

Suddenly slapped within my grasp
—sliding—shapeless—

like a baby bird collected from the sidewalk—
a freshly incised gallbladder.

It reeked of red earth.
I held it gratefully before surrendering it.

CELIA BROWN

My First Journey Abroad

I was a well-rounded bottle washer by the time I signed up for a nursing scholarship in England. Call it destiny if you like. Industrial Britain seemed little more than a slag heap in the late fifties. From the insides of our nostrils to the outsides of row houses, from Victorian facades to market squares, everything looked blackened and sooty. I'd grown up in Ireland, the oldest of ten. I'd had an early mentor—it was with great admiration that I watched Nurse O'Malley come once a year to help Dr. McGreal deliver the newest member of our family. This went on like the war, or until there were too many of us for the size of our sprawling farmhouse. Mostly I was a water carrier and firewood bringer and the general watcher who took care of the other siblings.

My mother would describe me (a little too blithely perhaps) as someone who had missed out on childhood. Even at the age of seven I was consulted in an adult manner about many things. I rejected dolls, preferring to write and draw. Sometimes I borrowed the novels my mother rarely got around to finishing—whether they were meant for children or adults made no difference to me. That was how I introduced myself to *Gone with the Wind, Wuthering Heights,* and the lively pages of D. H. Lawrence.

For an Irish girl coming to Stoke, many adjustments were required. My teachers at home had already decided that my future would be better served as a scholar, and several of them were vocal in their disappointment. Some felt that I at least should have chosen a career in public teaching, objecting, as was expected, to the perceived stigma of a nursing career for one of their possible university candidates. Nobody, not even my mother, seemed to understand that a nursing career, however improbable my choice, presented me, the oldest of ten, with a readymade job. I was already a family caregiver; it was on that basis that I chose nursing.

I remember most clearly my initial feelings upon entering nursing school. First came the tears, the separation anxiety, the yoke of a daily starched uniform, the new and arcane textbooks, classrooms that smelled of yellow soap and disinfectant, as well as a whole cast of mismatched people in an English teaching hospital, all of whom would be memorized by name, habit, accent, or inclination: doctors, patients, sisters, staff nurses, assistants, orderlies, lab persons, and fellow student nurses. I was suddenly rule-ridden, lonely, and much too busy. Nursing not only represented a changing status and a whole range of new disciplines but also would alter my ideas about culture.

Although I was entering a school of learning, in no sense did it carry the trappings of an academic setting. I would live in a dorm with the luxury of my own room. I was responsible for buying my own black shoes and stockings; everything else was provided. Each morning or night I walked to the various departments depending on my shift, and tried to make sense of the world of the sick. Falling into bed after long, confusing workdays I came to realize that for no good reason I'd been entrusted with the endless care of others for little or no pay. I'd never felt poor before, but here I was in a big city with its dull smog and grit swirling beyond my newly stratified enclosures. On my one day off, there were few places to go and no cash to spend. Outdoors, if I blew my nose, my hankie turned black with soot.

The skyline nearby was stacked with urns that we called the "potteries." Our one big town spilled into five smaller ones with names like Burslem, Fenton, Hanley, Longton, and Tunstall, towns still famous for the manufacture of Spode, Wedgwood, Minton, and Royal Doulton. These towns were places where people

Celia (Kelly) Brown (seated lower right next to skeleton) *with her fellow nursing school graduates, Stoke-on-Trent Preliminary Training School, England, 1959. Courtesy Celia Kelly Brown.*

called you "Duck" and said words like "summat" ("somewhat"). These were towns where female painters put a single leaf of gold or shiny rims on plates; places where kiln workers turned gray under the skin. I witnessed many deaths related to dust from coal mines and pottery factories at my hospital, a huge brick building that overlooked the rumble of London Road.

That first month I felt like a wartime recruit, shipped to fronts that included the suicide unit, the geriatric wing, and the theater. My best hope was to remain on a surgical ward where patients came in to get something removed and then went home. In that respect, my wish had somewhat been granted. But something was wrong with Ward One, my first surgical unit. I never forgot that ward, or my first ward sister who never forgot my mistakes: dropping urinals, spilling glasses, bringing her the wrong-sized catheter.

"I have no gift for this," I told the stainless steel sterilizers. But they only bubbled back and tried to burn me.

And who could forget Sully, the surgeon? More like God really, with the morning pinned to his breast pocket. I still remember dawns that were as harried as his thunderous brow, because little in life delighted him. There was continuous disdain for the coffee brewed for him and impatience for the smallest clinical fumble. There were lyrical times too on Ward One, when Sully was simply "away" and life was forced to plow forward without him. And there was that one day on Ward One that I recall as both better and worse than all the others.

Sully had come too early to do rounds. That made Sister cross. Orderlies were banished with their trays. Cleaners were asked to take their wax pots elsewhere, lab techs would have to return later, and the bed making would simply be deferred. Solid silence reigned on Ward One. Only then might the surgical cortege wend its way too early and too soon from belly to belly in order to check sutures that didn't need checking or shorten drains that should have been left alone. This was why other doctors were wont to call Sully "Mr. Cross-Infection Himself."

Rounds might take an hour or longer, depending on his whim. But on this one morning, fate took an unexpected turn. Perhaps because it was still too early in the day to remove stitches, or because nobody saw the thick, red swatch of wax on the ward floor until Sully slithered and swerved and finally flattened himself out with solitary grace. Smith, the nearest hernia patient, could have burst his stitches, literally, as he bent over to chuckle. Sister rushed to Sully's side in an effort to get him up, but he shook her off like a flea. Residents and interns of the entourage held fists in their mouths; students near the door escaped to the corridor. I was standing too close and didn't dare to smile. Waxed from shoulder to shoe, Sully rose like a miracle, his buttonholed elegance a travesty, but his dignity never in question. Grand rounds would go on without further delay—just then, a wary-looking cleaner was spotted scuttling about in waxy gloves. Sully gave her the stare of God and began to swear in God's accent. The woman bellowed loudly in Italian that it wasn't her fault. Then she raised her right hand and made the sign of the cross.

My first hospital bestowed on me the kind of raw realism that I appreciated—later—as I pondered the Big Questions (not to mention the ethics of sticking things out). How else would I have come to realize that happiness is often no more or less than the absence of pain? Ward One was like a second baptism (perhaps by bedpan). I was often homesick. Mostly I was broke. And yet there was nowhere to be for three more years but in the heart of Stoke.

Thankfully, I survived. All other wards would seem less menacing. Indeed, most of my ward experiences were places of learning, friendship, and fulfillment. But I will never forget Ward One, Sully, or the exacting Sister who so often criticized me. However, after so many years, I can also forgive them.

KATHLEEN GOLDBACH

Dirty Utility Room

University of Iowa Hospitals, 1961

The deep sink looms, faucets glisten,
brushes bristling, pink soap poised
to drip. Clean, stacked bedpans reflect

an orange daybreak sky just flaring up
behind tall, squared windows.
We gather here in blue student dresses,

starched white aprons crossed in back,
folded caps carefully pinned in place,
sturdy shoes whitewashed the night before.

The breakfast cart grumbles past the door,
carrying its steamy cream-of-wheat smell
that mingles with odors of alcohol,

urine, and sleep-soaked old men.
Armed with patient notes, we march out
to two long rows of facing beds,

each bedside waiting for one of us
for morning care. Each task
leads us back to this room:

Kathleen (Morgan) Goldbach, University of Iowa, 1961. Courtesy Kathleen Goldbach.

to pile used towels and bed linens
into hampers, pour out cooled water
from bed baths, dump full bedpans

into the hopper, then wash them,
toss serum-soaked dressings,
scrape and rinse viscous sputum and

rancid vomit from kidney-shaped basins,
take a brush to crusty dentures
soaking in cloudy water, by far

our most stomach-churning chore.
Between each contact, we scrub our hands
with Phisoderm for fifteen seconds.

By afternoon our hands are raw from scouring,
aprons damp from sweat and sink leaning,
name tags knocked sideways.

Under the faucets' gush, the hopper's flush,
we nod and murmur, careful not to say
first names, should the head nurse walk in.

We are beginning to sense
other shadows working among us.
Our mothers stuck us into laundry tubs

to wash away our Midwest dust
and summer stickiness with Lava soap,
poured vinegar through our squeaky hair

over the kitchen sink. Our grandmothers
emptied slop pots from morning bedrooms
into swill barrows for pig troughs, tossed

scoopfuls of lime into outhouse holes.
Our great-grandmothers made their own soap
from fat and lye, found water holes along

westward trails; beside their horses
they drank and washed clothes,
soaked blistered feet, cooled a parent's

fevered limbs, baptized a baby just born.
We know this room in our bones. For years
we have squirmed in rows of classroom desks;

now these rows of beds will be our true
teachers, these deep sinks we surround
still cradle tomorrow's world.

JAMES GULIANO

Sacred Values, Soothing Silence

It is so important to tell the stories of how we became health-care professionals. Documenting these journeys brings to life the often-untold experiences that were necessary for us to learn to treat others with dignity and compassion and to master the human experience from our unique vantage points. With each new experience, our confidence grew and memories accumulated. Such memories should not be forgotten, or left untold.

We looked up to those professionals we called "registered nurses" and longed for the day that we would be honored to bear such a title. They were angels in white, often wearing their cap and always their school pin. We learned that these were not merely cumbersome uniform requirements but, rather, symbols of core values that were held sacred.

We were taught by example first and then by required readings, lectures, and clinical learning. What did their examples teach us? They taught us to be present, truly present in order to see our patients in their entirety, not merely their diagnosis. They taught us to regard every detail as having the potential to impact our next decision, which it usually did. What is known today as "bundles of care" became an inherent part of our education. We were taught how to practice nursing, not merely work in a hospital.

We walked the path that our patients walked and we saw, heard, tasted, touched, and smelled the world through the patient's perspective. We were required to know the whole person, and, I believe that, in doing so, we gained more than merely a diploma in nursing.

We were sent into the patient's room to interact—that was all. Our first encounter as aspiring health-care professionals seemed easy enough since talking to people came naturally to us. We were to introduce ourselves and use therapeutic communication, which we studied at length. Then, after de-identifying the script,

James V. Guliano, 2015. Courtesy Ohio Hospital Association.

we were to document a narrative of the interaction, known as a "process record-ing" for analysis of our technique. The patients I met relayed their needs to me and were engaging, despite their ailments. They spoke of their pain, their fears, their disappointments, and their hopes. With each conversation, I encountered a different reaction, ranging from nervous hand-wringing to uncomfortable squirming to a smile that conveyed how grateful the patient was to have com-pany. In that early foray into my professional pursuit, I realized that my agenda was my patients' agenda and that I would need to develop the tools to be able to meet their needs. Privately, I reflected on whether I would be able to become the health-care professional they needed. What I learned over time was that I belonged in this profession.

Rigorous, didactic learning was something that we heard about from our upper-classmates. The tales of their struggles frightened some while challenged others. But the practical experience of being in a diploma program was a gift that has been invaluable to me and, I believe, to those for whom I provided care over the years. Before we entered the elevator and approached the patient care areas, better known as "the floors," we students were required to follow specific mandates when it came to our uniforms, hair length, grooming, and cleanliness—mandates we held sacred. They were rites of passage into a sacred space—the patient's bedside, the patient's world. Donning the uniform was almost as much a privilege as be-ing accepted into the nursing program. White shoe polish became a staple in our assigned lockers.

We reported to the floor the evening prior to our assigned clinical shift to re-search our patient's needs, and we were required to respond to any and all questions about our patients when called upon during our shift. Being able to paraphrase the pathophysiology of a diagnosis, the side effects of medications, the potential interactions, and our proposed care plan was only the beginning. What we thought was a grueling requirement for school actually taught us to be engaged and present. Never was a person known as merely a diagnosis. We were taught to see the entire picture—not only the clinical side but also the patient's. We heard the gurgling sounds that resulted from acute congestive heart failure, we touched the clammy and cold skin of a dying grandmother, and we felt the dignity of a retired chief executive officer who now relied on others for hygienic care.

A surgical clinical learning experience meant being with the patient from the preoperative phase until returning to the floor so that we could fully grasp what the patient's and family's needs entailed. These were lenses through which most of us had never had the opportunity to see. All the while, the science of nursing was blended with the art of nursing and never were they to be separated.

Martha was a mother of three young adults and the wife of a loving husband. She was scheduled for an exploratory surgery after having a mass detected. In-

James V. Guliano, St. Thomas Medical Center School of Nursing graduate, 1986. Courtesy James V. Guliano. Photo by Carmen Studios.

cluded in the routine of preparing a patient for surgery was also the responsibility of preparing a family for that same surgery, something that was only alluded to in our textbooks. Her young adult children were noticeably quiet as I reviewed the preoperative instructions, practicing coughing and deep breathing and splinting. After all, postoperative pneumonia or any other hospital-acquired condition was simply not an option. Her son, in particular, would lower his head and not make eye contact. Her husband paced the hallways, while her daughter dutifully took notes. They were a textbook family, it seemed. The next day was Martha's scheduled surgery. I reported to her room on the surgical unit and administered her preoperative medication. As we approached the cold hallway and wheeled her gurney into the elevator toward the operating room, I watched closely as her family kissed her quickly and bravely. I witnessed the fear of her children who forced their smiles and held back their tears. Her husband tapped me on the shoulder and said nervously, "Take good care of her, now."

I observed her surgery and followed her into the recovery room, as it was then known. There I learned to manage her airway and support her as she awoke from the anesthesia. Meanwhile, I was given the opportunity to join the surgeon in meeting with the family members to discuss the findings, which were a high likelihood of malignancy, pending biopsy confirmation. Martha's son was crushed, her daughter tearful, and her husband stoic. After the surgeon completed her explanation and then left the room, the entire family stared at me.

My support consisted of allowing silence. The silence was deafening at first but soon became soothing. We had connected because we journeyed together. Finally, we returned to the original room on the surgical floor, hearing each footstep on the freshly waxed flooring. Overhead pages interrupted the silence that seemed so necessary. Sounds of infusion pump alarms beeping coupled with occasional call light signals reminded us that we were back in the "real world" where the next phase began and where I learned to manage Martha's and her family's pain.

We did not realize it then, but we truly learned how to provide seamless care.

PATRICIA HARMAN

My Patients, My Teachers

"So, how you doing?" I ask Verona Jenkins, a fifty-year-old high school teacher. Her straight brown-gray hair is cut in a bob and she sits on the end of the exam table, swinging her legs like a girl. She has a few small red varicose veins on her calf, but her ankles are tan and slim.

"Okay, I guess. Better." This interests me, and now that I'm in my last year of nurse midwifery school I have time to listen.

"What's your stress level lately, between one and ten?" I smile. "Ten means you are about to check into the psych hospital."

"It was eleven last year, but I'd say only a seven now," the patient gives me a short laugh, indicating this is a joke. That's when our real conversation begins.

The exam room is like a classroom, a place I learn countless lessons, and these women are my teachers. I study Verona's face as I palpate her lower pelvis, "Any pain?" She shakes her head no. Occasionally I find a tender ovary or uterus that needs further attention, but more often in these routine exams I find "pain" in the heart.

I finish the internal exam, take off my sterile gloves and settle myself on the rolling stool. The patient sits up and straightens her exam gown. "Last year, I was a real mess. My seventeen-year-old daughter was out of control. She'd dropped out of school and moved in with her boyfriend. I was so scared; this was my baby, now out of reach, running hell-bent toward disaster. She was using drugs—marijuana and ecstasy. She told me right to my face . . . no birth control. She *wanted* to get pregnant."

Verona stops and tucks a strand of her hair behind her ear. "I was so frightened for her. We were fighting all the time, and my husband was no help. He just

Patricia Harman, University of Minnesota Midwifery Program graduate, 1984. Courtesy Patricia Harman. Photo by Tom Harman.

withdrew into his work, even told me once, if I mellowed out and got off her case, things would be better."

"And now?"

Verona smiles, exhales, and wipes a few tears with the back of her hand. I reach over and offer her a tissue. "We're doing better. The boyfriend didn't last long and she came home. She was treated for an STD at the health department, but never got pregnant, thank God."

"So is she back in school and everything's all right?" I'm waiting for a happy ending.

"No."

"Home school?"

"No." Verona tips her head to the side with a little regret. "She doesn't do much of anything. Sleeps late, watches TV, reads a little; sometimes she cooks."

I squint. "So isn't that hard for you?"

"At first it was, but I was just so glad to have her home and safe, I decided to give up on the lectures and just accept her for who she is." The voice in my head goes quiet. *Just accept her for who she is.*

"And guess what?" the patient goes on. "The other day, the three of us went out to dinner and Kayla said to us, 'You know, Mom and Dad. You're my favorite people. You accept me unconditionally.' Twelve months ago we were wolverines at each other's throats. Just the way she said it, *unconditionally,* I knew my daughter had been reading—or maybe only watching Oprah—but she was going to be okay."

Now I have tears in my eyes. *Just accept them for who they are.* I've read of the miracles it brings when you just love someone unconditionally. I do that with my patients, but with my almost grown boys, I am constantly shepherding, trying, with my wooden crook, to steer them away from cliffs, lead them down into the green valleys. And does it work? No. I just meet resistance.

I pull out a handout on the importance of calcium in the diet and give Verona a hug. The woman doesn't know the gift she's given me. Outside in the hall, I place my hand on the exam room door, palm open, fingers spread. I look both ways, and seeing no one, bow low from the waist.

HELEN ALBERT

*Helen Albert, First Black Registered Nurse Hired
in Trumbull County, Ohio*

An oral history interview, January 15, 2005

"Miss Helen, I have your yearbook, *The Crusader,* on loan from Norwood Hospital," I say. "I thought we could look at it together and you can tell me stories about the hospital, your training there, and these people in the photographs." (Helen's tired and having pain in her face and neck and in her left shoulder and arm. She says it's a rotator cuff deteriorating, pressing on a nerve. There's little to be done other than pain patches and medication.)

"I'm trying to bear up," she tells me. I say I can leave, but she doesn't want that. She is not afraid to die. She says this every time we meet. She says none of us are to be upset when she does die, for it will be a great reunion in heaven. She looks away for a minute, and I think she means a reunion with her mama, her dead son, and husband. She can almost see them now—I can feel it in her voice, how it trails off. I've been conducting oral history interviews with Helen since 1997, and today I've asked specifically about her education as a black woman during the 1940s in Alabama. I want to know how Helen got to Norwood Hospital where she trained. Who dropped her off in a place so far from home? Here's what she says:

Well, the hospital was about an hour away, and Dr. and Mrs. Martin took me to register, because I had helped them, you know, cleaned their house and cooked and helped with their children for years. And they were interested in me becoming a nurse. They contacted Dr. C. M. Caraway. They were friends, and they asked him if he would please accept me to be a nursing student at Norwood Hospital.

*Helen (McClendon) Albert, freshman year, Norwood Hospital, Birmingham, Alabama, 1940.
Editor's collection.*

I took a couple of dresses. I have to mention the aprons that were part of our uniforms. We were unable to buy material to make the aprons for school, so one of Mama's neighbors, she was a good friend, she took the sheets off her bed and made my aprons to go with my uniform when I was ready to start training.

We had white hose and white shoes and my brothers and uncle, they helped to buy the shoes for me. We were poor. Our cabin was a shack, no windows or screens. Shutters, just shutters. We never did get running water. We got electricity in 1943, the year I graduated nurses training. Mama did not have the money to buy my shoes, so my brother went to a commissary [coal camp company store] there in Walker County and bought me a pair of shoes. My uncle gave money for them too.

I don't recall, you know, exactly how we got the money for school, but Dr. and Mrs. Martin, they helped me with financial assistance. I don't recall exactly what it was, but it was a small amount that they did give to them [Norwood Hospital School of Nursing in Birmingham, Alabama].

I think it was about six months into training [when] we received our caps. You see, we did not receive our caps until we'd gone through a probationary period. And I got the school pin after probation. They said that they wanted to make sure we were going to remain with the nursing program.

Oh, our training, it was really something. We would get up and go to chapel before we started on the day shift. And there's where we would have prayer and then we would go out to the units, the colored ward, down in the basement of the hospital. But, they [the instructors] were wonderful to give us training. We had to give the patients their bath and feed them, and not only did we give baths, we had to help clean. We didn't have aids and housekeepers and all then. We nurses would take a part in the cleaning and all, and we served the trays when they brought the trays from the kitchen.

We would wash the beds down and clean the bedside stands and see that the linen was changed. The hospital would bring a cart into the unit and we would get the linens off. We did not wash the linens. No, we changed the patients and all, and we would collect the trays after they brought them from the kitchen to our unit.

We had class during the day. Our shifts were twelve hours, but our days were almost fourteen hours long. We would have an hour off during the day and have classroom study. And then, we would have an hour in the evening after we finished work. That would be about seven thirty or eight thirty. It was lights out at ten o'clock. In our second year, we worked four-hour shifts at the Norwood Clinic, not for pay, just learning how to be nurses. The poorest whites and blacks came there.

We had a washer in the basement of the dormitory for our clothes and uniforms. The white students, they were upstairs on the first and second floors. And the black nurses, we were down in the basement. Sometimes, we'd sneak out to

go watch boxing. It was so exciting. We thought the housemother knew, but she didn't make trouble. We would go home maybe once or twice a month, because we didn't have the money. And we didn't have cars, so we just didn't get a chance to visit that often. When we did get to go home, there was a Greyhound bus that we would get, catch it outside the hospital and go home. It wasn't very much. It was under a dollar.

The first year was real exciting. We got to meet the patients and families and it was rewarding, because they felt that they were going to get better, because we went overboard trying to make them happy and assure them that they could get better, treated with the right medication. The first year, we did not take care of the white patients. We were merely downstairs, but I do remember when Dr. Martin's wife was in and they [Dr. and Mrs. Martin] got permission for me to come in and help with Mrs. Martin. She was having a baby. After I helped Mrs. Martin, they started letting the black students help with white mothers in labor.

I think it was the second year we started to help with white patients, but not very often. In surgery, we didn't do much with the patients either. It was limited. We just observed the doctors and nurses. We stood by, and then, I spoke out and said *I want to do some real nursing, not just clean up after the surgery and watch.*

I would like to assist. And they saw that I was interested and started to let us scrub in more. It was really a challenge to be able to assist with the instruments and to take part in the nursing part of it. Yes, surgery was very exciting.

We had our own maternity ward on the unit where we were being taught how to observe labor, how the pains would come and go, and you could tell when those contractions were getting harder. And we also had to set up for delivery. We had the unit that was sterilized after each patient. We would set up the unit and had to be prepared to take care of the newborns. You have to aspirate them and see that they are all right. And then we were excited when the placenta was delivered. They told us to watch so that we would not have excessive bleeding and all. It was strange to see some of the babies, how when they didn't cry, the doctors would give them a little smack to stimulate them to cry and get their lungs expanded.

Our community nursing, that came later. I got quite a bit of experience after I graduated from Norwood Hospital. There was a maternity hospital, Slossfield Memorial, two miles from Norwood. When the family would call into the hospital, we would get the doctor's delivery bag and go to the homes. These home deliveries were very exciting. Before, the mothers would come in and we would teach them all they needed to prepare for a delivery at home. When they would go into labor, they'd notify us, and we'd notify the doctors. Sometimes, we would travel two or three miles. It was in the suburbs, and there was a large population there. They'd come in and get the prenatal training to know what to do when the labor started.

At Slossfield, I was hired in for seventy-five dollars a month. And it was quite a challenge. After a while, I went to look for my uncle and found him here, in Warren, Ohio. The rate here [for nurses] was $125 a month, so I was quite impressed to come here to work.

As far as I know, the white nurses and black nurses had the same certificates when we graduated, but we had our graduation ceremony at different churches. The white nurses had their exercises at a white church, and the black nurses had their graduation at a black church. The first time I took state boards, I did not pass. I cried and cried. I'm no test taker, but the next time, I passed—I'm no quitter, thank God. I don't remember the church, but I can remember it was quite a challenge, because all the congregation was there to witness the ceremony.

The one nursing instructor who stood out was Mrs. Turner. She was very blunt. She just didn't treat us exactly like you would hope. And I also remember Mrs. Barney Roberts. She was our director of nursing, and she was very strict. She really let you know that sometimes if you spoke out, she would tell you that you don't speak like *that.*

All of us students were in the same classroom. And the nurses that were in training, we all were very happy. It was like a family. We ate in the basement though; they ate upstairs. The white students recognized us, and we recognized them. It was just working together, because the main objective was to take good care of the patients, helping them to get better. Yes, it was sad we had to graduate separate. Yes it was. And we cried and hugged each other. It was the custom, and it takes quite a bit to change that sort of custom.

Helen Albert, Nurse-Humanitarian, 1921–2009

PART IV

———— ∞✦∞ ————

I came to this life with serious hands.

SONYA SANCHEZ, "AAAAYEE BABO [PRAISE GOD]"

And the baby's head emerges, his hair dark and wet
like the earth after rain.

Yes, that's my roommate washing her white hose in the bathroom sink. We miss our moms, and we're learning so much about water. We witness baptism in its many forms. Instruments must be soaked in water, also certain bandages. Our bodies' composition? Mostly water. When we get sick? We need more or less water. If we have excessive thirst? It means our body's suffering: dehydration, hemorrhage, lack of water. Babies swim in amniotic fluid (which is, well, water). Nursing students learn to time contractions and comfort laboring mothers. Often, they wet a cloth with warm water and wash the mother's face. With every witnessed birth, instructors/students are also reborn. Salty fluid leaking down our cheeks? Water. As nurses we are always washing our hands, but not everything gets rinsed away.

RITA MARIA MAGDALENO

May Snapshot, 1966

It was May when I posed for him. Posed in a pale lime-green swimsuit, Caribbean white designs swirled across the lime. Like little waves. Like something sweet and naive. Like me. A one-piece suit that didn't show off a girl's navel. Discreet like the girls we were supposed to be. Student nurses training under the stern eye of the Sisters of Mercy, St. Joseph's Nursing School in Phoenix, Arizona.

My auburn hair shining in sunlight. Auburn hair cut blunt. Pageboy style and my bangs falling softly. Dark brown sunglasses, my big wide smile. I was posing for him, Airman 1/C stationed in Cam Ran Bay, Vietnam. My new pen pal. He had already mailed a small black-and-white snapshot to me. Inside that square-white border, he stood in fatigues and black boots, military tank glaring in the background.

It was May, a warm breeze drifting over the pool. The tidy-white sundeck. The soft-drink machine humming. A little oasis for the student body. All women. A mild day, already climbing into the nineties, in the heart of Phoenix. This is where the nursing school stood. Right behind our mother hospital, St. Joseph's. All around, palm trees swayed like lazy dreams against solid blue sky. It felt like hula girls and orchids. And success—our first year nearly complete. Summer vacation around the corner.

I was nineteen and felt that anything was possible. I dreamed of working in San Francisco after graduation. Army recruiters had already visited our nursing school. Recruiters held out visions of MASH units, starting grade of captain, smart uniforms, world travel, and all tuition paid. But it was my Hispanic father who balked at the notion of me in the army. He fretted, "Don't wait too long, *mijita!* Dear girl, you know that life is like a carousel ride." He waved his hand in circles, "Yes, that brass ring only comes around once and you'd better grab

Rita Maria Magdaleno, St. Joseph's Nursing School, 1968. Courtesy Rita Maria Magdaleno.

148

it!" My papa was sure that I needed to get engaged, that I needed to catch one of those soldier boys coming home. That marriage was the smart thing to do.

Sure, I wanted to be engaged. A few of the girls in my nursing class were already showing off their rings. There were showy *ooh-la-la-las,* glimmer of diamonds on left ring fingers. Mostly tiny stones. Like chips of light faintly pricking a dark sea. Still, I wanted one. I wore my bangs thick and sleek above my eyebrows. Above my movie-star dark sunglasses. I wanted glamor. I wanted to convey a feeling of casual mystery. Like Karen Carpenter, her soft-loose hair, her lanky beauty.

And I wanted to be like my roommate, Sylvia. Confident, shining black hair. Sylvia who always had a boyfriend or two. She was my roommate during our first year of training. We were all required to live in the nursing dorm. Sylvia, my roomie from a small Arizona mining town. Sylvia, my roomie who would be dropped from nursing school by the end of our second semester. Sylvia, who would stand on her twin bed and bang her tambourine, who loved Mick Jagger, and would sing, "Everybody must get stoned." Sylvia, who was pretty and liked to have fun. Sure, I wanted to be like her.

It was May and I posed on the diving board, cupped my chin into my right hand, and smiled into the camera. I smiled above the warm turquoise water of the pool. "Look casual," the photographer called out. It must have been Kathy or Diane or Patsy who took my photo. They all had boyfriends.

It was the photo I'd mail to that Airman First Class, Cam Ran Bay, Vietnam. A year later, he'd drive a white Mustang to Phoenix and we'd get engaged by Christmas 1967. I'd graduate from nursing school in June 1968 and we'd get married that September. We'd have two kids, a boy and a girl, a cream-white house with red trim in west Phoenix. And it would be good, for a while. Then we'd split and I'd burn all his love letters from 'Nam.

But in 1966, I mailed that photo of me posed on the diving board. Because the airman who asked for my photo had become my pen pal. Because he had sent a second photo of himself. There he was. Climbing out of the sea, dark and wet and good looking in his swim trunks. Climbing out of the water at Cam Ran Bay, black and white. Wasn't it always supposed to be black and white?

. . .

A lot of the girls, especially the upperclassmen, got camouflage shirts from 'Nam. The shirts had their soldier's name sewn on a black strip above the left shirt pocket. Status. Pure status to walk the hallway—barefoot and in your panties—in a soldier's shirt with his name riding above your left breast. Very hot.

When the soldier's shirt arrived in the mail, it was time for another picture. This one a bit more suggestive. This one taken in our dorm room. Two options: nice girl leaning against her closet door, or a bolder girl relaxing on her twin bed—just panties and bra under that fatigue shirt. For her Vietnam pen pal. Perhaps for a future husband. Or a heartbreak yet to come. Still, we sent those snapshots and kept writing.

Little gifts I remember: red silk from Saigon; a dozen yellow roses wired to the dorm; tiny brass cups from Thailand. Red silk and yellow roses. I fell in love with that airman. And the rest is history. But perhaps that's not the point. Years later, my father admitted, "Oh, it's my fault to be such a romantic. I just wanted the best for you." My failed marriage; no Army nursing career for me.

"Yes, I felt rushed!" I told him. But I had believed my papa and I didn't want to miss my "brass ring." For sure, I didn't want to be the only one in our dorm without my own fatigue shirt. So I got my shirt, got my ring. But I did not accept the army's offer to enlist and become a captain. To travel and find the brass rings of my own life.

CELIA BROWN

The First Hour

*The lie is longitudinal, the attitude is one of flexion, the presentation is vertex,
the position is left occipito-anterior.*
  —*Textbook for Midwives,* by Margaret F. Myles

This will never happen to me
I vowed, shocked the first time
I saw a head pushing out
after a slight show and water
spurting, the attitude, right
and the vertex coming at me—
just like it said in Maggie Miles.

Push! I urged, sweating harder
than the woman I was trying to deliver
who wasn't listening at all
but swearing out loud
and ranting about red tomatoes
and someone stealing
out of her garden. Push!
I said it again, but by then
it didn't matter, the head
had come out and the shoulder
was presenting on its own,
the little body slithered
I grabbed the greasy pole of it
upside down, clearing the airway.

Cut the cord, and don't panic
I coached myself, clamping
down hard in two places to sever
the ropey tube and catch
the blue, howling vigor
of that first hour in my two hands . . .
my shaky, learning hands.

VIRGINIA RUTH

Mr. Magoo of Nursing School

I was the female version of Mr. Magoo when I attended Salisbury State College Nursing School. A "Miss Naive," I traveled through my school experiences surrounded by chaos and worldliness, yet I never seemed to be affected by it. I might have been in the path of danger or trouble, but somehow I breezed right through. Even though Mr. Magoo didn't see well with his coke-bottle glasses, he seemed to have insight and a naïveté coupled with the reliance on the goodness of people and situations. Just as his naïveté spared him, I think my naïveté spared me as well.

On one occasion, our school clinical assignment was to prepare and present a health education program for a Wicomico County public school classroom. My chosen topic was drug use prevention, specifically addressing cocaine and its effects on health. I spent hours researching in the library, searching periodicals, drug manuals, and contacting public health departments for pamphlets and age-appropriate information. I also researched the developmental aspects of ten-year-old learners. We student nurses were to provide a lesson that children could understand, and we were expected to include role-playing and strategies to enable them to "say no" to drug use.

As I contemplated this assignment and the best way to go about teaching, I deferred to my nursing plan process: assessment, diagnosis, goals, implementation, and evaluation. In my naive thinking I figured the fourth graders should see what crack cocaine actually looked like. I thought that would be a good start to the assessment; you should know what you are encountering.

Of course, I had no idea what crack or any other drug looked like except for what I saw on TV shows like *Magnum PI* or *Miami Vice*. The internet wouldn't be publicly available for another fifteen years. For some reason, I had it in my mind that crack would look similar to a brownish sugar cube. I figured since cocaine

Virginia Ruth, Salisbury State College graduate, 1988. Courtesy Virginia Ruth.

could sometimes be made in "crack kitchens" that I could whip up something that looked like it in my student apartment kitchen. I tried coloring a couple of sugar cubes and I tried baking some, but I mostly only created a sticky mess.

"What are you doing?" my roommate Linda asked as she entered our narrow galley apartment kitchen, sidestepping the brownish granular blobs plopped on our tile floor. "Because you are making a royal mess."

"Trying to make fake crack for my class," I replied, moving a crusted-over pan of hardened sugar so that she could find a place on the counter for her coffee cup.

"What? Whatever." She trailed out of the kitchen dismissing me with a wave of her hand.

Linda peeked into the kitchen doorway carrying her key fob and books on her way to class. "You know, you should see if the police station has some you could borrow."

I'm sure now that Linda's suggestion was a joke, or maybe a way to get me into trouble, but being Miss Naive, I thought her suggestion was a great idea.

I rode my reliable, old ten-speed bicycle to the Salisbury police station in the small college town where I attended school. Dutifully, I locked my bike to a "Parking for the Sergeant on Duty" post. Repositioning my backpack over my left shoulder, I tentatively walked up the brick steps to the heavy glass front doors. There was an older police officer assigned to the reception desk; he looked up when he heard the thump of the door closing. When he saw me with my bike helmet in hand, he pushed up his half-moon glasses, smiled, and gave a nod to indicate that I should approach his gray metal, government-issued desk.

Never having been inside a police station before, I was surprised by how quiet it appeared. My heart was pounding in my chest; I was sure he could hear it.

"I'm a nursing student at Salisbury State," I nervously explained. There was a loud crash resounding on the linoleum floor as my bike helmet slipped out of my fingers. "I was wondering if I could borrow some crack cocaine for an education project that I am doing at the local elementary school?"

My voice trailed up as I bent down to pick up my helmet.

"I'm sorry dear," the officer replied, stroking his mustache with his thumb and forefinger. "Could you repeat that?"

He kept his hand over his mouth as if he were politely squelching a belch.

I repeated my request, emphasizing my need to show the students what crack looked like. God love that gentleman for not laughing in my face and kicking me out. He must have seen a glimmer of sincerity written on my face. Gripping his desk as he arose, he excused himself to get the officer on duty. As he pushed through the back hallway door, I heard him say, "This one's a first."

While I waited, I focused on the room around me. It didn't resemble anything like TV police stations. First, it was as quiet as the college's library. The only sound was a light hum of activity punctuated by a burst of laughter coming from behind closed doors that said *Police Personnel Only*, the room the desk sergeant had entered. There was a faint smell of stale cigarettes coming from beneath the door. To the front of the room, I saw dust particles floating on the light rays coming through the smeared glass of the outside wall's high windows. I wandered closer, following the light rays. Tacked to a bulletin board under the windows was a slightly off-center poster of the dog McGruff and the slogan, "Take a Bite Out of Crime." Just below were some old wanted flyers, sketches of snarling-lipped faces. I began reading "Wanted for Armed Robbery" when I heard the clomp, clomp of shoes on the worn linoleum tiles.

"Well, miss, what are you trying to do?" I spun around at the sound of a bass voice and saw one of the largest men I'd ever seen. He seemed to fill the doorway as he came through. His khaki twill shirt was pressed and taut over an impressive muscular chest. A gold square name badge, "MacKenzie," almost popped off his left breast pocket.

Fiddling with my helmet strap, but careful to hold on, I nervously explained my assignment and what I wanted to do. The longer I tried to explain, the more I wondered *was this such a good idea?* I wondered if any of the wanted flyers contained a curly headed nursing student looking for crack.

Patiently, Officer MacKenzie explained that he couldn't let me have any samples of crack or cocaine but he did have something he could give me.

"Here's a video we use when we do our outreach programs to the youth clubs. You're welcome to borrow it." He handed me the video and shook my hand. "I'll be interested in hearing how it goes."

I released my hand from his giant paw, thanked him, promising to return it after my lesson, and hurried outside before he changed his mind. I carefully tucked the videotape in the bottom of my backpack.

"You what?" my nursing friends exclaimed. They looked at each other, some shaking their heads while others just rolled their eyes. "We can't believe they even talked to you much less gave you something."

"Are you crazy?" questioned my non-nursing friends. "You were lucky they didn't arrest you." On what charge no one said, but still, the consensus was that I wasn't playing with a full deck.

My teaching day arrived. I showed up thirty minutes earlier than the planned meeting time with my nursing instructor, Ms. Brandon. I waited in one of two desk chairs that doubled as the reception area in the small lobby of the elementary school. The hum of chattering was in the air. In the distance, I heard squeaks from the students' shoes as they played basketball in the gymnasium. Various-sized children shuffled down the hall carrying a laminated "bathroom pass" sign. When Ms. Brandon arrived, I'd checked and rechecked my bags and their

154

contents five times: my teaching lesson plan that I'd hand to Ms. Brandon while I spoke, my index card notes for reference, the antidrug posters I'd received from the Drug Enforcement Agency, and the police video.

"Are you ready? Once we sign in, we'll go directly to the classroom." Ms. Brandon gave me an encouraging smile. "You'll do fine."

Mrs. Radebaugh, the fourth-grade teacher, stood to the right of the chalkboard.

"Boys and girls. Today we have a treat. Ms. Ruth, a nursing student from Salisbury State, is going to help us with our drug unit."

As soon as she introduced me she returned to her desk at the back of the room.

"Good morning. Does anyone know what this is?" I had taped the poster of crack to the chalkboard.

"Popcorn?" called a voice from the back.

"Powder?" called another voice.

"Drruuggs," came the voice of the freckle-faced redhead boy in the front row. He glanced behind him as he said it, as if he were trying to drum up a cheer.

"Right," I nodded to him. I thought I'd better engage this guy before he took over the class. "What's your name?"

"Jimmy" came the reply.

"Okay, Jimmy, good answer. But do you know what kind of drug? Do you know what happens to your body when you take it?"

Thus began my lesson. I would ask questions, listen to the students' answers, and then proceed to tell them about the dangers of crack and cocaine—what it was, how it was made and used, physical and social side effects. I divided the children into groups of four. They did some role-playing, and then I ended my lesson by showing them the police video.

Ms. Brandon and Mrs. Radebaugh gave me big congratulatory smiles. "Boy, you were a natural," Mrs. Radebaugh said. "Have you thought about being a teacher?"

I thanked her and said, "No, there are enough educators in my family already."

When I think back to my student nurse days and to my naïveté, I'm grateful for all the people I encountered: my nursing instructors, the policemen from the Salisbury station, and the countless patients and staff members of the hospitals, clinics, companies, doctors' offices, and health departments where we did our practicums. So many were so kind, patient, and understanding of a sincere young woman who only wanted to learn.

· · ·

The nursing process starts with assessment. We investigate our patients' states of health or illness by checking signs, symptoms, and then interpreting data. The kind adults who helped me along the way must have seen me as a well-meaning, creative student (albeit one who had a different outlook and path than their other

155

students). They guided and shielded me through my student nurse journey as I gained experience in the world of community health.

Because of their actions, I try to recognize the motives and intentions of others, and I have a soft spot for the other "Mr. Magoos" or "Miss Naives" I encounter along the way. I try to give everyone the benefit of the doubt, listen to their ideas, help them with any activities, and provide feedback. I hope to provide them the opportunities that others gave me. I want to help them grow. After all, isn't that what the nursing process is all about?

GEOFFREY BOWE

Student Nurse on a Bus

I am a student nurse
on my first day.

The bus trundles
past blue English lakes.
sways as we pass
along green leafy lanes.

I am young and naive
I want to help people.

My mother bought me a fob watch,
a first-day present.

Pulling into the station
alighting from the bus
drops of rain begin to fall.

As I walk past unfamiliar shops
a hundred questions
fill my head.

I've never seen blood!
Will vomit make me squirm?
Am I clever enough to pass the exams?

Down the street
the school of nursing beckons—I go,
I go inside.

MURIEL MURCH

The Bed Bath

1. LEARNING: THE PROCEDURE

In 1961, twenty-four young women came together in the classroom of The Royal Surrey County Hospital in Guildford, Surrey. We were entering our three-month period of preliminary nurse training. With its completion, we could begin our official journey to become state registered nurses. But first we had to pass through Sister Tutor Cartwright's schoolroom, her capable hands, and caring heart. Only twenty students emerged from her classroom. By the end of our three years, we were a graduating class of sixteen.

During those three month, we had mastered making beds, managing bedpans and urinals, washing hands, carrying and placing meal trays, even cooking egg custard, and we were now ready, on this day, for one of our final important classroom lessons, The Bed Bath.

Sister Cartwright stood beside one of the four beds in her schoolroom. Her clean hair was, as always, rolled neatly up around her head and secured by unseen bobby pins. The brunette color now held a few wisps of gray. That made her, to us, already old. Her delicate, though starched, laced cap never moved from her head. Her sweet twinkling eyes were already decorated with laugh lines, for her countenance held a smile more easily than a frown. She moved with a brisk yet unhurried pace, one we came to learn ourselves. Her blue uniform fitted snuggly over yearning (we imagined) virginal breasts held back by the pinned bodice of her freshly laundered white apron.

Once she had our attention (and it didn't take much, so eager were we all), she looked down at the Raggedy Ann life-sized doll reposing with toy-like surrender in the bed. Sister Cartwright stroked back the doll's wispy hair, thereby bringing her to life, before turning to us.

"Today we are going to give Mrs. Jones a bed bath," she said.

Already Sister Cartwright had begun to instill in us the Girl Guide (and Boy Scout) mantra "Be prepared." It was one of the foundation blocks for a professional manner that would help subdue our own insecurities and fears while simultaneously bringing reassurance and comfort to our patients.

To prepare for the bed bath, Sister Cartwright began by asking, "What do we need on our trolley?" Then, every procedure's needs were laid out on a "trolley" to bring to the patient's bedside. By this time, some of us could answer, "A basin of hot water, face and body washcloths, a towel, maybe soap, if the patient does not have their own, talc powder and cream for massaging the skin." We were, with some prodding, able to add a clean gown, a mug for water, and small basin for teeth cleaning. And oh, since this could be when we changed the patient's bed, bed linens would be good to have also, wouldn't they?

With the gentle insistence of a mother hen, Sister Cartwright guided us through the procedure, emphasizing the patient's need for comfort and warmth, both physical and spiritual, alongside cleanliness. She showed us how to keep our patient warm and modest, safe from chill or embarrassment. We learned about using two washcloths, beginning with the face, moving down along the body, allowing the patient to clean their most private and vulnerable areas if they could. We understood the need to stimulate and refresh toes and feet and return circulation to the back and buttocks with long strokes from our hands. We learned to help those who were able to brush their hair. And we learned to leave our patients, whatever their illness, feeling a little bit better than before

Muriel A. (Slater) Murch, The Royal Surrey County Hospital, Guilford, Surrey, 1964. Courtesy Muriel A. Murch. Photo by W. Dennett Press & General Photographer.

Muriel A. (Slater) Murch (middle row, far left) *with fellow nursing school graduates, Guilford, Surrey, 1964. Courtesy Muriel A. Murch. Photo by W. Dennett Press & General Photographer.*

we had come to their bedside. It was a new intimacy for us and for our patients, and we were grateful to have the docile Mrs. Jones allow us to care for her.

It was not long before we were let loose on the wards, our learned preparedness doing more than we realized to mask our fear. When I was assigned to bathe a real live Mrs. Jones, she lay curled up in a tight fetal position, hiding her face from life, possibly praying for a lift off into Christ's promised kingdom. Gently pulling back the bedsheet, I was thrown into confusion by the soft shiny protuberance lying placidly between her buttocks and thighs. I didn't know enough of female or male anatomy to recognize the structure, but I wondered if this was, in fact, a Mr. Jones. I hastily drew the bedsheet back over her and went to find a senior student nurse.

"Oh, don't worry, that is only her prolapsed cervix. Just try to keep her dry and comfortable."

I returned to Mrs. Jones, humbled at my first lesson as to how the body can fail us while the spirit endures. Taking far longer than my allotted time, I gave her the best bed bath I could. During our first months on the wards, we all became proficient at bed bathing skills and did indeed leave our patients feeling more comfortable from our care. We survived the leering, "Look at what I got for you nurse," and then the displays of penile engorgements from the beer-drinking, motorcycle-riding patients.

We came, too, to care for the little children and their two-dozen-a-week tonsil-lectomies. We grieved over young and old who did not survive under our care. We stayed after our shift's ending to complete the last laying out of a patient before accompanying them to the morgue. We learned to let go of those patients we had come to know a little, and sometimes wondered what about them we would never know.

2. LEARNING A CULTURE

In the autumn of 1964 while sitting on my mother's bed one night, before I left to get "that Wild American Boy" out of my system, my mother, rather nervously, tried to offer advice.

"Don't forget, they may speak the same language but they are still foreigners."

How could she say such a thing? I bit back a retort. But not a month later her words ran through my mind when I joined my Irish flatmates in cultural mum-bling and grumbling. We were the cheap labor of the day, and in 1964 we had come to the United States by the planeload with completed green card applications. A group of twenty plus nurses poured into White Plains Hospital in Westchester County and were packed neatly away in an apartment building located just a few minutes' walk across the parking lot to the hospital. Our month of orientation was led by a stick-thin, gum-chewing, Texas-drawling nurse. We were lectured about *how we do it here,* walked through wards and departments, and ogled, as the fresh meat we were, by the young, mostly married, doctors. It didn't take us long, one month of tutored orientation, another month of days with the American nurses, before we were let loose, working what we chose, the evening and night shifts. Here we could work in our own familiar rhythms, using the skills we had brought with us.

We formed our own band of "jolly chums" and mumbled about our strange colleagues and grumbled about our complaining patients. We had never heard of "doctor's orders" in relation to nursing procedures and were, frankly, rather appalled by them. What on earth did doctors have to say about getting patients out of bed, relieving flatulence, and monitoring fluids? Luckily, the hospitals also pulled interns from the same pool of postwar Europeans striving for a better life. There were Polish and Czechoslovakian doctors, learning English as they cared for patients and worked alongside us. Unless something really untoward or pharmaceutical was needed, we would phone the attending physicians at ten at night and let them know what we had done with their patients, then ask if they wanted to write an order for that procedure. They always said yes.

After the nursing report and shift change, we walked our wards, checking on our patients, making sure our orderlies knew their assignments, and coordinating where we would need to help each other with the sicker or more difficult patients. This team approach took the orderlies a while to get used to, but as we worked alongside them, asking if we could help them, those young Negro (because it was the sixties) men began to take us under their wings.

The orderlies quickly took to our small group, three Irish and one English nurse (me), who shared an apartment. We always needed an hour or two to unwind after the work shift, although not Mary Rose. She worked nights and had given herself one year in which to earn enough money for her and her fiancé to set up a bakery together back in Ireland. But Etna, Anne, and I were restless and in need of talk, pizza, a light beer, and a late night movie to unwind. Soon those Irish girls had attracted a following from their explorations of White Plains. Often young men, who would soon, one by one, be shipped off to the war in Vietnam, joined us. Our orderlies came too, coffee and nut-brown young men who took the train north from 125th Street up to work in White Plains. They brought the pizza, the beer, and the stories. They taught us how to navigate Manhattan. One night they explained to us why, and how, I had frightened Mr. Wilson so.

It was Louis who found me out. That evening while doing my rounds I entered Mr. Wilson's room. It was his second postsurgical day, often more uncomfortable than the first, which can pass in a haze of anesthesia. By day two, a glimmer of reality returns, accompanied by pain and its dancing companion, pain medication. Mr. Wilson was in a muddle, with twisted bedsheets, which highlighted the blanching of his dark face, as he struggled, restlessly and now in pain. Looking at his chart and at him, it appeared that the day shift had let him sleep, often a good thing, and forgone his bed bath. But now Mr. Wilson was awake and one of the things that could make him more comfortable would be that bath. I put him on my list to care for as soon as I could.

Within an hour I was back at Mr. Wilson's bedside and, with a smile, told him I would be giving him a bath. His eyes widened and so I asked, would he maybe like some pain medication before we began? He shook his head but said nothing. I gathered all that I would need and soon set about gently bathing him. His eyes were still glazed and he said nothing as we began. But slowly, as I worked gently with his body, he seemed to relax a little. I was pleased with how the bath was progressing. I even managed to have him roll onto his side so I could wash his back and his buttocks as he clung to the side rail with tight-knuckled fists. Louis walked by at that moment and quickly came in to help me. I missed the look of relief that passed across Mr. Wilson's face when Louis held him and uttered soothing words to him. (I also missed the fact that while Louis could be called coffee-caramel in color, Mr. Wilson was a dark-mahogany brown.) Louis and I finished the bed bath and sheet change, and Mr. Wilson was indeed more comfortable than before. It was not until that evening, back in our apartment, a beer and slice of pizza in hand, that Louis sat shaking his head.

"Man oh man, woman, don't never do that again without me by your side." So said Louis, and we all learned a little more about the history of the country we had come to. This was not the history book lesson that we learned for our high school equivalency exams prior to taking our American nursing finals, but the history of the birth of a nation that America built on the backs of Mr. Wilson's parents and grandparents. His fear was not of the pain, but of a man faced with the body of a white woman threatening his safe haven of subjugation. Another lesson had been learned.

3. LEARNING TO RECEIVE

In the late 1960s, as pregnant nurses, we stayed away from those doctors who caught us in the ward's medicine room and, slipping a hand neatly around our waist, hissed, "When you are at five centimeters and writhing in pain, you will wish you had come to me." We were claiming back our bodies, our lives, even our minds, and giving birth was a good place to begin. We came of age when reproductive freedom was becoming a reality for many women. Choices were becoming available: to prevent pregnancy, to conceive or not, to carry a pregnancy to term or not. Could we control our child birthing experiences as well? We sought out, and found, obstetricians who would at least give lip service to our desires to "go natural," who listened, sometimes with a smile, but also said, "This is your baby; you can do what you want." They were not really convinced that we would or could manage without their help but were willing to let us try. We went about it, in our sensible American way, read all we could, and took classes in "Prepared Childbirth." We vacillated between total insecurity and unfounded confidence expressed as, "Well, this is exciting, of course I can do this" and "How on earth will I be able to get that baby out of here?"

For many women, nurses in particular, labor and giving birth became an adventure to look forward to, a mountain to climb, a physical challenge. Those of us committed, for whatever reason, to a natural birth, as if we had just discovered it, were determined to peel back the layers of masculine science that was designed to fix "our problem."

And so we proceeded, measurably growing bigger each month, taking classes, speaking with any other mothers we could—those who had given birth before, those with horror stories of restraining straps, vaginal tears, forceps high and low, and those few who had proudly made it through *sans* medication.

Every labor is different. And the birthing stories that we heard all bore truth to that statement. There is not one story, not one, that can tell you how this will be for you. As my labor picked up in the evening, my husband and I drove a friend's rusty, trusty VW bus to the Good Samaritan Hospital in Los Angeles County. At one-centimeter dilation and a slight pelvic engagement, I was admitted, my husband carrying our bag of every-thing-we-might-need-tonight with us.

As labor continued through the night, my dilation progressed slowly. At around five centimeters, my husband found that reading Kurt Vonnegut's *Cat's Cradle* aloud to me soothed him. Engrossed in the book, he would occasionally stroke my stomach. By the time I was ready to snap at him, he was saved by the entrance of Betsy. Betsy was big and round, wearing an untied green gown that flowed easily over her scrubs. She had come to check how the young first-time mother in room three was coming along. Immediately she saw where we both were and, bless her heart, did not scold my husband out loud. Instead, she bustled him out of the room with the firm words, "Now I'm going to give the young mother a nice bath." I couldn't think of anything worse than a bath but had not yet reached the irritability of transition to protest. I was tired and messy and quickly slipping out of that all-important control.

Betsy gathered everything she needed, just as I did when bathing a patient, and placed it close beside us. She covered my chest with a towel. Her dark hands entered the water and she drew out the washcloth and squeezed it almost dry before beginning to wipe my face. Betsy's touch was firm, gentle, and reassuring. I relaxed into her safe care and the sisterhood of nurses. I lay back and listened as she hummed to me. When she finished, I was indeed clean and refreshed. Soon my labor intensified, and I become focused anew on the rhythm of my body. I had reached seven centimeters when Betsy let my husband back into the room and quietly confiscated Vonnegut. The obstetrician popped his head in for a cheery good morning and "It won't be long now. How about a little shot of Demerol?"

"I don't think she will need it, Doctor," replied Betsy softly, for our ears as much as his. Within another three hours our firstborn left the comfort of my womb and traveled into this world.

From Betsy I learned again the mysteries and wonders of the bed bath, the strength of a nurse's touch, and how professionalism and love can come together to be given, and received.

PATTAMA ULRICH

Human Anatomy Class

Oh yes, I met a kind woman
I peeled back her skin, counted her bones
She has a name: *Forever*
I will remember her
I will remember her

CORTNEY DAVIS

Wednesday's Child

It was a Wednesday in late spring, 1972, and I was in my final months of training, eagerly awaiting graduation. When I'd arrived on the maternity ward that morning, my nursing instructor told me that I'd be caring for a baby, only hours old, with special needs. I thought she'd send me to the neonatal ICU. Instead, to my surprise, she motioned toward the linen closet, its doors tightly closed.

"The baby was born without a complete brain," she said. "A condition called anencephaly. He can't see or hear. And," she added, "they don't expect he'll live out the day. So try not to get attached."

The nursing-care plan was concise: "You don't need to do anything other than observe his breathing, turn him occasionally, change his diaper, and bathe him."

Hearing these instructions, so different from the nursing care I'd seen given to other special-needs infants, I felt both curious—*why is this baby hidden away in a linen closet?*—and a bit frightened.

Cautiously, heart pounding, I opened the closet door.

The steel linen rack had been shoved aside to make room for a single isolette. It held a sleeping newborn boy. There was no card proclaiming his birth date, weight, or name. I had expected to see a monster. Instead, I saw an infant with a compressed forehead, tightly closed eyes, and perfectly chiseled lips and chin. His skull was steeply sloped and covered with blond hair.

I stood and watched him sleeping. From some angles, he looked like an elderly man. If I turned him just a bit, he looked like a perfect, beautiful infant. My apprehension melted away. I touched his cheek and smoothed his hair. Maybe he would die within the day, but for now, I would pretend he was like any other newborn.

As I bathed him, I named him Baby Boy, trying to acknowledge the reality of his life, even if, as my instructor's cool instructions implied, his life was worthless. At the same time, I struggled not to "get attached," although keeping an emotional distance was already beginning to seem impossible. After his bath, I picked him up and rocked him, although that wasn't in the care plan. I sang to him, even though I knew he couldn't hear.

When I returned from my break and found the linen-closet light turned off, leaving Baby Boy alone in the dark, I felt a stab of anger and went in search of the charge nurse.

"Shouldn't we leave a light on?" I asked, hoping that my tone didn't reveal my agitation.

166

"Do you think a light would make any difference?" she replied.

"Might his mother want to hold him?" I persisted.

"Enough," she said. "It's a tragedy."

One by one, the other students stopped by to see Baby Boy. Some wanted to hold him. A few shook their heads and said that it would be a blessing if he died. We all wondered about his mother—why wasn't she involved in his care? We decided to do a bit of snooping.

We discovered that his mother's room was just down the hall. One of the delivery-room aides told us that the baby had been whisked away at birth, before his mother awoke from anesthesia. At her husband's urging, the doctors had told her that the baby was stillborn. She'd never seen or held him. She didn't know that he was only a short walk away.

We students ambled past the mother's room, peeking in to see her face. Her cheeks were flushed and her eyes puffy. She looked as if she hadn't stopped crying.

"What if she *could* hold him?" one student asked our instructor. "Would that help to give her some closure?"

"Or would it simply increase her sorrow?" she responded.

As the afternoon wore on, I wondered if I'd been assigned to Baby Boy because he was considered a lost cause—even a bumbling nursing student couldn't harm him. Wanting to do *something,* I asked if I might offer him some water.

"I suppose you could try," my instructor said, "but I doubt there will be any sucking response. Remember, the doctors don't expect him to live."

Did he respond to the water bottle I offered? It seemed to me that he did: I saw his lips close around the nipple. Did he respond to my rocking? I thought that he did: he settled into my arms like any newborn might. A part of me hoped that the doctors were wrong.

Again, I approached the charge nurse.

"Could I try some formula?"

She rolled her eyes. "Really, I doubt the doctors would want to prolong the inevitable."

On Thursday, when I returned for my eight-hour shift, Baby Boy was still alive. As I opened the linen-closet door, he began to cry, a high-pitched, agonizing whine.

The charge nurse saw me coming.

"Okay," she said. "Try some formula."

His lips smacked and his cheeks tried to suck, but the formula just dribbled out of his mouth. I tried again and again, but there was no further response. I gave up and held him, rocking him as he cried. In that moment, I resigned myself to Baby Boy's certain death, but I couldn't close my heart.

When his keening persisted, the nurses worried that his mother might hear and, responding to some primal recognition, try to investigate. They moved her further down the hall, and that afternoon the doctors sent her home. I wondered how long it would take her to stop crying over a baby she'd never seen, or how her husband lived with the knowledge that he'd left his boy in the hospital to take, in one doctor's words, "way too long to die."

On Friday, Baby Boy settled into a resigned stupor. His mouth worked in the pantomime of nursing. His fists curled and uncurled. His eyelids—did I imagine this?—opened, and his unseeing eyes seemed to search my face.

The following Monday, when I returned to the maternity floor, the closet held only linen. Baby Boy had died, alone, sometime on Saturday afternoon. He died before the advent of grief counseling, before the time when his parents would have held him, taken his photograph and tied a lock of his hair in a blue ribbon. He died before we understood how necessary it is for families to gather together to welcome such a child and then to accompany him gently to his death.

Back then, despite my own reaction to Baby Boy's situation, I accepted that such disregard for life, such secrecy and denial of grief, was the norm. But here I am, all these years later, writing about him.

Through his birth, his short life spent in the dark, and his death, surely he touched his parents' lives—and that of an awkward nursing student as well. Looking back, I know that we couldn't have saved him. I only wish that we'd known then what we know now about honoring the impact of even the smallest, briefest lives upon our own.

KRISTINE GARCIA-CROSS

Student Nurse: Last Clinical Day, OB, Block 3

Spring in Phoenix. The end of April. Labor and delivery, my patient Gravida 4, first boy. Ultrasound tech verifying, "Oh, yes! He's going to have a lot of hair."

On the imaging screen, I could see the baby, his hair waving like a wild little ocean.

My patient smiling, "Blonde, brown, red. Yes, all three of my girls had a different color at birth! All preemies."

My patient is waiting for induction. Thirty-seven weeks. Estimated weight: 6 lbs. Doc felt good about this.

"I feel like my baby will have brown hair, too," my patient says.

My duties: help her feel comfortable, talk with her, help her breathe through contractions.

After the AROM, artificial rupture of membranes, I have a lot of cleaning up to do.

Pitocin running. Contractions and dilation steadily increasing. "Set up two boluses of IV fluids," my preceptor nurse directs me. Then the epidural is placed as my patient sits on the edge of the bed. And I face her, snug her head on my chest, rub her shoulders, and speak calmly. "Just keep breathing," as the anesthesiologist threads a needle and catheter into her spine.

"You're doing great," I tell her.

Now, position my patient, reposition my patient. With the peanut birthing ball; then without the peanut. Tocometer, Foley catheter, fundus like an air balloon, EFM tracking tiny heartbeats. 150. Tiny racing heartbeats. Sounds like a superfast clock. Time racing forward. "Breathe, breathe."

The baby at +2 and my patient now pushing. And I'm counting to ten during each contraction and I'm right there, holding her right leg. Her husband embracing her left.

Kristine Garcia-Cross, Glendale Community College graduate, 2016. Courtesy Kristine Garcia-Cross.

Until the crowning. And the baby's head emerges, his hair dark and wet like the earth after rain.

"You were right! It's brown," I tell her. And she keeps pushing until the full head emerges, the cord pulsing around her baby's neck. A nuchal cord. But the doctor easily pulls it over, releases it. No damage done.

Amazing to see new life enter this world. Amazing to be a part of this birthing experience. Hoping I made a difference, today, in this patient's life.

PART V

For death comes to friends, to parents, to sisters. Death comes with its bagful of pain yet they do not curse the key they were given to hold.

ANNE SEXTON, "FOURTH PSALM"

He cradles his sax, gone the rush of his breath through the reed.

Oh, those? They're African violets. Lucy's. See how she presses her finger in the dirt to check moisture? How she puts the violets inches away from our curtains, careful of direct sunlight? Dirt, earth is also big part of a nursing student's learning curve. Earth has a way of hanging around: fingernails, toenails, soles of feet. And it has breath and depth. When the body is finished with whatever we feed it, dung is expelled, and dung looks a lot like wet earth, like mud. Earth is sensible and manages, finally, to balance inequities people have suffered. We can wrestle death and sometimes cheat it, but it waits for us and earth's small helpers, the worms, will surely carry all of us home.

NANCY KERRIGAN

Ward 24

St. Patrick's Day, 1966

Mental hospitals and snake pits, synonymous,
when I began graduate training. Stairwells smelled
of Lysol. Patients lay on the dew covered
lawns, their dormitory bedrooms padlocked
all day long to prevent napping. Eight hundred
milligrams of Thorazine made walking feel
like trudging through deep mud.

Women slept coiled on communal bathroom floors,
guarding handbags, pictures of children,
a fork for a weapon. Hems of hospital housedresses,
fabric worn thinner than tissues, wiped away
the few tears that managed to escape
this overmedicated state.

Come to my group, my plea, as I knelt offering
filtered cigarettes as free admission tickets.
In empty silence, we sat on single beds, arranged
in a square, in a room as cavernous as an airplane hangar.
What was my hurry? Most had lived there twenty years.
Hardly a word dropped into the atmosphere

Nancy Kerrigan, Loyola University of Chicago graduate, 1965. Courtesy Nancy Kerrigan. Photo by Austen Field.

until St. Patrick's Day, when I presented
a single green carnation to each woman in the group.
Anna sniffed the blossom; Edna placed it between
her breasts. Rose wore hers over her ear.
Vivian shared a memory about the feel of seeds
in her hands when she gardened. The oldest patient,
Lillian, who had a lobotomy, watered
the blossom with her drool.

LINDA MAURER TUTHILL

Visiting Nurse (1963)

Public Health duty takes senior students
into the city, past housing projects
and row houses standing shoulder to shoulder.
A flowing blue cape tops my uniform.
Initials JHH blaze from the collar, branding me:
Hospital Property. Please respect.

Regulation brown oxfords and a bag
of medical supplies announce my status
as I search for addresses, rap on doors
that often don't choose to open.

I visit one row house daily to give
Miz Fanny a morning dose of insulin,
her sight too dim to read the syringe.
She never fails to answer my knock,
her smile warmer than my navy cloak.

When she opens the door one morning,
the air feels shifty, her face strained.
She nods toward the couch, knowing,
of course, but not ready to admit,
her cancer-wracked husband,
has passed in the night.

After calling the morgue, I sit next to her
gazing at the photos of her bluesman.
He cradles his sax,   gone
the rush of his breath through the reed.

KATHLEEN CADMUS

The Novice

I retreated to the hospital cafeteria for a break—to sit alone, have some tea, and escape the eyes of a soon-to-be widow. I pushed back the wisps of hair that brushed against my face and neck. I had started my shift with my long dark hair piled neatly atop my head, and now just a few hours later, my hair and I were coming undone.

It was Sunday evening, and it was New Year's Eve. At the age of twenty-two, I had grown accustomed to feeling celebratory and hopeful on New Year's Eve, not inadequate and lonely. I was feeling cheated and a bit sorry for myself.

It wasn't that I didn't also feel grateful. As a nursing student eight months from graduation, I appreciated being able to work as a nursing assistant over winter break. It meant gaining valuable experience without the pressures of being graded or having an instructor micromanage my every move. My husband and I were both students, leaning on the help of college loans, part-time jobs, and the benevolence of parents. Working, especially weekends and holidays, meant fewer hotdogs and boxes of mac and cheese.

Friday and Saturday evenings I worked with patients on a hospital medical unit. After Mr. Meyer, one of my assigned patients, was diagnosed with meningitis, he was transferred—along with me—to an isolation room.

In a private room, with one wall made of floor-to-ceiling glass, I became his one-on-one nurse. My job was to monitor his vital signs, keep an eye on his IVs, and report his progress to the *real* nurses. Before I arrived at the hospital on Sunday evening, Mr. Meyer had slipped into a coma. It was 1967—his New Year's Eve, too.

Musicians sang the praises of abundant hair and free love, the U.S. Freedom of Information Act was enacted, more than 474,000 U.S. soldiers were stationed in Vietnam, and President Johnson called Martin Luther King Jr. "that goddam nigger preacher" after King denounced the war.

Kathleen (English) Cadmus, Ohio State University College of Nursing graduate, 1968. Courtesy Kathleen Cadmus.

Inside hospital walls, nurses—who were almost exclusively women—tied up their long hair so as to not touch their collars, then placed white caps on their heads. Glass IV bottles were attached to lines delivering fluids and medications, patient labs and data were recorded by punching holes in stiff seven-by-three-inch cards, and all charts were made on paper. The patient's improvement or decline was documented in handwritten notes, black ink for A.M. hours and red ink for P.M. hours. Death was spoken about in hushed tones and rarely with the patient present.

The switch from glass IV bottles to plastic IV bags would occur over the next few years, but computerized documentation of nursing notes would take decades to implement. *On Death and Dying,* by Dr. Elisabeth Kübler-Ross, had not yet been published. For years her book would be considered one of the most important works written in the Western world on the care of the dying.

Glass IV bottles raised my anxiety, pertinent lab values refused to stick in my brain, and I relied solely on intuition when dealing with emotions triggered by impending death. During a previous semester, my psychiatric nursing instructor had told me, "You have good intuition, Kathleen. Use it. But read and become more knowledgeable about theory too."

I was a novice at everything nursing. Except for my fat ballpoint pen that I could change from black to red ink with a flick of my thumb, I was ill equipped for my isolated New Year's Eve.

Before my break, I had taken Mr. Meyer's blood pressure, wiped his face with a cool cloth, and moistened his lips to soften their dryness, actions that would not make a difference in whether my patient would live or die. I spoke his name and softly told him what I was doing. *Could he even hear me?* I wanted to believe he could.

"In a few hours it will be a new year, Mr. Meyer."

Feeling as useless as a camera without a lens, I was just waiting for Mr. Meyer to die. Knowing that filled me with guilt. *Should I even be paid for this?* A lump formed in my throat. My eyes were stinging. I blinked and swallowed hard, then blinked again and continued to chart his journey to death in black and red.

In the middle of the cafeteria, I found a seat and savored the open space. Like an intimate café nearing closing time, the room was dimly lit. The small white holiday lights provided a comforting glow and a reprieve from the bright, intrusive glare I had left behind in Mr. Meyer's sterile isolation room. I breathed deeply, replacing the antiseptic smell clinging to my nostrils with the earthy warm scent of brewing coffee and sugary-cinnamon pastries. Wearing washed-out gray hospital scrubs, I was anonymous. No one could see my student nurse, novice status. I was simply part of the hospital team, appearing useful and helpful and knowledgeable.

I shuddered at the thought of returning to my unit, putting on the gown and mask and gloves and entering the cramped isolation room. I had forgotten—with all the gowning and masking and gloving, was I protecting *me* from *him* or *him* from *me?*

Stirring sugar into my tea, I checked my watch to see how much time remained in my break. Then looking up, I saw Mrs. Meyer walking toward me. *Oh God, no. Not now. Not here.* She was wearing the same woeful eyes that had followed me earlier like a protective watchdog, staring at me through the sliding isolation doors of her husband's private room.

As my eyes met hers, I thought about how she had been at her husband's side every moment during his weeklong hospital stay, until his meningitis forced him into isolation and forced her to view him through glass. I thought about how she kept watch over her husband, studying his face as I rearranged his pillows or moved his arms when I checked his IV. Had she been looking for a smile or a gesture or any sign from him to confirm he was the same man who had talked and laughed and held her hand only a few short days ago? And when she focused her gaze on me—my arms reaching around his shoulders, pulling him toward me, rolling him on his side to reposition him—what was she thinking? Did she resent that someone else, a stranger, was caring for her husband? Maybe she felt grateful.

Sitting in the middle of the almost empty cafeteria, I had been easy to spot. The cafeteria of a university medical center was not a place that drew the crowds that flocked to Disney World or Times Square on New Year's Eve.

Mrs. Meyer was short and thin and appeared to be, like her husband, in her early seventies The softness of her face and her kind smile reminded me of my great aunt Mae. She wore her hair in a modified bouffant, a style made popular several years earlier and worn by Lady Bird Johnson. But Mrs. Meyer's hair was shorter and gray. Meticulously styled, the one thing in her life right now she could control.

She placed her hand on the chair's back across from me. I nodded to save her the words. The metal chair's scrape echoed throughout the room, giving me a chill. I wished I were anyplace else. *What if she asked me questions? Pushed for answers I didn't have?*

But sitting down, she became more diminutive. Fragile. Like a small child needing a hug. Her fingers interlocked in prayer.

"Do you think he has a chance?"

"He is very ill."

She must've known time was running out, because she didn't ask me again about her husband. She told me about her husband, her words spilling out between sips of coffee.

"He's a retired English professor, you know. Loved his students. But travel was the best thing about him retiring, next to our grandchildren, of course."

She rested both arms on the table, leaning forward as she spoke. And softly, her words pulled me closer.

"We just got back from the shore with all six of them." She smiled. "Ten days of walking the beach, every day ending with him reading them a bedtime story."

I tilted my head, watched her face, and forced myself not to look away from her pain. I couldn't help her husband, but maybe my listening would give her some comfort.

"We've been married over fifty years," she said.

More than many people's lifetimes, I thought. An eternity, it seemed to my naive mind, to spend with one person. I was a novice at love as well as loss.

"I don't want to stay away too long," she murmured, pulling us out of the brief celebration of his life into the reality of his pending death.

We left the cafeteria. Two women, far apart in age—I in my white nursing shoes, her in her black winter boots—walked slowly and silently together back to the isolation area. The doors slid open. Her hands still linked in prayer, she reached out, touched my arm, then took her place outside the glass doors, ten feet from the love of her life. I felt relieved to be free of her voice and thankful my eyes could focus on a task and not on her tearstained face behind the glass door.

Before the New Year, Mr. Meyer was gone. Only then was his wife allowed at his side. She slipped her hand in his, placed her other hand on his forehead, and kissed his cheek. Like a shadow, I moved away and slipped out quietly. My shift was over.

I removed my gloves, my mask, my gown. Time had passed into this new year without a dance, a hug, or a kiss for me. I was almost home before I released my tears, allowing them to flow freely, crying as much for me as for the Meyers.

. . .

It was June, six months into 1968, my first day back at college after my father's funeral and two months until I would graduate. Thankfully, I knew more about IV bottles and lab values by now. I was no expert, but the insecurity of being a novice was lessening.

My nursing instructor assigned Mr. Williams to me. He was admitted to our general medical unit with vague neurological symptoms, but his condition had rapidly declined. Mr. Williams was in his midfifties, the same age as my dad. And, like my dad, he died unexpectedly and too young. I talked with his wife and told her I was sorry for her loss. Having spent only a few hours with Mr. Williams before he died, I didn't get to know him or his wife. I felt like an intruder in her grief. But I wanted to show her compassion, for she was my patient too. And I saw my mother's eyes in her face.

My nursing instructor knew my absence from clinical the prior week was due to my father's death, yet she never acknowledged his passing. Acknowledged my loss. She had assigned Mr. Williams to me, a critically ill and dying man. Did she not consider how difficult this might be for me? To me, my instructor seemed like a novice at empathy and compassion. Or maybe she thought my caring for Mr. Williams would be a good fit since I had been so close to men dying and close to their widow's painful journey.

I felt useless. I felt angry. There was nothing I could have done to help this man, having been introduced into his life only as he was dying. As with my father, when I had been called home after he had died in the ER of a massive heart attack, I was just standing on his exit ramp.

Over the following weeks, I tried to shut out the image of Mrs. Williams and the small silver cross she had clasped as it dangled from her neck. Had that given her strength? I buried my head in medical information to gain clinical understanding of Mr. Williams's death.

I watched my mother as she sorted through my father's belongings.

"Should I give this away to someone who could use it?" she questioned as she sorted into piles, touching each object, each piece of clothing as if sacred, then returning the item back to his dresser, his closet. I listened to my mother, over and over repeating the memories of their life together, reliving each scene as if for the first time, working through her grief.

My mother's grief—a wife's grief—had been more complicated and intense than my own, though we were grieving the loss of the same man. I felt sad, while my mother had deep sorrow. I missed my dad's voice on the phone during my weekly calls home, but she yearned for his voice, his touch every minute of every day. I picked up my life and moved toward the future; she struggled to get through each day and not live in memories of the past.

For me, that world without my father was like being on a trip in a foreign land, having lost a guide. It meant relying on my memories of his wit, his love, and his endless capacity to believe I could do anything I chose to do with my life. It was a highway with fewer road signs, that world without my dad, Mr. Meyer, and Mr. Williams.

.   .   .

Eight months into the new year, I took the Florence Nightingale pledge to "devote myself to the welfare of those committed to my care" and received my bachelor of science in nursing. My mother, my husband, and I were celebratory and hopeful about my future. As I walked across the stage at the Ohio State University, my thoughts were on mental health nursing. I wanted to care for those who were physically healthy, not those who were sick and dying. I knew suicide was always a risk for the mentally ill, but my focus would be on prevention.

As I studied for my Ohio nursing board exams, I devoted my time mostly to mental health nursing, since I'd accepted a position in an inpatient psychiatric setting, and to maternal-child nursing, since I was in the early weeks of my first pregnancy. I did not study concerns of death and dying.

I don't recall being taught anything during my nursing education about how people experienced the last moments of their lives or how those moments affected those around them. I don't recall readings focused on grief, group discussions about grief, or one-on-one talks with my nursing instructors centered on handling the dying and the moments after death. I remember learning about what makes people ill and what makes them better, and I was taught how to document thoroughly, objectively, and clearly if a patient I was caring for would die.

Life and living have taught me about grief. But it was three wives-becoming-widows who were my mentors during my student nurse years, Mrs. Meyer, Mrs. Williams, and my mother.

All three women's grief showed me we can't step away from the unfixable. Death is not failure. They taught me to stand in the midst of someone else's pain, even when I didn't understand.

"I know he's not really dead," my mother had said when I arrived at her home in the predawn hours after my father's death. "They have to be lying."

Her words frightened me. Had she lost her mind? Mom had called me three hours earlier. Her first words when I answered the phone were, "Daddy's dead." Tearfully, she told me how my father arrived home from work with chest pain, was taken to the ER, and then died while being treated for a heart attack. And she was with him at Aultman Hospital when he died.

I know he's not really dead. For me, my mom's words were like icicles falling from a rooftop and smashing to the ground. I took a deep breath. She talked. I listened. The closer I stood to her grief, the more I understood. Each of us is a novice.

Sometimes being still *is* doing something, and sometimes saying nothing *is* being useful. Being present is the best anyone can offer another during loss and sorrow. Grief is the universal price we pay for loving. It lets us know we did it right.

MURIEL MURCH

Brookwood Female Geriatric

In the days before
urinary catheters
made wrist restraints
standard care
for geriatric, psychotic patients

women lay
row upon row
in beds,
fetal curled inward to death.
Their hands reached down
to pull the skeletal mons raw.
Crying out.
Not with demented imaginings
of sexual penetration
but with crystal memories
of birth emerging.

In the days before
urinary catheters
made wrist restraints
standard procedure
for geriatric, psychiatric nurses.

BEVERLY MITCHELL

Rabbit Hole

"But I don't want to go among mad people," Alice remarked.
"Oh, you can't help that," said the Cat.
"We're all mad here. I'm mad. You're mad."
"How do you know I'm mad?" asked Alice.
"You must be," said the cat. "Or you wouldn't have come here."

Working in Acute Psych is a tricky thing. Entering a locked ward is a bit like going down a rabbit hole or through the looking glass. While the Bellevue unit I trained in has windows and a good deal of natural light, I always emerged from the hospital a little surprised to find the world unchanged. It made me wonder what it was like to emerge as a patient.

My rotation in psych was a short one, just five Fridays of clinical exposure. In New York City, Bellevue is synonymous with psychiatric care, although this institution—the oldest public hospital in the United States—boasts a wide array of other services and specialties. It's known to house a traditionally underserved population, but the patients I've seen in the halls and elevators represent diversity of every kind. Patients on my assigned unit included a philosophy professor, inmate transfers from Rikers Island, folks arriving from and returning to shelters, medical professionals, Ivy League college students, an Olympic athlete, and an international tourist. Many believe they shouldn't be there; for others, it's the closest thing to a home they've known.

Medically speaking, there are lots of reasons patients are admitted to the psych unit. Most have chronic mental illness, some have a new onset mental illness, some are experiencing a drug-induced psychosis and require detox and rehab, and a very few have suffered a brain trauma, altering their personality and/or cognition. When I arrived on the unit, the big surprise for me was that twenty-five of the twenty-nine patients in that day's census were born in the seventies and eighties. Initial onset of mental illness often takes place during our twenties, with the following years being a time of difficult adaptation as the patient accepts (or doesn't accept) their diagnosis and makes a decision whether or not to comply with treatment. Acute psych is a revolving door specialty, because the most prevalent reason for admission is relapse. And the most common cause of relapse is noncompliance with medication.

I worked predominantly with one patient during my rotation. He was a student at a local, prestigious university, twenty years old, and a rising junior from a family of means. During the summer, Lance had his first manic episode, which included erratic behavior, excessive spending, interpersonal meltdowns, binge drinking, and dangerous activities. Friends brought him to Bellevue after they discovered him skateboarding against traffic on the Williamsburg Bridge. His parents had arrived within twenty-four hours of Lance's admission, and although in the outside world they were sophisticated, well-heeled grown-ups, on this side of the looking glass they were Hansel and Gretel, lost in the forest, disoriented, their eyes glazed at the wonders they beheld. Their son's diagnosis was Bipolar I.

Lance was a handsome kid with a shock of chestnut hair that swept to one side, though he insistently pushed it to the other. His smile was gleaming white and his irises green as glass, but the dark shadows beneath his eyes betrayed his Prince Charming glow. To talk to him I almost began to wonder if a mistake had been made. In my previous career I'd spent a good deal of time with twenty-year-old rising juniors, and I vividly remembered being one. Erratic behavior, alcohol and drugs, issues with identity and doing everything possible to punch parental buttons is hardly innovative behavior. As we spoke, however, Lance's grandiose delusions began to emerge and I immediately recognized that his mind was on a different plane from any student I'd ever encountered. He had no insight into his illness (typical for new onset) and believed he had been admitted because he was "too arrogant." Lance and I spoke for a few hours over the Fridays we were both at Bellevue and I struggled to imagine what kind of person he'd been on the "outside." He was medicated nearly to the point of sedation, yet his mind continued to spin faster and harder than would seem possible. On my third Friday, Lance was discharged. He had been quickly "stabilized" and stayed only three weeks, rather than the typical eight or twelve.

His parents came to retrieve him and return with him to the West Coast in the hopes he could return to school the following term. I told him goodbye and stood back to watch the scene as he hugged a few patients and nurses. Among these patients were those who, like Lance, had just begun this journey and, with misunderstood camaraderie, imagined there could only be healing and redemption. Then there was also the old guard, a couple of graying men and a grandmotherly woman who had walked this path for years and who knew, with painful accuracy, the journey that likely lay ahead for Lance. They were neither optimistic nor

discouraging, but held him in an embrace that spoke of hope and fraternity. He was now one of their tribe, and though he might travel alone, he would never be without companions.

The charge nurse, a stoic young woman with tattooed wrists, pierced nose, and a beleaguered look that can only mean one is at the end, not the beginning, of a twelve-hour shift, began returning Lance's property to him: cell phone, iPod, wallet, shoelaces—it was the shoelaces that got me. Or, not so much the shoelaces, as the look on his mother's face as he accepted them. It seemed as if, in that moment, I watched his mother age not in years, but in hues, as she quietly realized all that had been lost and all that had been gained by her beautiful boy, whom she had sent into the world with all of her hopes and dreams for him set upon his head like a crown.

I've known for many years that we all, at times, may circle the edge of a rabbit hole. The fortunate ones peer down or draw near by accident and manage to grab hold of a branch or a root before tumbling. The blessed have taken a long free fall, lucky to claw their way onto stable footing and climb out. The unlucky, like young Alice, fall down, down, down. If we do find ourselves at the hole's bottom (with a *thump*) and are brave enough to open our eyes, what might we find? It might be the padded isolation room on a wing of the twentieth floor at Bellevue. I assure you, this place is no Wonderland.

Seventeen blocks from Bellevue's front door is where I live. The week after finishing my psych rotation, I was on my way to the gym on a Wednesday morning.

As I rounded the corner onto 14th Street, I noticed a man panhandling outside a cell phone store. It was 9:00 A.M., and he didn't appear sober. Wrapped in a scratchy, gray wool blanket, he sang softly and rocked back and forth, looking very much like a small child. He looked up at me, as if to seek the comfort of my gaze and then, without settling his eyes, peered straight through me. I immediately recognized him as a patient discharged during the second week of my rotation. His diagnosis was undifferentiated schizophrenia, and we had spoken briefly about his happiness at being released after what had been his third stay at Bellevue. He told me he planned to sleep on a friend's couch until he could get back on his feet. His social worker had enrolled him in an outpatient day program. When I'd met him, he'd been eight weeks sober and was looking forward to returning to the AA community.

As I passed him on the sidewalk, I struggled to keep my feet moving, not knowing what would be appropriate if I were to approach him. On that sunny August afternoon, when I felt more like a self-conscious New Yorker than a doting student nurse, he seemed to me a goblin whose touch or song might turn me to dust. Four weeks earlier, he'd been a man on the brink, and now here he stood in a discarded blanket with the demons circling, trapping him in the revolving door.

Several yards past him, I glanced back over my shoulder, almost expecting a hole in the sidewalk to open beneath him.

JEANNE BRYNER

There Is Mud Here

and in a past life maybe I was a nun
not a woman learning to be a nurse,
not the daughter of a boy who spidered
coal mines at age fourteen. I mean

it's a wonder, the grizzlies we'll face
to clear a path, how much crap we swallow
in the name of prophets. The way a knife
gets folded, handed down, how I just told

a man older than my Papaw *Please roll over,
face your beige wall* while my finger fishes
your butt, snakes its warm tunnels, claws
circles inside your body, scoops a harvest

of dried brown dung. My gloves are thin,
the color of flesh and his knees, hulls bent
against his chest to pray. He whimpers,
a gun-shy dog who shakes, tries his best

to get away. I mean this must get done,
so I scrape my finger's find over the bed
pan's silver lips until fresh poop falls.
I discover small rubies, blood streaks

on chocolate rocks I drag from his cave.
He weeps softly, an all-day rain,
so I pat his thigh as if to say
Good boy, stay, stay.

Listen, my clinical instructor's no swish.
I'm twenty-six, married, two kids, a car,
just now, a house, so there's mud here.
This guy, gray as a collie, paws against his cage.

And I want to lift the hook as he pushes
his weight against the latch,
but I need my grade to be an A.
I stroke and rub his flank and hip.

    Good boy, stay, please stay.

JEANNE BRYNER

Men's Ward, Psych Rotation, 1978

They finger comb their hair,
In faded jeans, the herd paces.
No mother's song is there.

Hollow cheeks, eyes lost in pairs.
Heads down, no belts or laces.
They finger comb their hair,

Count floor slats, ants in prayer,
The bowl's last cornflake, clay faces.
No father's hand was there.

They beg smokes, do not care.
Shaky palms, brown teeth cases.
They finger comb their hair.

We aren't allowed to stare.
For them, no rose in vases.
No mother's song is there.

Shod feet tacked by chairs.
Broken stallions, no races.
They finger comb their hair.
No father's hand was there.

MADELEINE MYSKO

The Sister on the Chronic Ward

I entered my three-month rotation at Seton Psychiatric Institute through a leafy drive, a pastel tunnel of old trees and flowering shrubs. I was nineteen years old and eager to leave behind the dark and creaky nurses' residence in downtown Baltimore. Seton was a welcome escape, with its sloping lawn and the distant, treeless hill where the home for elderly nuns gleamed.

Even the "chronic ward"—as it was called in 1966—had a wholesome, scrubbed charm, not unlike a nursery suite tucked under the eaves of a Victorian mansion. It was on the top floor of the hospital, a low-ceilinged space checkered by light from a row of dormer windows.

The patients on the ward had severe dementia, confined mostly to chairs or beds. We student nurses were kept busy there, where it was back to the very basic principles and practices of nursing—wash basins, toothbrushes, towels, and sheets. The psychiatric interviewing techniques we had learned downstairs on the acute wing seemed no longer to apply. On the chronic ward, we were more concerned with getting our patients to open their mouths for the spoon.

On the first day of our chronic ward rotation, each student was assigned a patient. Mine was a large woman with a broad face and pale blue, empty eyes. Her shoulder-length hair was the color of an old linen tablecloth, much like my grandmother's hair.

She never spoke, never made a sound. Feeding her breakfast was a long and miserable affair over a bowl of thinned oatmeal. "Would you like another taste of your oatmeal?" I asked. "How about a sip of your juice?" I even mentioned the weather. After a while I gave up this one-sided conversation, putting my energy into helping her finish the meal. Sometimes she opened her lips when I prodded with the spoon. Other times she did not.

I felt more comfortable providing morning care, which required only diligence and a firm hand on the washcloth. I threw myself into it, taking my time, for she was my only patient and I didn't know what else to do. When at last I emptied the washbasin, I could say with satisfaction that she was clean. Even the few teeth in her mouth were shining: I had managed to swab them thoroughly.

I decided I ought to do something about her hair. I brushed and brushed, delighting in the simple busyness of it. Beyond the windows of the chronic ward, the morning was pretty as a Disney fairy tale, but I was looking forward to the afternoon when my boyfriend would arrive and take me out for a ride. I got out the comb, made a sharp part down the center of my patient's head. She was as unresponsive as a mannequin.

I wonder now where I'd found the ribbons. Perhaps they weren't ribbons at all, but strips of bandage gauze? Whatever they were, I used them—tied into two prominent bows—to anchor the woman's hair in stiff ponytails on either side of her head. When I was finished, I took her by the shoulders, righted her, and stepped back to appraise the effect. She gazed past me with her dull blue eyes and listed to the side again. She looked like a very old baby doll.

There was a Sister of Charity in charge of the chronic ward. Silently, from around a corner of the chronic ward, she appeared, sweetly saying hello to my patient and to me. Then she lightly pressed a finger to the shoulder of my starched bib and asked me to follow her.

"Why did you tie her hair in bows?" she asked. Nearly forty years later I still remember her words. "She's a grown woman. Why did you fix her up like a little girl?" She was smiling at me as she spoke, her eyes kind but ineluctable.

I was stung, embarrassed. I don't remember how I responded, but I know I saw at once what those two perky bows really meant: I had made that woman into nothing more than a project for the morning.

Over the years, memories of that afternoon with the Sister of Charity on the chronic ward have returned to me many times. She taught me how easily dignity is robbed from the sick and vulnerable. She taught me that a good nurse is often the last defense—the nurse who calls you sweetly by name and combs your hair with the dignity you deserve.

VENETA MASSON

Morning Report

Standing at attention
in the damp dawn
of my novitiate
I take down
everything I need to know
about his deteriorating condition—
scheduled labs and consults
the machines and their quirks
the tubes, meds, and procedures that
    please God
will keep him alive,
at least through my shift.

But nothing of what I was told
has prepared me for what I find
in the hectic clutter of sheets—
    a man
a small man
with rheumy eyes
and sleep-creased cheeks.
I stand watching, drenched in unease.
Wait! He stirs,
slowly at first
then jerks a shaking hand
from some hidden fold.

Veneta Masson, Pasadena City College graduate, 1963. Courtesy Veneta Masson.

Bang! You're dead,
he says with a grin
through cracked lips,
trigger finger leveled
straight at my head.
I snap to life at this morning report
and the burden of dread falls away.
Face to face with vitality
still venting itself
from this body of death,
I am struck by the force
I must reckon with.

VENETA MASSON

Passages

Tragic! the day shift said that afternoon when I came on duty.
She's 35 and dying of uterine cancer.
Yes, he's still there, sitting beside her—
    he seems to want us to leave them alone.
Imagine how he must feel, after all
    a gynecologist
    watching his wife
    die on account of his impotence.
At least she's too far gone to feel the pain.

Tragic! I echoed, looked down at my feet
    stuffed my notes and my hands into pockets.
At 20, I was a novice still
    and ill at ease
    with the celebration
    of mysteries.
Reluctantly, I began my rounds, knowing that door
    at the end of the hall
    was one I had to open.

The moment came. I knocked lightly and entered.
First I saw her, or rather the barely perceptible
    rise and fall
    of the caul
    of luminous sheets.
Then I saw him, eyes fixed on the IV drip
    as if on an hourglass
    watching the last few
    grains of sand run through.

I want to talk with you, he said as I worked
then followed me out when I left the room.
Where in God's name have you been? he exploded.

195

For hours no one has opened that door!
  And then in a small
  and stubbed out voice
How do you know if she's dead or alive?
There's nobody with her but me.
  I'm sorry, I said, and stood there.

He was 40, a physician, and powerless
  to stop this traitor womb
  from giving birth to death.
I wanted to say, but hadn't the words
  What can I do?
  You are the healer.
I didn't know then the things I know now about how it is
  that nurses heal
  and healers fail
  and face the face of loss again and again.
Many times I've wanted to find him, touch him
  as I couldn't do then
  let his eyes sink into mine
  hear him down to the roots of his words
  practice now familiar rites of nurturance.
And yet, if he asked, I would have to confess
  I am 40, a healer, and still don't know
  a remedy for despair.

FRANCES SMALKOWSKI

The Silent Treatment

Last year, while enjoying a two-week tour of the cultural capitals of China, I was amazed by how at home I felt. Searching my memory for the reasons behind this unexpected state of mind, I suddenly remembered Mr. Loy.

We met more than forty years ago. I was in my third year as a nursing student, doing a semester-long rotation in a large psychiatric hospital. Each student was assigned a patient for the semester, and Mr. Loy was mine. We were expected to forge a therapeutic relationship with our patients. This was a tall order; most of our patients were diagnosed with some form of persistent schizophrenia, and few spoke in any coherent fashion, if they spoke at all.

Mr. Loy was no exception. A short man in his late sixties with raggedly balding hair, he made frequent references to "the machine on my head." His bald spots marked his attempts to remove the machine. The machine, he said, had commanded him to kill his son. Because he'd actually tried to do so, using a large knife, he'd been hospitalized as criminally insane.

Before our first meeting, I read Mr. Loy's medical history. Thanks to the psychiatric nursing education I'd received, I understood about hallucinations and delusions, and on a basic level I felt prepared to talk with him. I made a tentative plan to ask him about his life story while accepting in some way his regular references to the machine. In this fashion, I hoped that I could uncover and affirm some positive aspects of his life and make our time together a beneficial experience for him.

But I wasn't prepared for the fear that struck me during our first encounter—not fear of someone who'd been labeled as criminally insane but fear of a Chinese person. The neighborhood I'd grown up in, Jamaica, New York, was fairly diverse in race, color, and creed, but no Asian people lived there. My images of Asians came from the television shows I'd seen, in which they were depicted, in the usual stereotypical way, as sinister bad guys.

This fear made it hard for me to relate to my new patient, although this probably wouldn't have been noticeable to anyone else. Someone looking at us would

Sr. Frances Smalkowski with school-children in Kennedy Playground, WDC, the Catholic University of America graduate, 1968. Courtesy Sr. Frances Smalkowski.

have seen Mr. Loy and me sitting side by side in silence. Occasionally I'd make attempts at conversation. Most of the topics I broached—his work, his home and family—sparked barely any response.

These long periods of silence, as it turned out, were therapeutic—for me.

Being outgoing by nature, I found sitting with Mr. Loy difficult, even painful. But sitting beside him, I could see how irrational my fears were. Unlike the Asians on TV, Mr. Loy projected nothing sinister at all. (I viewed his psychiatric diagnosis as a separate issue entirely.) I took comfort that he seemed very accepting of my presence. Even early on, when I would come to the unit for a session, he would stay seated next to me instead of getting up and pacing, and soon he began to smile when he saw me come in.

His acceptance of me, and my self-awareness, combined to allow me to see what my issues were. Little by little, I felt my fear peel away.

Then, one day when we were planning a St. Patrick's Day party for the patients, I had a major breakthrough with Mr. Loy.

"Do you have a favorite song?" I asked him.

To my surprise and delight, he answered!

"Yes," he said.

"What is it?" I asked.

"'How Much Is That Doggie in the Window?'" he replied. (I was so pleased that he'd spoken that I didn't think to ask him how this particular tune had become his favorite.)

The day of the party arrived.

Strumming my guitar, I led the singing—beginning with Mr. Loy's favorite. He beamed from ear to ear, and I marveled at how little it took to touch his heart.

This seemingly small connection made all the difference. From that time forward, Mr. Loy began to talk more in our one-on-one sessions. He also became noticeably protective of me. During fire drills, for instance, if he saw another patient acting disrespectfully to me, or anywhere nearby, he would frown at the person or point in the time-honored "get lost" gesture.

For me, the highlight of our relationship occurred when my turn came to lead the small-group session.

We students dreaded this experience. Under our teacher's eye, we'd sit in a circle with seven or eight patients and do our best to get them to speak about their thoughts and feelings—a nerve-wracking challenge. Halting initiatives by the student were met with awkward silences; and after a few minutes, one by one, our patients would get up and wander off.

Soon after I opened the session, Mr. Loy stood up. Going to each patient in turn, he pointed and said, "You!"

To my thrilled astonishment, many of them responded, in words ranging from "you" or "my baby" to "leave me alone," "get out of here," and "shut up." The exchanges were brief—and yet, it was the most active group I'd seen in all of my time at the hospital. Afterward, my psychiatric nursing professor was very congratulatory—and at semester's end, she recommended me for a National Institute of Mental Health traineeship.

It was a sad day for me when, after weeks of preparation, I had to terminate my therapeutic relationship with Mr. Loy. I approached him gingerly.

"As I've told you before," I said, "I'm only a student so I only get to stay here a short time—and today is my last day."

He looked at me and I looked at him, not knowing what else to say, sensing our bond, knowing that he had so little company, if any, and feeling guilty that I was deserting an old friend.

To this day, I have him to thank for helping me through the opening stages of my successful thirty-five-year psychiatric nursing career as a clinical specialist and private-practice therapist.

Visiting Mr. Loy's homeland, I felt his spirit with me in a special way, and I had a sense that he understood the gratitude I've felt to him all these years. It made me realize that we didn't say "goodbye," only "so long." Such treasured encounters are never really forgotten. Their imprints in our hearts and minds remain, a testament to the powerful—and mutual—bonds that form between ourselves and our patients whenever healing takes place.

JUDY SCHAEFER

Early Days of Shift Work

I start the morning with orange juice
and coffee—and then toast smeared
with peanut butter and finish
with a well-ripened yellow banana.
It is not *Sunday Morning* but I think
of that Wallace Stevens poem while I eat.
Do I tell you this to show that I am
accustomed to a shift routine? No, because
I'm new at working shifts and have no routine
but can happily tell you that I'm off today,

that it rained early this morning before sunrise.
The neighbors and I are happy about the rain,
not that we declare it, we simply show it
in routine on-the-way-to-work waves.
The small green gardens in blue patio pots
need the rain. The need is discussed briefly
in small passing hellos, as if we knew
what it was to depend upon the fruits of the soil.

So we unwittingly bend our heads to each other
and to a past dark with broken nails on calloused hands.
Peanuts pulled moist from the ground,
oranges pulled from exotic trees,
coffee beans collected and roasted brown.
Bananas gathered and carried on the heads
of girls in yellow dresses to a black diesel train.
Ah, a routine life with the purchase of florist moss
the rattle of galvanized sprinkling cans
and the sweet smell of betadine.

CORTNEY DAVIS

The Nurse's First Autopsy

The senior students said *Don't*
look at the face.

This was a test: weaker girls who
fainted were dismissed. I held my place,
allowed my thoughts to drift

while I observed the race
between two residents who cut
their corpses neatly and with grace.
Organs, scooped out,

sank in stainless bowls. Blood,
once hot, chased
through tortured veins, now stopped.
The doctors drained the heart with ease.
I wondered what

this patient did when living, and yet,
I loved him less
than I was fascinated. Taught well
to separate myself from feeling, I fought

to care for but not about. Out
came bone from flesh,
the muscles lax, devoid of heat.
I think my eyes burned—then the corpse
was sutured shut.

CORTNEY DAVIS

Surgical Rotation

He was my first, first death, first cold palm on my heart
hand of frost, pulse of fear, he was only thirty-five, his wife
waiting in the family area, he was in for a nothing surgery
bunion of all things, knobby growth not cancer not tumor
the anesthesiologist gave him the sleepy juice, the patient
went out easy, surgery progressed, skin cut, bone rasp
snips and grinding, nothing, then the gas man gave a little *uh*
and the surgeon looked up, we all looked up, *BP tanking*
then the storm dam burst, spewed panic like ice
circulating nurse she hit the button and all hell broke, docs
and residents running, me flat against the wall, held breath
bam bam code cart, sparks and the flash of needles, blood stink
names of meds in my ears like static, like shiny wires screeching
then absolute hush, blank eyes, death like a building fell
death dust rose and settled, everything quiet and gritty
everyone with their particular duty, nurses here, there
the senior resident given the task, long walk to the waiting room
speaking the wife's name in his Bombay lilt, her
scream shot all the way back to OR 3 where I stood
struck dumb, enthralled, all of me bright with this
hard desire, *let this be, let this be, let this be my life's work*

PART VI

But the wind is our teacher.

AUDRE LORDE, "HUGO I"

Most of us need a teacher, someone who has
traveled this way before.

We run through puddles, our shoes fill like boats. We tuck care plans and anatomy books under our jackets, a sudden summer storm, thunder, lightning, and wind, so much wind. See how the trees bend in its gale? How it howls as if it's somehow wounded? Wind has a voice, be it breeze or hurricane, and its weight shapes whatever it touches. Our beloved mentors and teachers, the women and men who lectured and tested and saw our many hungers, were and are the winds who made us competent nurses. They set a high bar and expected excellence. Critical thinking was not based on regurgitation of facts, but creativity and being able to function when chaos came uninvited to your unit (and it always appeared). At this table, let us hold hands and remember the beautiful and terrible wind as grace.

NANCY KERRIGAN

A Nursing Remedy for Earaches

Tell me your nurse stories, my daughter, age nine, sobbed through earache pain. Hearing them was the cure she prescribed. You mean when Mary Ellen, Barb and I flew down Lake Shore Drive, with white, wet nylons that you called *broken pantyhose,* flapping like nursing flags out the windows of my black VW Beetle?

Or do you want the morning I forgot my garter belt? To hold up my nylons, I tied my shoelaces around my thighs. Nylons later puddled around my ankles as I stood on a stool, observing neck surgery. A medical student standing behind me, alerted me by running his gloved finger up and down my leg where my seams should have been.

Or do you want the time Barb and I, charged to set up for a 2:00 A.M. delivery, were caught by Miss Bracegirdle at the grand finale of a bubblegum-blowing contest? The sterility of this room's everyday miracles fatally compromised by our breath and ungloved hands. Bracegirdle's eyebrows spoke their own language: *start over.*

No, no! I want the one with the linen chute. Oh, the day Mar forgot her white size 5 oxfords at the dorm. Size 8 whites, the smallest we could find in the hospital lockers. After a discharge, her arms laden with dirty linens, an emesis basin, urinal, and bedpan, all stainless utensils clanged down the metal chute when her size 8s flipped off the pedal.

Was the bedpan full? The question delighted Ellen each telling and cleared her eustachian tubes. *No.* Mary Ellen ran, her size 8s flopping like Bozo the clown, to report the incident to the head nurse, who without lifting her eyes from her chart noted, *laundry already knows what's coming.*

ELAYNE CLIFT

Whiteout

In a cloistered convent of blue-frocked novitiates
wearing starched white caps in place of veils,
I tiptoed through curfewed terrors
in the early weeks of nursing school.
"He's an inguinal aneurysm,"
the head nurse said of my first patient.
"If it blows, press on it, hard,
and yell for help."
I looked at the shriveled old man
who had no idea he could erupt
into a bleeding geyser and wondered
What am I doing here?
Sick with worry, mistakes being murder,
I became ill. "I caught a chill," I said.
"Don't you know you get colds from germs?"
the RN snapped. "And you, a nursing student!"
Depressed, I sought counseling.
The mousy shrink with a flat affect
accused me of transference,
and so I transferred, left nursing.

All these years and several careers later,
I regret it still, and wonder
what might have been,
had I had the courage of cap and veil.

Elayne Clift, volunteering in Greece, holds a Syrian baby, May 2017. Courtesy Elayne Clift. Photo by Brigitte Dunais, MD.

AMANDA ANDERSON

Learning to Care

I never imagined that I would learn more about the art of caring from a coffee shop than from nursing school.

Literature and philosophy stopped making sense during the second semester of my second year of college, so I procrastinated, spending chilly spring afternoons zipping across rural roads in my friend Joy's battered Saturn sedan, procrastinating and listening to jam bands on the radio. One day, she took me to a town in the north that people from our conservative college only spoke of in hushed voices.

Joe's Cappuccinos was a small coffee shop in the center of this new, small, liberal town, marked with a huge neon cup in the window. It was here, from my perch in the corner of a dirty green-and-white-checkered couch, amid Frank Sinatra posters and blaring music, that I met David, the larger-than-life coffee shop manager, from whom I would begin to learn the art of caring.

On that first day at Joe's, the wind felt cool, but the sun coming through the windows hit my back with a touch of warmth. I felt a bit rebellious, managing far more distraction than comprehension for the huge book for my honors philosophy class I'd brought along with me.

A bald man waltzed halfway into the shop's open door wearing a flower-patterned skirt and Lucite Birkenstocks with sagging socks. Creamy clumps of white makeup were slabbed in patches over his face and shaven skull. It wasn't his red lipstick or brightest-blue eye shadow that got me staring, although these were things I'd never before seen on a man. There was something sweet-turned-sour in his dance of indecision at the threshold, just feet from where I sat. When he finally entered, I watched, mesmerized, and a little apprehensive, to see how David, from behind the counter, would greet this man.

"Steeeeeeeevie Wonderrrrrrrrr!" David boomed above the music, with the same smile he seemed to give to everyone who walked into the store in search of cof-

Amanda Anderson, Cedarville University, 2007. Courtesy Amanda Anderson.

fee, and perhaps also to bask in his effervescent, feel-good attention. I watched David's flashy grin, unchanged, as Steven reached his dirty left hand to the back of his head, rubbing one of the thick slabs of cream-colored makeup across it like butter on bread. His fingernails were long and dirty with chipped pink nail polish.

I don't remember what he said to David, but a cup of hot coffee appeared on the counter, along with an exchange of crumpled, oily money. Steven's mouth twitched with the tics of unborn words, and his body's jerking movements sloshed the coffee in his cup, a splash smacking the dingy linoleum floor. Somehow, he added sugar to the cup's remains and left, his odd smell sweeping with him into the spring wind. I was embarrassed at how shocked I was. No one else had even glanced up.

Our first afternoon at Joe's, where I was exposed to a world of humanity I'd never imagined, turned into every afternoon at Joe's. Joy and I said we were studying, but instead we drank coffee and talked, watching the town take its turn at David's counter. My motivation for the theories of sixteenth-century English literature and honors philosophy plummeted, inversely related to my love of this forbidden town and its intriguing people.

It was at Joe's one night, when the store was closed and lit with neon glow, that I first had the inkling that perhaps I was destined not for literature and philosophy, but for nursing. David invited Joy and me to stay late, listen to music, and eat Indian food with one of the regulars, an older, near-blind local man named Peter, whose entire face seemed to squint behind the dark glasses he always wore.

I'd never had Indian food before and David was eager to teach me all the "best" things that I'd missed in my sheltered, conservative youth. This meant free food, free coffee, and my first experiences with diverse and colorful worlds far from my usual experience. We sat together, eating with our hands, the buttery naan slipping from my fingers as I tried to scoop up the hot curry rice. Then Peter said something that came back to me weeks later, sparking the decision to change my life and pursue nursing: "Everyone should always have a trade," he said. "At some point in your life, a trade is necessary to take you where you want to go."

Over spring break, Peter's words reappeared in my mind, as did the images of the people that I'd come to know in Yellow Springs. These people had deep convictions, they knew their ways and adhered to them, and they had battled things, seen things, lived through things that the conservative folk of my school and my childhood hadn't. And so, on a patio in a sunny alley of a western New York coffee shop over spring break, I was struck with a new purpose: nursing.

If someone had been looking over my shoulder as I wrote in the journal I still wish I could find, they might have seen my thoughts turning to actions on the page; *what will I do with my life* turned into, on Peter's advice, *I want a trade,* which quickly concluded with, *I think I should become a nurse.* By the end of my cup of coffee, I resolved to dedicate myself to a profession about which I had no earthly idea.

And I did. I drove home, down that straight-shot road with that lone stop sign that I never had the guts to blow, through the twisting streets of my parents' suburban neighborhood. I parked my car in the driveway, walked in the door, and told my mother, who stood at the turquoise-colored kitchen island, "I've decided to become a nurse."

I don't recall her response. I only remember sitting down with the dean of the nursing program as soon as I returned to school. Miraculously, my nursing classes fit into six semesters. And so I began.

Naturally, I wanted to live in the same town as Joe's. If I had to stay at my rural school for three more years to accomplish my new goal, I'd have to find my sanity in the place that I loved. I asked David for a job, told him I wanted to move to town. I met Joe, the grouchy-kind owner of the coffee shop, and he hired me part time.

My work at Joe's began ceremoniously. Foaming milk was my first job, and I did this for hours, until my shoes and my jeans were covered with sticky, cooked liquid and I could create the perfect, lightest, foam for the pickiest customer.

At that point, I must have wanted this job more than I wanted nursing school. I was eager to fit in as a "local," eager to shake my conservative view of the world. But my dedication to my barista work caused my performance in my first semester of nursing, packed to the brim with anatomy, physiology, and pharmacology, to slip.

Up against final exams that threatened failing grades, I realized that I had to study for the first time in my life. My brains, my intellect, which had always gotten me high averages in high school and my first two years of college, were now facing a monster challenge—nursing—with me not knowing what the hell I was doing and no longer able to fake it.

I started to use my "new family" to help me. I woke up early, rode my rusty blue Schwinn to the shop, and made Joe quiz me on body parts and drugs while he waited for his opening-shift customers. I returned to the shop after my shifts, grabbing the lopsided table lamp from the back room and studying under the neon glow well into the morning, music softly playing, industrial refrigerators cranking on and off every so often. Once, I fell asleep, waking only to the chilly creep of the early morning air, whatever album I had chosen long gone silent. I spent some time in the library at school, but mostly I sat craned at the front window, poring over big books of muscles and generic drug names, as David brought me hot cups of caffeine and plates of whatever gourmet lunch he had used his tips to purchase that day.

I passed both classes, despite a lower GPA than I had ever received. Joe, the owner of the coffee shop, took us all out for Christmas dinner to a five-star restaurant in the nearby city where he lived. It felt like a celebration for my success at school, not just the shop holiday party. It was around this table that I realized, for the first time in my life, that I knew *who* I was and how it felt to work to reach a goal.

When I returned from winter break for my first semester of pathophysiology, I was ready to take my studies to the next level. This was no longer a solo quest, as it had been when I was a literature major, slogging through poetry and analysis alone, trapped by a constant worry of lack of purpose and lost meaning of life. This was a family matter now.

Every one of Joe's customers knew my mission and asked me about it. The mailmen, who came before the store opened every morning, talked to me about my progress in nursing as I zipped up and down the purple step to the convection oven to make muffins, fill the baked goods case, and drip the first drops of coffee into the scratched metal carafes.

The Friday night wine-tasting crew gave me extra tips for my "stethoscopes and scrubs fund." Joe and I bonded over the etiology of illnesses, the ethics of the Terri Schiavo case, and the science of bed making. When I slept in, missing our morning flash card sessions, he'd squawk, "What the hell, Anderson? You trying to fail?" More often than not, I got up, dragging myself to my stool behind the counter, and sipped on the perfect latte that he'd make me without a word. Flash cards turned to stories and to friendship.

Joe, a former college football player turned small-town coffeehouse god, was my biggest supporter of all. But it was through his prickly side, his cranky mornings and his fiery grudges, that I first learned the importance of never taking offense, a skill that would never fail me at the bedside.

The deep friendship I had with David and Joe gave way to the understanding that the care of a nurse is as unconditional as the love for a friend, even when that friend is difficult. In the end, it never mattered how many mornings Joe screamed at me for missing a pile of crumbs under the fridge the night before. I always knew that the latte would appear, along with his stern, "Wake up, Anderson. Tell me what 'a number of small swellings in the lymphatic system where lymph is filtered and lymphocytes are formed' means, already." In short, my success in nursing was not my own success. I was now part of a village that was rooting for me.

I moved out of Yellow Springs my senior year. I still worked at Joe's, but now I also worked at the hospital fulfilling my clinical requirement, seeing patients, learning skills that held no likeness to frothing milk or cleaning coffee mugs. But the longer I spent in the hospital, the more I felt that my patients weren't so different from my customers at Joe's. They often had the same look in their eyes that my patients did, and their eager want of conversation was not much differ-ent from my patients' white-knuckled grasp on their call bells or their anxious happiness to see me arrive at their bedsides.

I quickly found that my patients responded to my attention the same way my customers at Joe's did. When I perched on the corner of a patient's bed, chatting the same way I talked to my coffee drinkers, giving them a little bit more of me, they tended to calm.

Of course there were difficult moments at Joe's. I was often tired and needed to study. Sometimes the pesky tourists, the over-radical university students, the old men who asked me too many questions about bed baths, got to me. Often, I wanted to sit in the back next to the sticky convection oven and memorize maternal health terms. Instead, I had to jump at the sound of the squeaky front door, the bell ever ringing at the counter.

It wasn't until years later that I realized that these sour moments were just glimmers of what I would see and feel at the bedside—aggravations I learned to ward against because of my persistence at Joe's. I'd never waste time or frustra-tion bringing a cup of water to a patient without also bringing the straw I knew they'd want, too. Never would I leave the room before placing all items close by, including the television remote, the call bell, or before adjusting the blanket just so. Never would I stomp about, hurting the feelings of another human because of my own stress and hurt as I had too often done with coffee in hand. I didn't remember many lectures about handling stress during nursing school, but I often recalled the tactics I used to stay calm when Joe's was full to the door with a line of customers demanding Caramel Snowstorms.

Somehow, I managed, finding a balance between the craze of learning a new trade in the hospital and focusing on my customers at work. Spring came again, and I secured my first nursing position in an intensive care unit in a big city. Toward the end of my time at Joe's, I began to see the glistening beauty of what my work there had taught me about my new career, and about myself. At nursing school I learned the recognition and treatment of illnesses, how to make a bed with a patient in it, and when to worry about vital signs. But it was at Joe's, over coffee and espresso and wholesale muffins, that I learned how to connect with patients as people and how to accept everyone I met—bedside or bar—as valued and valid.

The confessions of infidelity, financial ruin, abuse, and loneliness that passed over that scratched Plexiglas counter into my young student ears prepared me for the same at the bedside. At the bedside, I learned to create comfort and quickly found that asking my patients about their homes, their lives, their romantic stories, the same way that I had spoken to customers at Joe's, was a way to clothe them against the shocking nudity of illness.

At Joe's I learned when to be nice and when to stand my ground. I never had to call the police during my three years of working there, but I left knowing how to call a bluff and when to spot sincerity. I spoke firmly to customers asking me to bend rules or those trying to rip off my boss, and I gave away drinks to those looking like they might otherwise go home and cry.

I carried these skills to clinicals and to all the bedsides of my career, remembering the Stevens of the world, ignoring the "he's just f---ing crazy" or "he will talk your ear off, be careful" that I sometimes heard in report. No one was turned away from Joe's. Why turn away a person who is different from you in a hospital?

I saw Steven again, only once, almost three years after that first day at Joe's. He came into the store on a Sunday morning. Gone was his flower skirt, gone was his makeup. His neat gray sweater zipped at the front. "Small black coffee, please," he said, quietly. "Hi, Steven," I said. He took two crisp dollar bills from his wallet, waited for me to take them, and walked very slowly away with his coffee.

We are all patients, some of us for our entire lives, some of us only at the beginning and the end. Much of our time as patients happens far away from sterile white sheets and hospital halls. I first learned this from behind a sticky counter, next to a life-sized poster of Dean Martin, dancing to the music of Prince and David Bowie, while talking to burned-out hippies and relapsed psych patients, pumping them full of caffeine in a grimy Italian-style coffee shop.

GOEFFREY BOWE

Student Nurse in a Jail Cell: A Birthday to Remember

Okay
it was me.

Chased
down badly lit side streets
arrested in Barrow-In-Furness
by Sergeant Dimwiddy,
I'd thrown a brick
through an out-of-focus
bookshop window.

My 22nd birthday,
empty bottles of pilsner,
a platoon of soldiers on the bar—
I'd downed the lot!

Vera, the sergeant's wife,
worked on Ward One
as a domestic.
Over bacon and eggs
she casually mentioned
the failure of a certain student
to turn up.

The sergeant
dipped bread and butter
into the runny yolk.
"Last night I arrested one."

I should have phoned out
but my head was spinning,
I could smell the jail cell toilets;
I was due in court,

I hung my head.
The magistrate didn't lift his,
gave me a fifty quid fine
and I was broke till payday.

I lived on biscuits
three each at mealtimes
for a week.

JEANNE BRYNER

Passage

For Dr. Durandetta

No life jacket, no maps. College.
Nursing school. Ladies in wool suits

smart as TV lawyers stand, chalk dust
like pollen in the air. You're twenty-

five, married seven years, laundry
stacked in your damp cellar.

This professor, his neat tie bordered
by periodic elements? A pilot, blue sky

in his eyes. Heaven's wind. He tries
to keep you afloat, reads a pupil's terror.

The 65%, your first Chem I test? Red
slashes like someone almost died

on your paper? Your stomach aches
not porch talks after chores nor catching

bugs in a jar. No. No starry nights,
but the prof holds his smile, a lantern

near the shed. The rest of the world
did not care spit about your hurts,

meatloaf smell on your husband's flannel
shirt, your hair tumbling loose, never quite

right. Your professor? The lone thing
he saw was how fear held its blade

to your throat. *Just dive and row,* his words
fell like two-inch squares, patching doubt

to hope,
made you a sail for a drifting boat.

STEPHANIE L. EZELL

Forgiveness

We tell ourselves stories in order to live. The princess is caged in the consulate. The man with the candy will lead the children into the sea. The naked woman on the ledge outside the window on the sixteenth floor is a victim of accidie, or the naked woman is an exhibitionist, and it would be "interesting" to know which. We tell ourselves that it makes some difference.
—Joan Didion, *The White Album*

In the middle of my master's coursework, a nurse for less than two years, I presented, at a conference, my tenderfooted thoughts about where our profession was headed.

I have learned something about disparity in a graduate nursing program. Pursuits such as research funding, rankings, and the power of leadership supply information we need to know in order to advance health care. But most of this course work is online, so I rarely have to interact with other future leaders. Nor do I need to watch professors cope in real time with patients and what it means to be human. Flowcharts and algorithms will care for them when they are old; they will not need me. Instead, I will have read their randomized-control trials, advanced through their PowerPoints, and quilted creations of evidence-based support. They will have pruned my ideas and so forced the buds of critical thinking. Their co-faculty will have fought mightily for tenure, struggled to build community. For them, I will be "stuck" caring, not as a leader, but as a grateful student.

Now, though, through the reflection of my earliest clinical rotations, I am not sure which translation of who I thought I was is more accurate, either in spirit or letter.

It was the last day of my final clinical rotation on a hospice unit, the objective of which was to teach me something about leadership. As the amateur to whom the cosmos had given a flick, I finally relaxed and did what I was there to do. I comforted. I had touched and spoken softly and nodded in time and rhythm with illness-shrouded faces for fourteen months. As I stepped off the elevator, with bagels for the unit, I realized for the first time I would be doing this for a while.

On the unit, one man and two women were dying, and their children and brothers and aunts were moving through the halls and around the nurses' station, as if they could not decide whether to stay to the right or hurry by on the left. The unit had 18 rooms, 18 windows that illuminated different family portraits, 18 openings through which hundreds of ragged, gurgling breaths would usher out the last of the heart sounds. But these three patients held the entire floor together with a magnetic pressure. I set the bagels on the back room counter, as if they had anything to do with how much I appreciated my faculty, who seemed to be fractured and yet united, for teaching me what might, or might not, matter.

The emphasis on leadership still shakes my conscience. We lead by looking, alongside our patients, for ways to cope. At times we remind them to hang back and sift through the remnants of memory, to cherish those exquisite moments of their lives that, at the time, might have seemed only dull bits of "home," now sublimated by the blasts of illness, age, and social disparity. We try to help them find a sensible mediation, a connection between past and present.

When I was told to give a seizure-level dose of an anxiolytic to someone who was agitated, and I did not look it up and then was encouraged to document what might have been rather than what was, I learned not only what would make me rightfully frantic but also what I would not do. I broke stride—not because I cared about my license or an incident report, but because there were scores of patients and family

Stephanie Ezell, University of Illinois at Chicago graduate, 2012, with niece, Maggie Loar. Courtesy Stephanie Ezell.

members who were waiting for someone to bring medication that would help and not hurt. And in spite of the tension that resulted from my refusal to go along, my refusal to chart words that served to justify an incorrect dosage, I persisted—because I have a professor and friend who sat vigil with me that week and dozens of times since, recounting the constellations of all that goes into nursing, including honoring our mistakes and unveiling what rises from forgiveness. She explained that all my experiences, even the difficult ones, were certain to make me a better nurse—that it is essential for our patients and our nursing profession to wrestle with such situations rather than to shrug them off defensively as simply the side effects of a haggard system over which we have no control.

Even when I cannot find my phone or remember all the details of what I thought was my life, I will have my notes. "Lie on the bad side so that the good lung can still do its work." The small things that make up our life force can break apart under friction, and sometimes this shattering lets go of more than we thought possible. Though it might not heal us in the strictest sense, such a release might make us feel better. Less tense. More comfortable. Rolling and turning, healing takes on so many different guises that sometimes we do not recognize them. But leadership—its aim does not always jibe with its scope.

I rang the bell, nobody came, and so I lifted the woman from the bedside commode and laid her down on the bed. I drained 650 ml of fluid from her abdomen (the chart noted that no one had been able to drain any fluid for a few days). Maybe it had been the moist towel I had held there for a few minutes. Maybe no one else had bothered to drain the fluid completely. But probably I was just forcing the jar lid past the last thread after a lot of others had gotten it going. I'd been told how to determine when and why you need to worry about draining too large an amount of fluid at one time. In the bladder, the danger is blood vessels collapsing and rupturing. In the lungs, removing too much fluid can cause a rapid drop in blood pressure. In the abdomen, the space is so large, "it doesn't really matter." Or so the physician, dropping by, had said. The patient smiled, I think, and then closed her eyes.

From these patients, and from the nurses and professors who have taken care of them before me, comes the truest education. Patients might spend the ends of their lives or the ends of their mothers' or partners' lives depending on me to offer some small peace or stay ahead of the pain or ease the timing between the acts. And because of them, I will pull out my talents a little faster and try to be less clumsy the next time. Knowing and teaching come from the dust of comets whose orbits trailed thousands of lifetimes ago and from the gravity of moons with no names.

In the first week of that final rotation, I nodded passively when I was told to stay in the room after a gentleman had been "taken off the vent." And because I did not ask his friends if they would like to be alone with him (because I did as I was told), I learned to pay closer attention to what is important. Long after it was over, after the nurses asked the patient's religion, and laughed before explaining to me how to remove the tubes, late into that night—late into every night since, and even into sun-sharpened days—the loud, vibrating quietness of that room came to represent everything else, so that eventually I realized what I had not allowed in: a movement of contours with no borders, space with no edge, the emptiness between the rise and fall of breaths. He had two friends, and that was important. It was sacred. I watched the patient, but I also desperately tried not to watch his friends. From the ceiling, from outside the window, from the space beside the beds where I stood, from anywhere in the room that I could be, I was trying to not watch. But my intention and stillness took up their space, disrupted the air.

When it all began, removing that patient from the ventilator, there was a woman silently playing a guitar and five or fifteen or thirty-eight people in lab coats or scrubs gliding around the room without moving. Respiratory therapists gloved themselves and looked for nothing on monitors that had been dragged into the room, asking unspoken questions of everyone who was receiving the patient and everyone who was giving him up. All these people had the playbook, but I am fairly sure they all were aware they really knew nothing. That day I felt as if I were looking at the individual windows on the reel of a View-Master, trying to figure out their origins. I was far beyond the space in which I could take the time to think of what the previous two scenes were, much less which should come next.

Discussing her latest novel, which largely reflects the dynamics in her family, Miriam Toews explains to Alice O'Keeffe in *The Guardian* (2015), "Yes, there were serious issues, and there was tragedy, but there was a lot of love." Somehow a story that circles the foundations of, and responses to, suicide in a family, parallels what nursing requires of us. Toews offers her resolution: "I wanted people to not be afraid of the subject matter . . . to get the tone right . . . off the top, and get the readers' trust, so we could come out together in some other, less dark place"

When I held the tape and tongue depressors just right so that the respiratory thera-pist could strap them to the denture-less cheeks of a ninety-four-year-old woman whose hands were restrained to the bedrails to keep the goddamn tubes intact, I learned about the limits of existential angst. When I sat quietly at the nurses' sta-tion, listening to the seventy-year-old daughters of another patient sing "Eres Tu" and "Cielito Lindo," I smiled and let go my own resentments, breaking the static of those at the nurses' station who rolled their eyes at such singing. I knew the reason. I heard choirs of angels.

I found a dim but constant light that casts an angle of clarity somewhere in the dark room of the Lithuanian woman who, though tiring of my questions, still keeps me around. "You know what I want? I want to die." And just as I begin to think that I am taking up too much space, she finishes her thought: "And I think you can help me do that." An artist, she has been here since 1951, strung together with a few of her family, their final steps away from the German occupation. Sharp and gruff, her words do not soften for a few long days. And she conserves them as if she has already packed too many precious pieces of home into a bag that will need to be hidden. She asked me "What?" again and again, but now my drawl has straightened up. And a little at a time, she shrugs, telling so much more than she ever felt safe to share. When she realizes it, as I knew she would, her eyes close. She stops talking for another day or two, lying beside her pain and unsettled fears. Before she stopped, though, I got a glimpse of the middle ground.

In *Tribe,* author Sebastian Junger lines up the effects of our dissembling the community of our society. His focus is the everlasting casualty of war suffered by veterans. Nursing risks losing its sense of community. Health-care mergers, advancing technology, and an increasingly blurred focus on human connection play a part. Monitors and scans, dials and signals provide numbers and graphs for templates with checklists that reduce patients to numbers and dollars. And warped by speed and distance, this trajectory somehow holds while researchers, journalists, and advocates from other stops in life continue to cast light on one of our greatest needs: patient-centered care. Nurses, educators, and students work this conflict until it is dry and frayed, trying to imprint our practice with a more lasting image.

Two weeks ago, once again those lessons of time and space: discontinuing a life-sustaining treatment has residual, latent effects on those providing this *care*—not only in ethical considerations but also from the shifting pressure that moves the wind. In no coincidence, my first assignment as a nursing student in the leadership rotation was to stand by with the friends of the man who had been extubated. From that event and from all of those since and from every uncomfortable situation still to come, I work and rework the possibilities of what my part in patient-centered care will look like lifetimes from now.

Most of us need a teacher, someone who has traveled this way before, to point out what Brueghel, Auden, and others knew: as Icarus fell, a plowman unknowingly worked his field, bathers continued their tasks, life was unaware. The same compression occurs over and over but often needs context in our collective unconsciousness. Serious issues, tragedy, and love create a triptych that might explain the inattention of the world and how this happens—at a first but lasting glance—and not just why.

In this profession, we are fortunate because as nurses we look out for one another. Those I have come to trust—Sues One and Two, Fern and Margie and Eileen, Mandy—have all helped me understand what it means to be surrounded by suffering and loss and yet still retain all that is human, with a love for the world that can only be realized in the most tender and efficient nursing care and friendship. With this awareness, I have come back to each shift, clothed in resilience, knowing these trusted friends will be walking the floor with me, listening closely, and reminding me, when events begin to unravel, of why I still want to be here. And then Gerry and Tracy, Martha and Teresa, and Drs. Ferrans, DeVon, and Vincent—just as their co-faculty do for others—provide balance and tilt the plates on a fulcrum that often seems fixed. They have taught me that along with evidence and clinical skill, just as important are considering how to act ethically on behalf of patients, other nurses, and whole communities; why we need connection and touch; and how offering understanding and support to each other might provide answers to some of the most important questions coming our way. For them, and so many others, I will continue to be a grateful student—with a clearer take on my own translation.

From words, abstractions, and silence, we learn better what might help the next patient and family who are suffering. But we need others to ferry us through, to set the boundaries of the landscape, to let us know when to open our hearts a little more—even if to those in our care, we look less than assured. Some of us will plow, others will stop to paint or write and add to the learning of those who will get here later. Yet all of us, wrapped in context by caring teachers and patients, coworkers and friends, will help advance the art of nursing. And we will be left with a choice the next time a skeleton drops from the sky with charred wings broken by the wind, decomposing from wax melting in the friction, heat, and miscounts. Nursing helps us sustain that choice.

JEANNE BRYNER

Life Flight

I'm a cloud drifting past a window where I was a student nurse.
An avalanche of bodies bound in cotton, ceiling lights raining down.
Decades since I've run those stairs, steered my medicine cart,
its paper sails, tickets naming the sick, up the reef of beige halls.

I pour rainbow pills, a jug's water, shuffle needles
kept in shallow drawers. I am here to help the heart's fist
squeeze and twist its red mop. Pain's a forest. My hands?
Both ends of a two-man saw. My will's its blade.

I want to feel the knot of fear again as I did then,
mixing an insulin drip, holding Digoxin when the apical
was a lazy turtle, counting stacked breaths,
pushing morphine slowly, slow.

Let me, please, be starstruck again
—my afternoon charge nurse wearing her owl glasses
caught a granny, carried her, a clammy doll
safely to bed—comb Mrs. Byrd's white hair's puff,
smooth her gown's gauzy blue.

I want to be liquid as the doe I was then.
I want the moon to be a newborn
her life's at risk, and I'm the flight nurse. Down
the hall of gypsy nights, I am the steady wren.

I'm the one who brings her to her mother's arms.
I'm the one who sings her sweet face home.

THEODORE DEPPE

From Little Colloquium by the Sea *(a book-length poem)*

At the Boat Inn, in Oughterard, we are shown
    not to the usual café
        which is being restored (or "reborn"—what did

our waitress say?)
    but to a large, airy dining room where, in a corner,
        at an angle to our table,

there's a painting I can't quite see,
    but it's the red and gold of the icon
        I dreamed about last night.

A woman hangs her handbag on the back
    of a chair, then leaves it to greet
        the mother and daughter who sit beneath

my maybe icon. They form
    the sort of triangle
        Leonardo would have composed

and I'm "in the poem" again, everything
    shimmering in this place where no one
        would steal a purse, and when I order

Theodore Deppe, Berea College graduate, 1978, holds his infant son, Peter. Courtesy Theodore Deppe.

a pot of tea, no milk, no sugar please,
    the waitress walks off singing what sounds
        like "Will You Meet Me on Clare Island?"

My good friend, who is usually right,
    tells me not to include the word "poem"
        in a poem—*try*

to be less self-referential—
    but how else to explain
        what's happening?

Well, training as a nurse, I thought
    I must be suffering
        from each psychiatric condition

I studied, and this feels like
    what I'd guess hypomania must be.
        Or maybe it's too much like

the charming and doomed schizophrenic
    I once cared for in Connecticut
        who believed his life a movie.

Everyone was given their lines
    while he ad-libbed his, yet how grateful
        he was to be in such a fine film—

even if it would end sadly.
    Oh, as Father knew, everything ends sadly,
        though I seem to have inherited

his tragic optimism that things might go well
    until they can't.
        And more and more the everyday

seems charged with a heightened
    sense of details. I can be writing a student
        and look up to see wind lifting spume

from row upon row of waves
    and I'll be right back in it,
        unstoppable grief coming in

and gratefulness tossed up and blown
    toward the open sea.
        I'll pull on my father's jacket and set off

walking into the sunlit frenzy.
    But if anything can be part of the poem,
        surely there's a problem?

Or, maybe, not. Out of the Everything,
    luminous details keep emerging,
        like this morning on the beach when I met

the lady with two lapdogs.
    She lives abroad now, but since
        her stroke last spring

she's returned to the place she grew up
    to regain her balance, walking on sand.
        She's already fallen three times today

but is in good spirits—
    when she tosses a ball her dogs leap up
        and are carried a little down beach,

unable it seems to get enough of almost
    flying. I told her about my father
        and the swimming and she said

we all grieve in our own ways,
    for the first year give everyone a pass.
        But, I asked, *since all of us*

in any given year are grieving someone,
    don't we ever get to judge
        anyone? and she threw

the ball and the terriers
    named Tutu and Mandela took to their wings.
        Oh, excellent dogs that connect

to so many things I don't know
    where to turn next. Forty years ago
        after we'd heard Archbishop Tutu speak

I asked Annie to marry me.
    That was in September and she didn't answer
        until October, so this fall,

after Seamus Heaney died,
    we took his directive literally
        and drove out west to the Flaggy Shore

on the last day of September
    and found things just as he described,
        the ocean wild on one side

and the lake to our left "lit
    by the earthed lightning of a flock of swans."
        When we told our host, he said

Seamus and Marie stayed in the same room we did
    so we'd spent the night as well as the day
        inside his poem. On our way home

we stopped for lunch in Kinvara
    and got an email from the husband of my student
        saying she was in a coma.

A few weeks later her next assignment
    came in right on time
        and the only thing

she'd been aware of during five
    unconscious days was a man asking
        if she'd like to hear a poem.

GERALDINE GORMAN

Learning the Wisdom of Tea

When my bare feet hit the cold tile floor outside the shower stall in Door County, Wisconsin, I thought, *maybe I should be a nurse.* That was odd. I had never even remotely entertained nursing. In fact, coming of age on the crest of the second wave of feminism, there were two paths I knew with certainty I would never take: I would not enter the convent and I would not become a nurse. I was thirty-five years old with a master's in English lit and a job in social services. Pregnant with my second child, I was having a rugged first trimester.

The nursing flash was either intuition at its most sublime or hormones run amok. Since I had never before offered nursing any serious consideration, I decided not to change my game plan. Having done little to no research on different programs or educational routes, I chose the last diploma program remaining in Chicago simply because that was the fastest route to nursing. I already had a graduate degree and couldn't imagine going back for a second undergraduate degree. The diploma program was in a nearby Catholic hospital. I could bike to it. I applied, was accepted, and took a giant step backward into the pre–Vatican II era. Latin and incense still lingered in the hallways.

One week into the program the value of research, planning, and professional discernment became clearer. Beth L., our psych teacher, locked the classroom door precisely on the hour, allowing no one to straggle in thirty seconds late. Molly K., a nurse who had worked in the hospital for over forty years, ran the skills clinic like a white-haired Marine sergeant. "Nope, you broke sterility," she would announce as I tried to "don" the sterile gloves, sweating profusely and semi-paralyzed by performance anxiety. When she demanded I repeat this for the tenth time, I began to cry, which was, of course, the point. Molly, however, feigned surprise and wondered aloud how I would ever "manage on the floor."

Two semesters in, I'd had enough clinical experience that I needed to discover where the nurses' stories lived. I searched through the stacks in the school's small library, finding journals from every possible nursing specialty and ample multiple

Geraldine Gorman with volunteer for Afghan Youth for Peace/Voices for Creative Nonviolence, Emergency Hospital, Kabul, Afghanistan, August 2013. Courtesy Geraldine Gorman.

choice tests to accrue CEUs, but damned if I could find one first-person narrative by a nurse. I left the third floor and went downstairs to our director's office. "Where are the nursing journals that tell the nurses' stories?" I asked. She looked at me blankly. "First-person accounts of interactions with patients and families—what it felt like, what they learned," I continued. "I don't know of any," she said.

On the other hand, for there always is that other hand, I also met Vanessa W., my A&P teacher, who was tough but also a Mother Earth of sorts. She allowed me to sit in her office and wail when I discovered that my son had entered the world with an undescended testicle requiring surgery. She passed me tissues and didn't try to wrestle my hysteria into proportion. When he came through the procedure just fine, she rejoiced with me. And there was Liz Y., the nurse we all strove to be. She taught diabetes like she was born to it, and we nodded in gratitude as she so clearly explicated the mysterious pancreas and the dire consequences of uncontrolled diabetes. Her hands were ivory pure, as if she marinated them in bleach, and I wondered if one day I, too, would possess such hands—if perhaps after five, ten years of practice one just awoke to alabaster instruments of healing. (I'm still waiting.)

And there were moments of pristine absurdity: Attempting to transfer an elderly woman from wheelchair to bed in a skilled facility, my friend Denise on one side and I on the other. We underestimated both the extent to which our patient was able to help us "pivot" her and also the astonishing force of gravity. When we found we could not accomplish what the lab videos made look so effortless, the three of us fell backward on the bed together, laughing like third graders at a slumber party.

During my last year, I argued hard—as testy nursing students are wont to do—for a leadership placement in the intensive care unit. When I was turned down, I penned a manifesto detailing all the reasons this was both unfair and a pox on the profession. My weary clinical instructor regarded me with exasperation: "Gerry, just go to graduate school."

A time-honored tradition of the diploma program was the conferring of a cardiac fellowship on the most worthy maiden in the school. It was doled out by a notorious surgeon who was rumored to have a collection of antique cars of incalculable value. His reputation was legion: he raged, he tossed, he roared. And he also offered monetary bribes to any nurse who thought she could withstand his tantrums and theatrics. Whether we were interested or not, we were mandated to await his arrival in our nursing school lounge so that he could explain the potential good fortune he was to bestow. On the assigned date, he was held up in surgery; thirty minutes passed, then forty-five. None of us was allowed to leave. I had two small children in daycare and by that time I was pregnant with my third; sitting around waiting for a megalomaniac to grant an appearance was not high on my list. No matter. He arrived in blood-spattered scrubs, his mask atop his head, and plucked the fairest among us. None of us could leave until he did, and we were instructed to remain standing as he left the room. (I swear to God.)

And lastly, when the time came for graduation photos, I was eight months pregnant (I was to give birth to my daughter in my final maternity rotation; I was given one week maternity leave). In the last months of my diploma program I was tired, swollen, and decidedly non-perky. I balked at having to "don" the goofy nursing cap that no one actually wore. I was told that if I did not wear it in the photo, I would not graduate. The year was 1991.

.   .   .

Graduate school had to wait till I secured a BSN. This I did through an articulated RN to BSN program at the same Jesuit University from which I had attained my master's in English. By this time, I was a neophyte nurse, practicing on the oncology unit in the hospital where I had attended school. Everything stunned me—the brutal chemotherapy protocols under which people wasted and became wraithlike, the blue "protective" gown and industrial gloves we wore as we delivered the toxins, how the nurses on my unit never talked about the physical and emotional toll all this exacted. When patients died, their names were erased from the census board, the room was cleaned, and the next patient was admitted. I began to understand the lack of published stories—there was so much about which we held silent.

I would leave work, exhausted and disoriented, and arrive at the university. My classes were populated with experienced nurses, some older than me, some younger but all with five, ten, or fifteen years of experience. They were goddesses: poised, calm, utterly capable, and efficient. Nothing, it seemed, threw them. I was inexorably unraveling.

Then I met Connie, a university faculty member who was a grad of the Cook County Hospital School of Nursing. She told us that no matter what academic accolade she accrued, nothing made her more proud than to be told she was "a good nurse." This spoke to something buried so deeply within me I hadn't realized it was there, but I could feel it straining, wanting to be recognized and heard (*yes, I understand this*). Connie also bestowed the great gift of making us write—not research papers, not care plans, or concept maps but journals. She wanted to know what was happening in our practice, in our lives, and she listened. And responded. Although as an English major I had written many papers, this was the first time I wrote from that deep place, wrote because I needed to be heard, and yearned to express so much of what had been suppressed. In many ways, all that has happened in the following two decades was possible because Connie coaxed forth my voice and welcomed me.

The BSN completion program provided my first glimpse into the world of community-based nursing. The possibility of practicing outside a hospital was barely acknowledged in my diploma program. Yet here these women were calling themselves nurses, crisp in their creased navy blue pants and white Oxford shirts and blouses. Deirdre was a fierce public health advocate, a crusader to defeat respiratory disease. She took on the cigarette companies with glee, staging "die-ins" outside their headquarters, dressing her young sons up as Joe Camel, carrying signs with dire warnings. In class she spoke like a machine gun, talking for hours, without notes. I could not fathom that we shared a common species.

Miriam became my Lillian Wald. Tall and thin and elegant in her navy blues, she worked at Chicago's first hospice for people with AIDS. She extended her compassion for the vulnerable within our communities to her students. She invited us to her home, made us tea, listened to us with artistry. When I graduated, she gave me an inscribed copy of *Notes on Nursing*, thanking me for what she had learned from me. She was that kind of teacher.

Toward the end of the program, life and death on the oncology unit lurched and tilted. People were dying quickly and horribly. No one talked about it. My hands were raw, and red blotches ringed my eyes. As a still-so-new-nurse, I fell in love with almost every patient I touched and then they died, many of them angry from expectations raised and explanations and options not offered. A wonderland of distortions and chaos subsumed us. When my father ended up in one of our beds, diagnosed with rapidly advancing lung cancer, I took a leave from my position and sat vigil at his bed in the ICU. A month later, extubated and freed to die in the relative quiet of a designated hospice room, his death granted me permission to leave the hospital. I fled.

I knew I was leaving the oncology unit, the site of so much pain and such oppressive silence. I thought I was also leaving nursing. Despite my less than clear understanding of what had drawn me to the profession, the practice had taught me that what I wanted was to use my hands to offer tangible comfort. Oncology nursing demanded a complicity in suffering I could no longer abide. My hands had extended precious little comfort. Instead I hung poisonous bags of chemicals and then held emesis basins. Small wonder my skin protested. The pressure of all that had not been said felt volcanic.

When I approached the university to inform them of my decision to leave the program, my advisor offered a different option. I didn't know Mary well. She had always been warm and welcoming, but she dwelt high in the rarified realm of Olympus, having served twice as interim dean and actively involved in a plethora of professional and health-care organizations. She extended an alternative to permanent exile. A seminar was being offered in England on the national health-care system and hospice. It would provide respite, exposure to something new, time to think, to listen. Time for my hands to heal.

The three weeks I spent in the English countryside saved my nursing career. Accompanying the eight students were two community health faculty members, Janice and Maude, who had a home in England. They served as guides to a different way to care, one that was slower, less technological, based more on conversation and the sharing of tea. And they modeled the support that only nurses can offer one another. Their palpable appreciation of one another's gifts infused our time together. After we finished our classroom and clinical experiences for the day, Janice and Maude led us on treks through the countryside, culminating in tea and scones or in ale shared by a warming hearth. I visited numerous freestanding hospices, saw how dying could unfold organically, how death could be marked not by erasure on a census blackboard but by a candle lit and floated in an atrium fountain. One afternoon I sat in the corner of a community clinic, witnessing the interactions between the general practitioner and her patients. What she offered was reassurance. "Now then," she would say, removing the blood pressure cuff from the arm of a local farmer, "we are fine. There is nothing sinister here."

And so the lava flowed. I put my hands to work and I wrote like the madwoman I was. I wrote in the morning and learned in the afternoons. I sat in the garden of the Lewis Carroll museum gazing at Alice, frozen in the looking glass. In the evenings we laughed and ate and drank, and I wrote more, writing to get Alice unstuck. When we returned to Chicago I placed all that I had written into the hands of my trusted faculty guides, and they read it. I wrote my first published article, a narrative of my father's death, and gave it to Mary. Her eyes met mine and shimmered.

I competed the BSN program and entered graduate school. Having left the hospital, I applied to the last remaining Visiting Nurse Association in the Chicago area, joining the daughters of Lillian Wald.

. . .

During my doctoral program, I learned that many consider nursing a "science." This revelation came during a qualitative research class when the professor referred to us as "nursing scientists." I thought she was kidding. I laughed. She was a disciple of the late great Martha Rogers who dreamed of nurse astronauts and cofounded the Space Nursing Society. I was to learn that Science is Serious Business in nursing academia.

Certainly I am no "denier." I realized that scientific principles are interwoven through nursing practice and education, but I felt no more kinship with nurse scientists than I did with nurse astronauts. Always it was the relationships that captivated and, yes, healed—those stories unfolding over a cup of tea. Because it was a Jesuit university with a strong tradition of humanities-based education, we had some flexibility. Nursing research had not yet cornered the market on what constituted rigor. We still talked about constructing the final "grand theory" that would render the cosmos containable. So we suffered through stats and measurement, but we also talked our faculty into an elective on nursing and metaphor. Back in the waning years of the twentieth century, we held to Florence's maxim that nursing is both science and art; indeed, it tilted toward the finest of arts.

The more ignoble side of nursing education also surfaced during graduate school. All disciplines have their peccadilloes, but finding paranoia and competition within a profession as relational as nursing proved jarring. Particularly brutal was a methods class taught by one of the school's most successful researchers. It was commonplace for several of the students—professional women in their forties and fifties with decades of practice behind them—to leave class in tears. We were required to write a massive paper that investigated a topic pertinent to the profession. I chose to examine evidence for the inclusion of humanities into nursing education. This struck a particularly raw nerve in our professor. She wrote with a red pen, sarcasm and invective dripping on every page. She crossed out each reference I made to poetry, advising me to "save such precious touches for your novel." Midway through the semester she suffered a myocardial infarction. Confined to the ICU, she dispatched her husband to our classroom to collect our final assignment, instructing him to wait no more than the allotted ten minutes she had allowed us as window. This adversarial relationship between teacher and students was puzzling and hurtful. It suggested a boot camp mentality so alien to professional ideals and to those aspiring toward holism and healing. Many of us limped out of graduate school, less confident than we were upon entering, despite our new titles.

My dissertation grew out of the ashes of the VNA. Midway through my program, Hillary Clinton's health-care reform package went down in flames and acquisition fever became epidemic. Community-based organizations toppled across the country, among them the Visiting Nurse Associations, midwifed by Wald and her Henry Street Settlement associates. I wrote the story, chronicling the proud tradition of the VNA movement and of our particular organization, sold out beneath us in the year of its centennial. I interviewed nurses with whom I had practiced, with whom I had fought to preserve the doomed nursing-led organization. The dissertation evolved as a hermeneutic exploration of feminist understanding and loss of innocence. No longer could strong women trust that they would be allowed to continue their work in good faith. A corporate mind-set gripped the land, and nurses needed to understand due diligence. The narrative of the VNA's demise provided my ticket out of graduate school, but it was a pyrrhic victory.

By the time graduation arrived, my marriage was floundering and my body was shrinking. At the commencement ceremony, Mary, my dissertation chair and adviser, scanned the ranks of regalia-clad middle-aged women but could not find me, though she passed within five feet as I ascended to the stage. One of the ushers hastily "hooded" me before I crossed to shake the university president's hand and accept my diploma. Later, at a celebration for the newly minted PhDs, we took turns at the microphone, announcing our names replete with our new titles. When finished, I found my brother among the seated audience. "Where were you?" he asked. "I was watching and I never saw you." This feminist scholar and faux nurse scientist had faded like the Cheshire cat, invisibility an unpredictable state.

. . .

Full circle back to the classroom. I used to stand in front, now I do more sitting, often in a circle. "So tell me," I often begin, "what made you want to be a nurse?" And then I encourage them to take seriously where their intuition leads. It has been quite a journey.

September 2001, my first postdoctoral faculty role. I faced my nursing students, a field of young, blonde-haired sophomores, away from their small Michigan towns for the first time. Ensnared by the vast uncertainty of that time, we knew only that something seemingly inviolate had shattered. Fifteen years later, I sit among my students at a large public university in Chicago. They come from everywhere: refugee camps and occupied territories and lands once encased behind an iron curtain, the surrounding suburbs and our own violence-ravaged neighborhoods.

They speak many languages, demand new pronouns to address their nonbinary identities. Their culture and knowledge arise from sources I barely understand, but I am trying.

They are fierce and beautiful. We never lock the door to our classroom.

When I urge them to tell their stories and seek the wisdom of those who came before them, I remember the resounding silence in the hospital library stacks, the sorrow choked back in the corridors of the oncology unit. I hold the students' words in my hands, their nascent nursing selves unfolding; I choose with care my response and the color of my ink. An occasional student still summons the "selfless" specter of nursing and I quickly warn of the sinister implications: *You need yourself. Treasure yourself. You are your instrument. Pay attention to the brain in your belly, your blessed nursing intuition*, I tell them. *Don't be selfless. Don't disappear. You are too precious. We need you too much.*

On weekends I practice as a hospice nurse. Frequently I bring students with me. Sometimes we sit at the table, share tea with the constellation of beloved that the dying call to formation. In such moments boundaries blur: between the living and the dying, practitioner and recipient, teacher and student. Hungry for connection, we pass stories around the table. We sip from our mugs. Only now, as a woman in my sixth decade, do I begin to understand what led my thirty-five-year-old self to nursing. Formal education offered signposts along the way. Students illuminate the path forward. A century ago, the aging Irish poet recognized the futility of parsing the *yin* from the *yang*:

O body swayed to music, O brightening glance,
How can we know the dancer from the dance?

We breathe, we learn. Our stories entwine.

NANCY KERRIGAN

From Beginning to End

For Larry, my first patient

. . . you don't mean shit to me, he shouted,
looking backwards, as his thirteen years, all swagger
strutted away from me, a thin adolescent—
Sam Cooke in a dirty, white undershirt
with a forbidden, rolled cigarette
hanging from his lips.
Our last therapy session, fifty years ago
during grad school. I chased him, an orphan,
a ward of the state, around hospital grounds
waited and waited
in damp offices with broken glass windows.
An hour, three days a week for three years—ours.
He grew,
went from wearing state-issued,
worn-thin hospital gowns required after restraint
to a blue button-down, a small-brimmed fedora
purchased for his nappy head.
Mailed cookies to jail in between
when he phoned from there.
The ebb and flow of psychotherapy washed over me,
while he yielded to the imperative
that living creatures
bend toward light.
How did I stop listening to his music
when his long-playing song
had just begun?
How did I say goodbye, when then
I became just another
45 record he didn't have?
I knew otherwise.

LINDA MAURER TUTHILL

Duty Bound

Starched white caps, bobby-pinned to our hair,
appeared to float like dainty sails from bed to bed.
But our feet, encased in sturdy brown oxfords,
furnished the power that kept us from capsizing.
We called our blocky shoes, with their regulation
eight eyelets, duty booties. Their leathery tongues
spoke a no-nonsense language, urging us onward.

All nursing stations contained a Procedure Manual
with step-by-step directions for any treatment
a doctor could order. Instructions for an enema solution
called for a temp. of 105–110 degrees F.
and a well-lubricated No. 28 to 32 French rectal tube,
destined to be inserted 4 to 5 inches.
We prayed the tubing would stay attached
to the enema can, lest our duty booties
become canal boats sinking in a wash of soapsuds.
To calm our nerves, we mouthed a code:
High, Hot, and a Hell of a lot.

When, with luck, we reached graduation,
we sailed across the stage wearing coveted
white from head to toe: organdy cap,
long-sleeved dress uniform, hose, and shoes.
Our oxfords, shabby and thin-soled,
endured an annual ritual, impaled
on a fence surrounding the nursing dorm.

I am still trying to untie the laces.

BELLE WARING

You Could Have Been Me

Just you walk out from that hospital air into the rasp edge of winter
when trees look fresh as a black lace hem
frayed in somebody's backseat.

Just walk out of the hospital, where grief is stripped and intricate
as winter trees.

I was fresh out of the sonogram room where they tilted a sensor
over and over a place in my breast.
You could have been me there—
a jacklighted deer
hearkening.

Ultrasound, imperceptible to anyone but bats,
will pass through liquid and bounce off solid
as sonar reveals a torpedo.
As it sees a malignant mass.

Doctors are whispering.

One looks over: *You mind us talking?*
Talk, I said. *Sing, if you feel like it.*

I walked straight out of that hospital
the moment the just-set-sun was casting a pearl shell over the city.

A man asked for change.
I told him the truth. I was out of work.

Belle Waring (far right, standing) with fellow nurse writers at Chapters Book Store, WDC, 1995. Northern Virginia Community College graduate, 1975. Editor's collection.

God bless you, he said, *come back tomorrow, I'll have money.*

My sonogram film now stood packed in with a thousand others.
When you rejoice, you forget the unspared ones.

You just watch that godlike blue between sunset and night,
blue laced with underlight curving around the shoulders of the earth
until it falls like a veil teased off—

and as a Chevy full of folks creaks down the way,
headlights swagging down the alley,
something shifts—inside me again is a perfectness.

No harm will come to us.
The street will not swallow us, the night not oppress us.

Something opens inside my chest—
a flower from a pellet in a glass of water, a toy
for a child so dumb with delight she's forgotten the difference
between herself and the one to be thanked
and the thanks, the very thanks.

CORTNEY DAVIS

I Want to Work in a Hospital

where it's okay
to climb into bed with patients
and hold them—
pre-op, before they lose
their legs or breasts, or after,
to tell them
they are still whole.

Or post-partum,
when they have just returned
from that strange garden,
or when they are dying,
as if somehow because I stay
they are free to go.

I want the daylight
I walk out into
to become the flashlight they carry,
waving it
as we go together
into their long night.

AFTERWORD

Cortney Davis

So here we are at the end of this journey—we have traveled a winding and some-times perilous, sometimes gorgeous road from the British Isles, from Germany to America, from Alabama and Virginia to the West Coast, from there to New England, from a midwestern coal town to city tenements, from classroom to hospital, from awkward first ministrations to life-saving miracles. And now we hold this book, this record of courage and desire, a treasure in our hands.

That shiny pocketknife of memory Jeanne Bryner mentioned in her introduc-tion has carved out poems and stories that stay in the mind, and in the heart. We have suffered with some nurses here, silent witnesses of the damage we humans might inflict on one another. We have triumphed and celebrated as well, mind-ful of how the spirit and the will might survive, of how tenaciously we grasp the falling branch, of how fast we run toward the fire, not away from it.

Above all, we speak of how we have been educated in our various nursing pro-grams *to stay.* Nurses stay at the bedside of the dying and the newly born: we stand by the angry patient, by the ones who would judge us, and by the ones who embrace us. We remain as the patient's advocate during the most horrific moments—the sights and sounds and smells of traumas that we can't shake, that can envelop us, heavy capes we might wear for the rest of our days. Sometimes, if we can put these darkest memories down in words, by that sharing we fling off those capes and rest in the sun. We also share moments of transcendence. Surely, reader, you know by now, and maybe from personal experience as well, how one nurse might change a life. Our patients change our lives too—we draw our strength from them.

The nurses you have met here, these writers, have earned their wisdom, their tears and laughter, and they have presented their stories and poems to us as gifts to be opened, often revealing what they have never revealed before. Let us be humble, and let us be thankful for the women and men who have studied, who still study, the mysteries of the body in order to tend us, to save us.

My profound gratitude to the writers who have shared the days and years of their nursing educations with us. I especially thank and applaud Jeanne Bryner, whose love for nursing and whose ability to look close and to listen deep have guided our journey. Jeanne and I now put down our pens, but we know that this journey will continue. We nurses carry so many wondrous tales. They spill from our pockets and they cling to our stethoscopes. We will keep writing about our lives and our patients long after these pages fade. Thank you for being good company along the way.

CONTRIBUTORS

Helen L. Albert, RN, was born March 30, 1921, in Argo, Alabama, the daughter of Lumas Stanford and Marcenia Haglar. She was the 1943 valedictorian of her Norwood Hospital School of Nursing graduation class in Birmingham and first practiced at Slossfield Maternity Hospital. In 1944 she married, and she and her husband were part of the Great Migration north. Her husband found employment in a steel mill, and she was the first black registered nurse hired in Trumbull County, Ohio. Born to lead, she eventually became supervisor of nursing at St. Joseph's Riverside Hospital, a role she held for fourteen years. In 1960, she founded and operated Albert's Nursing and Residential Facility before retiring in 1995 after fifty years of nursing. A woman of strong faith, she was a trustee for Grace AME Church in Warren, Ohio, served on countless community boards, and received awards locally, nationally, and internationally. Ever the humanitarian, Helen lived by the mantra of *loving, caring, and sharing*. She died in September 2009.

Amanda J. Anderson, MSN, MPA, RN, CCRN, is an award-winning critical care nurse, writer, policy scholar, and health-care administrator. Amanda worked as an intensive care nurse for many years before moving into administration, academia, and publishing. In addition to her work in hospital administration in New York City, Amanda directs a nurse-specific writing center at the Hunter-Bellevue School of Nursing, and she is founder of the Bedside Confessionals, a live narrative event for health-care professionals. Her writing credits include pieces in *Pulse: Voices from the Heart of Medicine; Off the Charts;* and the *American Journal of Nursing,* where she is a contributing editor, member of the editorial board, and coordinator for the column *Transition to Craft.* Her work as a nurse has been awarded the 2016 Hunter-Bellevue School of Nursing's Commitment to Clinical Excellence Award, and the 2008 Medstar Washington Hospital Center Nurse Leader Award. Amanda is a Macy Foundation Henry Biggs Health Policy Scholar, and a Senior Fellow of the Center for Health, Media & Policy at Hunter College.

Geoffrey Bowe, RN, trained as a general nurse in Cumbria, England, graduating in 1983. After training, he moved to Kent, England, and worked there on a variety of wards, including the orthopedic or surgical wards. His poetry and prose have appeared in the *Nursing Standard, Between the Heartbeats: Poetry and Prose by*

Nurses, and in *Intensive Care: More Poetry and Prose by Nurses.* In 2012, he became ill with necrotizing pancreatitis and spent a year in the hospital, experiencing what it is like on the other side of the sickbed. He is currently retired.

Barbara Broome, PhD, RN, FAAN, is currently the associate dean and chair for Community/Mental Health at the University of South Alabama College of Nursing. She previously taught at Kent State University and was instrumental in the development of the nursing program at the Trumbull Campus where she taught nursing. She maintains a clinical practice in continence therapy and is the developer of the Broome Pelvic Muscle Self-efficacy Scale©, which has been used in national and international studies and translated into several languages. She has developed continence clinics in Alabama and Ohio. She is a coeditor for the *Journal of Cultural Diversity* and associate editor for *Mental Health and Substance Abuse: Dual Diagnosis.* Barbara is the research chair for the Society of Urologic Nursing and interim secretary for the Association of Black Nursing Faculty. Her awards and honors include the Association of Black Nursing Faculty Young Publisher's Award, University of South Alabama College of Nursing Faculty Scholarship Award, Fellow of the American Academy of Nursing, Fellow of the NIH Summer Training Institute, and Ohio Board of Regents Fellow.

Celia Kelly Brown, RN, MA, is a native of Westport, County Mayo, Ireland. She trained as a registered nurse and midwife in England before immigrating to the United States in 1963. She began her U.S. nursing career in Boston's Beth Israel Hospital and then moved to Hanover, New Hampshire, and worked at Mary Hitchcock Hospital, as a school nurse in Lyme and Hanover, and as a volunteer for the Red Cross. She continued her nursing career in the Washington, D.C., area for the Red Cross and a diet agency. After devoting time to raising her two sons, Celia earned a BA at the New England College and an MA at Dartmouth College; she later received a Jenny McKean Fellowship to the George Washington University. Her publications include *Mending the Skies* and *Light.* Her poems and prose have been anthologized in *Between the Heartbeats: Poetry and Prose by Nurses* and in *Intensive Care: More Poetry and Prose by Nurses.* Brown's poems have appeared in numerous publications, including *The Seattle Review, American Journal of Nursing, An Anthology of Cape Women Writers, The Federal Poets,* and the *Salmon* in Ireland.

Jeanne Bryner, RN, BA, CEN, was born in Appalachia. She is a graduate of Trumbull Memorial Hospital's School of Nursing and Kent State University's Honors College. Jeanne worked as a staff nurse in pediatrics, med-surg, ICU, ER, immediate care, periop-pool, the IV team, and Vlad Pediatrics. Her books include *Breathless; Blind Horse; Smoke; Eclipse; Tenderly Lift Me: Nurses Honored, Celebrated, and*

Remembered; Early Farming Woman; and *The Wedding of Miss Meredith Mouse.* Her work has been awarded the 2011 Tillie Olsen Award from the Working Class Studies Association and an *American Journal of Nursing* Book of the Year award. Her poetry has been adapted for the stage, and her new play, "Foxglove Canyon," was first performed in Akron at Summa Healthcare's Humanities conference. Her nursing poetry has been adapted and performed by Verb Ballets, Cleveland, Ohio. Jeanne has received writing fellowships from Bucknell University, the Ohio Arts Council, and the Vermont Studio Center.

Kathleen English Cadmus, ANP-BC, CNS, is a board-certified adult nurse practitioner and psychiatric clinical nurse specialist in a private mental health practice in Columbus, Ohio. She received both her undergraduate and graduate degrees in nursing from the Ohio State University College of Nursing. Her nursing career has included maternal-child health, neonatal, and benign hematology (hemophilia) as well as mental health. Kathleen received an MFA in creative nonfiction writing from Ashland University in Ohio.

Minnie Brown Carter, RN, was born March 4, 1926, in Lynchburg, Virginia. She retired from nursing in 1988 after forty years of service. Minnie celebrated her ninetieth birthday in March 2016 with family and friends. The guest speaker for this event was Deputy Surgeon General Rear Admiral Sylvia Trent-Adams, PhD, RN, FAAN, of the U.S. Public Health Service, also a Hampton University Nursing School graduate, who presented Minnie with several awards of the highest honor for her service to nursing and the community. On September 17, 2016, Minnie Brown Carter was honored as a charter member of the new Smithsonian National Museum of African American History and Culture. She was asked to submit her life story and memorabilia to the museum for millions to see for years to come. Her historical story as a Cadet Nurse Corps graduate is also included in the Women's Memorial at Arlington National Cemetery in Washington, D.C. From very humble beginnings, Minnie Brown Carter has lived the life of a registered nurse to the fullest, truly a life of service to nursing and the community.

Joanne M. Clarkson, RN, came to nursing early—and late. She majored in nursing after high school, but was overwhelmed after losing her father and grandfather and haunted by the death of her infant sister. Instead, she studied English, then library science, teaching, and writing, and worked as a professional librarian for twenty-five years. After caring for her mother through a long illness until her death, she re-careered at fifty, becoming a home health and hospice RN. Her fourth poetry collection, *Believing the Body,* focuses on her beloved nursing work. Her website is http://JoanneClarkson.com.

Elayne Clift, MA, a Vermont Humanities Council Scholar, is an award-winning writer and journalist whose work has appeared in numerous publications. A regular columnist for the *Keene Sentinel*, a book reviewer for the *New York Journal of Books*, and a regular contributor to *Vermont Magazine* and Women's Feature Service, Elayne has had pieces published in the *Boston Globe*, the *Washington Post*, the *Christian Science Monitor*, the *Chronicle of Higher Education*, and international publications, among others. She published her first novel, *Hester's Daughters*, based on Nathaniel Hawthorne's *The Scarlet Letter*, in 2012. Her latest book of short stories, *Children of the Chalet*, won First Place/Fiction 2014 from Greyden Press and was published the following year. Her website is www.elayne-clift.com.

Cortney Davis, APRN, MA, was a nurse's aide and then a surgical technician before graduating from Norwalk Community College in Connecticut with an ASN. After working in the ICU and serving as head nurse on Danbury Hospital's first oncology unit, she returned to school, graduating from New York Hospital School of Nursing/Cornell University as an APRN. She also completed a BA and MA in English while working as an adult nurse practitioner in pulmonology and cardiology subspecialty practices and then for many years in an OB-GYN clinic that served uninsured women. Cortney is the author of five poetry collections, including the award-winning *Taking Care of Time* and *Leopold's Maneuvers*. Her works of nonfiction include *The Heart's Truth: Essays on the Art of Nursing* and *When the Nurse Becomes a Patient: A Story in Words and Images* (both from Kent State University Press). With Judy Schaefer, Cortney coedited *Between the Heartbeats: Poetry and Prose by Nurses* and *Intensive Care: More Poetry and Prose by Nurses*. Her honors include four American Journal of Nursing Books of the Year Awards, an NEA Poetry Fellowship, three Connecticut Commission on the Arts Poetry Grants, a Gold Medal Living Now Award in Nonfiction, an Independent Publishers' Silver Medal in Nonfiction, the Connecticut Center for the Book Nonfiction Prize, and a Benjamin Franklin Gold Medal in Nonfiction. In 2007 she received a Nightingale Award for excellence in Nursing.

Theodore Deppe, RN, received his BSN from Berea College and his MFA in poetry from Vermont College. He worked for twenty years in coronary care and psychiatric hospitals. He is the author of *Children of the Air*, *The Wanderer King*, *Cape Clear: New and Selected Poems*, *Orpheus on the Red Line*, *Beautiful Wheel*, and *Liminal Blue*. Ted is a recipient of two grants from the NEA and a Pushcart Prize, and he has been a writer in residence at the James Merrill House in Stonington, Connecticut; the Poet's House in Donegal, Ireland; and Phillips Academy in Andover, Massachusetts. Ted has taught creative writing in graduate programs in the United States, Ireland, and England. He is on the faculty of the Stonecoast

MFA program, and directs Stonecoast in Ireland. A dual citizen of the United States and Ireland, he has lived for the most part on the west coast of Ireland since 2000.

Stephanie Ezell, MSN, has been an RN for seven years, working solely on an in-patient hospice unit in the Chicago area. Having received master's degrees in nursing and public health in 2016, she is now a doctoral student in the College of Nursing at the University of Illinois at Chicago. She is thankful that Geraldine Gorman, PhD, RN, introduced her to the value of reflecting upon, and metabolizing, nursing experiences through narrative writing at the beginning of her graduate studies. Her research and practice interests are end-of-life care, bioethics, social determinants of health, and the trauma imposed by war and violence.

Heather Foster, RN, MFA, lives and writes on a corn and soybean farm in west Tennessee. She holds an MFA from Murray State University and a BSN from Union University. She works in as charge nurse in OB/GYN. She has stories featured in *Exigencies, Monkeybicycle,* and *Cream City Review.* Her poems have appeared in *Tampa Review, Third Coast, PANK, Weave Magazine, Cutthroat, Iron Horse Literary Review, Word Riot, RHINO,* and *Mead: The Magazine of Literature & Libations.*

Rachel Renee Gage, MA, BA, MSN, RN, entered nursing school from a background in the arts with a master's degree in music—she had been a cruise ship singer, traveling to seven continents. As a performer, Rachel did TV commercials, film, acting, dancing, and singing on stage. She has been a presenter as a Zumba Education Specialist for Zumba Fitness, and was a Schweitzer Fellow—her project involved using visual arts as a healing modality with high-risk youth in Humbolt Park. Rachel was recognized as a "Daisy in training" award winner and earned the chancellor's student service award for the four years of her nursing education. She is on the advisory council of the Hektoen Institute Nursing and Humanities.

Kristine Garcia-Cross, RN, grew up in Phoenix, Arizona. She received her bachelor's of science in sociology at Oklahoma State University, where she played college softball and received an athletic scholarship. She is married, has a daughter, and works full time. Kristine was also a full-time nursing student at Glendale Community College, graduating with honors in 2016 as a registered nurse. She was accepted into Alpha Delta Nu Nursing Honors Society at Glendale College and was elected treasurer of the honor society.

Mary Gavan RN, PhD, trained in a pioneer course at the Nursing Studies Department of Edinburgh University, Scotland, then specialized in psychosocial nursing in London. Her career focused on rehabilitation and palliative care in the community where she worked with distressed families on behalf of the health authority. In addition, she ran her own nursing business and was involved in setting up and nursing in the First AIDS Hospice in Canada. In describing her experiences, she more often uses her second profession: storytelling. Through stories, shows, and skits, she transmits the knowledge gleaned and gained from nursing along with her unique understanding of human nature, often expressed in Celtic ways. Mary was awarded a PhD in thanatology, the study of death and dying.

Kathleen Goldbach, BSN, graduated from the University of Iowa in 1964. She worked as a nurse in psychiatry and pediatrics before receiving a BA in music from San Jose State University in 1987. She raised four children in San Jose, and lived in Germany for five years in the 1990s. Her poems have been published in the *Vocabula Review, Eureka Literary Magazine, Poetalk,* and other publications. She lives with her husband in Campbell, California, where she teaches piano and writes poetry.

Geraldine Gorman, RN, PhD, is a clinical associate professor in the College of Nursing at the University of Illinois, Chicago. She also practices as a hospice nurse and is the mother of three children.

Miriam Crawford Grant, BSN, is a writer/actress and on-set registered nurse who has worked on several television shows and films. A native of the Charleston, South Carolina, area, Miriam's career in television began when she was a stand-in on ABC's *Army Wives.* She graduated from the Citadel Military College of South Carolina in 2006. The transition of the college from all male to coed shaped Miriam's perspective in a profound way, and that experience finds its way into her writings. Upon graduating from the military college, Miriam pursued a post baccalaureate in medicine at Brandeis University before returning to Charleston where her passion for helping people and for the medical sciences led her to the Medical University of South Carolina Nursing Program from which she graduated in 2010. Miriam has worked in various medical settings, lived, trained, and worked professionally as an actress in both NYC and currently in Los Angeles, California, where pursuing acting, writing, and industry set nursing is a daily adventure.

James V. Guliano, MSN, RN-BC, FACHE, currently serves as vice president, Quality Programs at the Ohio Hospital Association. In this role, he has oversight of the patient safety, quality, and public health programs within the state hospital association. Jim has held administrative positions, most recently as chief nursing officer, and has maintained a clinical practice. He is an adjunct instructor in a nursing undergraduate program. Jim earned his diploma in nursing from

St. Thomas Hospital Medical Center School of Nursing in Akron, Ohio. While practicing nursing in critical care settings, he then earned a master of science degree in nursing administration from the University of Akron. He is board certified in Nursing Professional Development by the American Nurses Credentialing Center. Jim is a fellow in the American College of Healthcare Executives.

Amy M. Haddad, MSN, PhD, RN, is the director of the Center for Health Policy and Ethics and the Dr. C. C. and Mabel L. Criss Endowed Chair in the Health Sciences at Creighton University. She received her BSN from Creighton University, her MSN from the University of Nebraska Medical Center, and her PhD in education from the University of Nebraska-Lincoln. Her poetry and short stories have appeared in the *American Journal of Nursing, Fetishes* (a literary journal of the University of Colorado Health Sciences Center), the *Journal of Medical Humanities, Touch, Janus Head, Reflections on Nursing Leadership,* the *Journal of Humanities in Rehabilitation,* and the *Bellevue Literary Review.* She is a coeditor of the *Arduous Touch: Women's Voices in Health Care.*

Patricia Harman, CNM, MSN, has ben published in the *Journal of Midwifery and Women's Health* and the *Journal of Sigma Theta Tau for Nursing Scholarship* as well as alternative publications. She is a regular presenter at national midwifery conferences and her novels have been *USA Today* best sellers. Patricia got her start as a lay midwife on the rural communes where she lived in the '60s and '70s, going on to become a nurse-midwife on the faculty of Ohio State University, Case Western Reserve University, and West Virginia University. She lives and works near Morgantown, West Virginia. She has two memoirs in print, *The Blue Cotton Gown* and *Arms Wide Open;* two historical novels, the award-winning *The Midwife of Hope River* and *The Reluctant Midwife;* and a third contemporary novel, *The Runaway Midwife.*

Patricia Kalas, RN, BSN, is from Gustavus Township in northeast Ohio's Trumbull County. She graduated from the University of Michigan and is a member of Sigma Theta Tau. She spent her nursing career at Trumbull Memorial Hospital in Warren, Ohio, where she worked in the intensive care unit for more than thirty years. She also worked as specialty director and in immediate care and the specialty pool, which included the wound care and hyperbaric unit. Pat truly loved her nursing career, especially "her" patients. This is her first publication.

Nancy Kerrigan, BSN. After graduating with a BSN from Loyola University of Chicago, where she received a National Institutes of Mental Health Traineeship, Nancy never looked back but gave her professional career over to psychiatric nursing. She has worked as a psychotherapist in private and public hospitals, community mental health settings, and in independent practice, and has taught psychiatric nursing at Loyola University, St. Xavier University, and Yale University. Kerrigan is an alumnus of Wesleyan University's Writers Week and of workshops at the Frost Place in Franconia, New Hampshire. Her poetry appears in *Nantucket: A Collection, Caduceus, Rattle, The Breath of Parted Lips: Voices from the Frost Place,* and *Everyone Says Hello.* Her chapbook *The Voices: The Poetry of Psychiatry* won a PEN New England Award. She is also the author of another chapbook, "High Heels & Sneakers: My Balance Myth."

Rev. Robert J. Kus, RN, PhD, a native of Cleveland, Ohio, is currently pastor of the Basilica Shrine of St. Mary in Wilmington, North Carolina, and a police chaplain for the Wilmington Police Department. He graduated from Cleveland Metropolitan General Hospital School of Nursing in 1966 and practiced GYN nursing for two years at the same hospital. He received a BA in sociology from Cleveland State University in 1968, a PhD in sociology from the University of Montana in 1981, an MS in Psychiatric-Mental Health Nursing from the University of Oklahoma Health Sciences Center in 1982, and an MDiv from St. Meinrad School of Theology in Indiana in 1998. Fr. Kus has practiced in many areas of nursing at Cleveland Metropolitan General Hospital, St. Patrick Hospital in Missoula, Harborview Medical Center in Seattle, and Baptist Medical Center in Oklahoma City. He has taught sociology, psychiatric-mental health nursing, and chemical dependency nursing in a variety of universities and has also served as a research scholar in Prague and Budapest in the areas of chemical dependency and human sexuality. He was ordained a priest of the Catholic Diocese of Raleigh in 1998. Fr. Kus's greatest love, besides being a parish priest, is writing. He is the author of several journals and books, including *Saintly Men of Nursing* and a book of essays on psychiatric-mental health nursing.

Jeanne LeVasseur, PhD, APRN, MFA, is professor of nursing at Quinnipiac University. She received her PhD in nursing from University of Connecticut and an MFA in writing from Vermont College. Her poetry has been published in *Nimrod, The Iowa Review,* the *American Journal of Nursing, Literature and Medicine,* and *JAMA,* among other journals. Her poetry has also appeared in the anthologies *Between the Heartbeats: Poetry and Prose by Nurses* and *Intensive Care: More Poetry by Nurses.* Jeanne's poetry collection is titled *Planetary Nights.*

Rita Maria Magdaleno, RN, was born in Augsburg, Germany. She immigrated with her war-bride mother to Arizona in December 1947 to be with her father's Mexican American family. Rita graduated from St. Joseph's Nursing School,

Phoenix, in 1968 and received her degrees in social psychology and English and creative writing at the University of Texas at El Paso. She has read poetry and presented "Poetry of the Borderlands" seminars at the University of Augsburg and the University of Bamberg, Germany. She has received fiction and poetry fellowships from the Arizona Commission on the Arts. Rita worked 1990–2004 as Poet-in-the-Schools for the Arizona Commission on the Arts and has been a writing fellow at the Vermont Studio Center, the Millay Colony for the Arts, the Ucross Center in Wyoming, and the Atlantic Center for the Arts. She currently lives in Tucson and teaches memoir writing workshops. Her first book of poetry, *Marlene Dietrich, Rita Hayworth, and My Mother,* was published in 2003.

Veneta Masson, RN, MA, is a nurse and writer living in Washington, D.C. She spent her last twenty years in practice as a family nurse practitioner and director of a small clinic in the heart of Washington, D.C. You can find more of her work—poems, online notebook entries, and a list of her books—at www.sage femmepress.com

M. Ben Melnykovich, RN, BSN, is a former paramedic who turned to nursing as his true calling. Having originally trained as a classical operatic tenor, he realized that this would not be the path life would take him. After spending eleven years as a paramedic, he graduated from the St. Elizabeth Medical Center School of Nursing with an RN diploma in 1981. He later completed his baccalaureate from Youngstown State University (YSU) ten years later. He began his nursing career in the emergency department and has worked almost entirely in that specialty area. He has been a limited service faculty member at YSU, has spoken on a variety of subjects throughout the United States, and has taught Trauma Nursing Core Course since 1987. He left the hospital setting in 1987 and worked for seven years at an emergency medicine staffing company, returning in 2004 to his home hospital, St. Elizabeth in Youngstown. He continues to work in their Level I Trauma Center as the trauma outreach/injury prevention coordinator. He resides in Lake Milton, Ohio, with his wife of twenty-nine years.

Beverly Mitchell, RN, BSN, CNOR, is a second career nurse, having worked in the theater for fifteen years before finding this path. She currently works as a perioperative nurse in the operating room at New York University Langone Medical Center, in Manhattan. A 2011 graduate of the NYU College of Nursing, Mitchell is currently at work on her master's degree in nursing administration, also at NYU. Bev has found her passion for theater, storytelling, and personal narrative to be a powerful tool in her work as a nurse, with both patients and colleagues.

Marilyn Mitchell, RN, BSN, is originally from New York and a graduate of SUNY Stony Brook's bachelor of science in nursing program. Her nursing experience is primarily in the field of women's health care. She received a master of advanced studies in health law from UCSD/California Western School of Law. Currently, she works for the VHA's National Center for Ethics in Health Care as the integrated ethics manager for ethics consultation. She has been writing prose since elementary school and is also an internationally exhibited visual artist.

Muriel A. Murch RN, BSN, was born and grew up in England, graduating nursing school in 1964. In 1965 she married Walter Murch in New York City, and in 1968 they motorcycled to Los Angeles, relocating to the Bay Area. Murch graduated from San Francisco State in 1991 with a BSN degree, a process she relates in *Journey in the Middle of the Road: One Woman's Journey through a Mid-Life Education.* Her short stories and poetry are included in *Between the Heart Beats; Poetry and Prose by Nurses; Intensive Care: More Poetry and Prose by Nurses;* and in *Stories of Illness and Healing: Women Write Their Bodies* (Kent State University Press). Her most recent book is *The Bell Lap: Stories for Compassionate Nursing Care.* Muriel continues to write while producing independent radio programs for KWMR.org. She and her husband divide their time between London and California. Her website is www.murielmurch.com.

Madeleine Mysko, RN, MA, is the author of two novels, *Bringing Vincent Home* and *Stone Harbor Bound.* Her poetry, stories, and essays have been published widely in literary journals, including *Smartish Pace,* the *Hudson Review, Shenandoah,* and *Bellevue Literary Review;* her op-ed pieces appear in *The Baltimore Sun.* A graduate of the Writing Seminars at Johns Hopkins University, she has taught creative writing in the Baltimore area for years. Presently she teaches at the George Washington Carver Center for Arts and Technology and serves as contributing editor at the *American Journal of Nursing.*

Stacy R. Nigliazzo, RN, is an emergency room nurse. She is a graduate of Texas A&M University and a recipient of the Elsevier Award for Nursing Excellence. Her debut poetry collection, *Scissored Moon,* was published in 2013. It was awarded first place in the *American Journal of Nursing*'s Book of the Year Awards (2014) and was also named a finalist for the Julie Suk Poetry Prize and the Texas Institute of Letters First Book Award for Poetry/Bob Bush Award. She serves as a reviewer for the *American Journal of Nursing* and the *Bellevue Literary Review.* Her website is www.srnigliazzo.com.

Lady Amaka Offodile, RN, MBA, MS Accounting, CPA, was born and grew up in Nigeria. She moved to the United States in 1988, had three children, and started a career in accounting by 1992. Later, she switched to nursing and graduated with a BSN in 2004. For the past twelve years, she has worked in med-surg, long-term acute care hospitals, a transitional care unit, and is now working in a skilled rehab center in Cleveland, Ohio. In 2016, she began taking classes toward her master of science in nursing (MSN) degree, while still practicing as an RN supervisor.

Yolanda Perez-Shulman, MSN, APRN-BC, is a board certified adult nurse practitioner in Boston, Massachusetts. Prior to nursing, she worked in urban planning. Yolanda received her nursing degree from the Massachusetts General Hospital Institute of Health Professions. Her nursing career includes working at a summer camp for girls with type 1 diabetes, an allergy and asthma clinic, and preoperative clinics.

Virginia Ruth is the pen name of Virginia V. Simms, BSN, RN, CWPD, CWWS, CWHC. She has been a blogger for several years, encouraging and inspiring others to live life well, and she has spoken locally and nationally on a variety of health and wellness topics. She has fond memories of her student nurse days at Salisbury State College (now Salisbury University). While at Salisbury, she was president of her class Student Nurses' Association and was actively involved in running the student nurses' learning lab. She posts inspirational vignettes three times a week on her website, www.wellofencouragement.com.

Rosa M. Goldschal Sacharin, RN, was born in Berlin, Germany, in 1925. Rosa was part of the 1938 *Kindertransport* project, which brought thousands of Jewish children to the UK. Only thirteen, she was moved again to Edinburgh, Scotland, that same year and worked as a domestic until March 1941. From March 1941 until the present, she has lived in Glasgow where she reentered and completed high school in 1943. Her professional education includes training at the Royal Hospital for Sick Children, 1943–46, where she earned an RSCN; then general nursing, 1947–49, where she earned an RGN; and finally Midwifery 1st and 2nd, 1949–1951, earning an SCM. A lifelong scholar, she received a diploma in nursing (London University) in 1973; Nurse Teacher Certificate (Glasgow) in 1975; Educational Enhancement, Glasgow University, 1962–66; and a BA in higher education, 1975. Retired after more than four decades of practice, she remains active as a lecturer, examiner for the General Nursing Council (National Board Scotland), and examiner for the Northern Ireland Board Assessor and Examinations. Rosa coauthored Scotland's first pediatric nursing textbooks, *Paediatric Nursing Procedures* (1964), and wrote

Principles of Paediatric Nursing (1980). Her poignant memoir, *The Unwanted Jew: A Struggle for Acceptance* (2014), recalls the story of her life inside a very dark chapter of world history.

Saundra Lee Sarsany is a 1960 graduate of Trumbull Memorial Hospital School of Nursing in Warren, Ohio. A lifelong learner and skilled critical care nurse, she spent the next fifty-five years practicing her art. After working in CCU, ICU, staff education, and nursing management positions, at age forty-seven, she fulfilled another dream to become a flight nurse on a life flight helicopter in Cleveland, Ohio. She flew 480 flights in four years and called her work the "Agony and Ecstasy," for it might be one or the other in a hair's width. A reviewer of and published author for *RN Magazine,* she wrote a series of articles on "How to Handle Bedside Emergencies." On community bloodmobile drives, she served as a Red Cross nurse. As a student, she cared for and later married one of her patients, Paul Sarsany. They were blessed with four children. An avid traveler in retirement, she has also been past president of the Harriet Taylor Upton Association and Trumbull Memorial Hospital retirees.

Judy Schaefer, RN, MA, whose most recent book is *Wild Onion Nurse* (2010), edited the first biographical/autobiographical work of English-speaking nurse-poets, *The Poetry of Nursing: Poems and Commentaries of Leading Nurse-Poets* (Kent State University Press) and coedited, with Cortney Davis, the first international anthology of creative writing by nurses, *Between the Heartbeats.* Her work appears in journals such as *Academic Medicine,* the *American Journal of Nursing,* and the *Lancet.* Memberships include the Kienle Center, Penn State University, College of Medicine, and Sigma Theta Tau International Nursing Honor Society. Judy volunteers at a local hospital and for the Harrisburg Symphony Orchestra. She is an avid amateur artist in watercolor and acrylics, and is the East Coast poetry editor for *Pulse: Voices from the Heart of Medicine* at www.pulsemagazine.org.

Paula Sergi, RN, MFA, holds a BSN from the University of Wisconsin, Madison. After a career in public health nursing, she obtained an MFA in creative writing from Vermont College. Her book publications include the anthologies *A Call to Nursing, Mediations on Hope,* and *Boomer Girls: Poems by Women from the Baby Boom Generation.* Original poetry collections include *Brother, Family Business,* and *Black Forest Love Songs.* The Wisconsin Academy of Sciences, Arts and Letters, along with the Hessen Literary Society, selected Paula as the 2005 cultural ambassador to Hessen, Germany, where she taught poetry in schools during a three-month residency. A recipient of a Wisconsin Arts Board Artist

Fellowship, Paula publishes regularly in such journals as *Witness, Crab Orchard Review, Rattle, Spoon River Poetry Review,* and the *American Journal of Nursing.*

Kelly Sievers, CRNA. Kelly's poems are anchored in her student days at St. Mary's Hospital School of Nursing, Rochester, Minnesota, class of 1968. Her career as a certified registered nurse anesthetist began after graduating from the Johns Hopkins School of Anesthesia for Nurses, Baltimore, in 1976. Her poems appear in anthologies such as *Between the Heart Beats: Poetry and Prose by Nurses; Intensive Care: More Poetry and Prose by Nurses; Boomer Girls; A Call to Nursing; The Poetry of Nursing* (Kent State University Press); *Prairie Hearts and Vacations;* and in journals, including *Ekphrasis, Passenger, Rattle, Prairie Schooner,* and *Poet Lore.* Her online poetry can be found in the Oregon Poetic Voices Project and the *Permanente Journal.*

Sr. Frances Smalkowski, CSFN, PMHCS-BC, BCC, has been a Sister of the Holy Family of Nazareth for fifty-five years. She graduated as an RN-BSN in 1968 and went on to become a certified psychiatric clinical specialist and a certified chaplain. Her clinical work has involved pediatrics, school nursing, psychiatric nursing, and geriatric nursing. Sr. Frances has also served as a general health and mental health educator/consultant in high school, college, and elementary school settings. Her poems and prose have appeared in journals and publications such as *Pulse: Voices from the Heart of Medicine, Sisters Today, Journal of Psychiatric Nursing and Mental Health, Free Association, Vision,* the *Journal of Psychosocial Nursing, Neurology Now, Praying,* and *Readings in Public Policy and Health Care.* Her poetry collection, *Panning for Gold,* was published in 2005.

Rosanne Trost, RN, MPH, lives in Houston, Texas. Her career included medical-surgical nursing, school nursing, and hospice nursing. In addition, she spent much of her career in oncology nursing research. Since retirement, she has realized her passion for creative writing. Her works have appeared in the anthologies *Inspiration for Nurses: 101 Stories of Appreciation* and *Wisdom and Temptation: A Sizzling, Sensual Guide to the Seven Deadly Sins.*

Linda Maurer Tuthill, RN, BSN, grew up in a Pennsylvania German farming community, attended Heidelberg College, and graduated from the Johns Hopkins Hospital School of Nursing in 1963. She worked on a urology unit and taught preclinical students at Johns Hopkins and medical nursing at St. Luke's in Cleveland. After time out to raise a family, she took a refresher course and worked in psychiatry. She helped launch and edited the *Connection,* a community newspaper, and wrote numerous features for *Shaker Magazine*. Her poems have appeared in *Pudding House* and *Cleveland Salon* anthologies and in the *Aurorean*. Now retired from nursing, Linda has facilitated poetry and nonfiction classes for more than fifteen years for Case Western Reserve University's lifelong learning program.

Ellen Hunter Ulken, RN, nursed in medical hospitals for several years and then became a flight attendant for a decade. After a refresher course in nursing, she worked part time in psychiatric hospitals, both in the clinical setting and in utilization review. In addition to stories published in journals, she has written *Beautiful Dreamer, The Life of Stephen Collins Foster* and *Silent Sisters: Profiles of the Short Lives of Karen Carpenter, Patsy Cline, Cass Elliot, Ruby Elzy, Janis Joplin and Selena Quintanilla-Perez*. Along with Rebecca Watts and Clarence Lyons, she contributed to a history of Peachtree City, Georgia. She is retired and lives in Peachtree City.

Pattama Ulrich, MPH, BSN, RN, is a lieutenant commander in the United States Public Health Services with more than twenty-five years of experience in this field. Her current assignment is with the National Institute for Occupation Safety and Health and the World Trade Center Health Program, where she combines her expertise in clinical and public health services, program management, and emergency management to support the program providing medical monitoring service and treatment for responders and survivors from the 9/11 terrorist attacks. She is currently pursuing a doctoral study program in environmental health science at the Ohio State University. She has received numerous awards and citations, including the Ann Magnusen Award from the American Red Cross and a Public Health Workforce Scholarship from the Center for Disease Control.

Eileen Valinoti BSN, MA, is retired after a varied career in oncology, nursing education, and school nursing. Her essays have appeared in *Pulse: Voices from the Heart of Medicine, ARS MEDICA,* the *Yale Journal for Humanities in Medicine, Blood and Thunder,* the *Healing Muse,* and *Confrontation*. Her work has also been anthologized in *Body and Soul: Narratives of Healing from ARS MEDICA, Meditations on Hope: Nurses' Stories about Motivation and Inspiration,* and *Pulse: Voices from the Heart of Medicine: Editors' Picks: A Third Anthology*.

Belle Waring, RN, lost a long battle with cancer on January 31, 2015. Early in her career she worked at Children's National Medical Center as a writer in residence and also spent nine years as a neonatal intensive care nurse at Georgetown University Hospital. Her observations during this time inspired much of her award-winning poetry. She joined the National Institutes of Health in 2002, and in 2006 became a writer-editor for the *NIH Record*. Belle's publications include

Refuge, winner of the Associated Writing Programs' Award for Poetry and the Washington Prize, cited by *Publishers Weekly* as one of the best books of 1990, and *Dark Blonde,* winner of the San Francisco State University Poetry Center Book Award and the Larry Levis Reading Prize. Her poems are widely published and anthologized, including in *Between the Heartbeats: Poetry and Prose by Nurses* and *Intensive Care: More Poetry and Prose by Nurses.*

Anne Webster, RN, worked twenty-five years as a staff nurse and administrator in Atlanta hospitals while writing in her spare time. Unfortunately, her nursing career ended when she was diagnosed with Crohn's disease. Anne's poetry collection, *A History of Nursing,* was a nominee for the 2009 National Book Award prior to its publication. Her poetry and essays have appeared in such journals as the *Southern Poetry Review,* the *New York Quarterly,* and *Rattle* and in anthologies such as *The Poetry of Nursing* (Kent State University Press). She is currently finishing a memoir titled *Gutshot* about her experience with inflammatory bowel disease.